# CHARLOTTE ATLEE WHITE ROWE

*The James N. Griffith Series in Baptist Studies*

This series on Baptist life and thought explores and investigates Baptist history, offers analyses of Baptist theologies, provides studies in hymnody, and examines the role of Baptists in societies and cultures around the world. The series also includes classics of Baptist literature, letters, diaries, and other writings. For a complete list of titles in the series, visit www.mupress.org and visit the series page.

—C. Douglas Weaver, Series Editor

# CHARLOTTE ATLEE WHITE ROWE

*The Story of America's First Appointed
Woman Missionary*

## Reid S. Trulson

MERCER UNIVERSITY PRESS
*Macon, Georgia*

MUP/ H1012

© 2021 by Mercer University Press
Published by Mercer University Press
1501 Mercer University Drive
Macon, Georgia 31207
All rights reserved

25 24 23 22 21      5 4 3 2 1

Books published by Mercer University Press are printed on acid-free paper
that meets the requirements of the American National Standard for
Information Sciences—Permanence of Paper for Printed Library Materials.

Printed and bound in the United States.

This book is set in Adobe Caslon Pro.

Cover/jacket design by Burt&Burt.

ISBN      978-0-88146-803-8
Cataloging-in-Publication Data is available from the Library of Congress

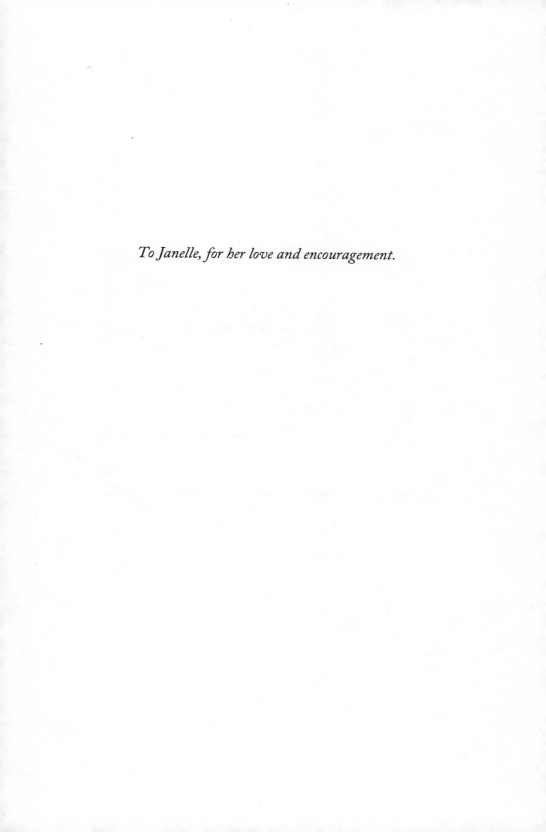

*To Janelle, for her love and encouragement.*

MERCER UNIVERSITY PRESS

*Endowed by*

TOM WATSON BROWN
*and*
THE WATSON-BROWN FOUNDATION, INC.

# CONTENTS

# PREFACE

First came the surprise. For three decades as I worked in several capacities in the American Baptist Foreign Mission Society, I studied mission history and researched documents in the society's archives. In 2014 while preparing for the society's bicentennial, I noticed an important detail: when the Baptist Board of Foreign Missions appointed its first missionaries in 1814, it only appointed Adoniram Judson and Luther Rice. Adoniram and Ann Judson were already serving in Burma at the time, and Baptists generally spoke of the Judsons as their first missionaries. The Board, however, did not appoint Adoniram's wife, Ann, but considered her and missionary wives following her to be volunteer "assistant missionaries" helping their husbands. I was taken aback!

Then came the intriguing discovery. In 1815, one year after Adoniram's appointment, the board appointed Mrs. Charlotte H. White to join the Judsons in the mission in Burma.

Then came the mystery. Charlotte White was the first American woman appointed by any sending body to serve in international, cross-cultural mission. But who was she? Her appointment was considered scandalous by some within and beyond the board, but what happened to her? There was no record that she ever served in Burma. Had the Board of Foreign Missions revoked her appointment? Did she serve elsewhere? If she did, then where, what, and how long was her ministry? When did she die? Where was she buried? And why is she largely unknown and almost completely absent from mission studies, Baptist histories, and women's studies?

Then came the search. I found abundant details about Charlotte Atlee White Rowe in previously unexplored source materials in England, India, and America. Her life's story emerged from documents in the Angus Library (Regent's Park College, Oxford, UK), the India Office Records (British Library, London, UK), the American Baptist Historical Society (Atlanta, Georgia), the Wheaton College Mission Research Center (Wheaton, Illinois), the Lancaster County Historical Society and St.

James Episcopal Church (Lancaster, Pennsylvania), the Historical Society of Pennsylvania, the Library Company of Philadelphia, and the American Philosophical Society (Philadelphia, Pennsylvania), along with journals and newspapers from Charlotte's time. The search culminated in the discovery of a remarkable woman.

Then came the conviction. Ann Judson was a truly heroic mission pioneer whose sacrificial service rightly continues to inform and inspire. However, it does no disservice to Ann for Charlotte White's story also to be known. Charlotte's life sheds light on the persistent gender bias that still influences women's opportunities and the valuing of women's accomplishments. Charlotte's ministry took place in the context of the progress and regress through which American Baptist women finally achieved full and equal missionary appointment with men.

This examination of Charlotte White's pioneering role seeks to make careful use of language. For instance, some have said that Charlotte was the first single woman missionary. Others, distinguishing between widows and women who had not previously married, have identified other persons as the first single woman missionary even though they were sent later than Charlotte. Rather than viewing Charlotte primarily with reference to her marital status, this study clarifies that she was the first American *woman* to be appointed as a missionary.

Why was *appointment* important? Appointment had organizational significance that established mutual obligations. Appointed missionaries were agents of the sending body from whom they received instructions and to whom they were accountable. Likewise, the sending body was accountable for the missionaries' wellbeing, including adequate financial support to enable missionaries to fulfill their work. In later years, sending agencies would provide for missionaries' medical care during their years of service, give attention to the unique needs of their "third culture" children, and assure a pension income for missionaries in retirement.

Appointment also had spiritual significance. Through it, the body of Christ publicly affirmed that God had called a particular individual into the ministry of mission. In that regard, the appointment of a missionary was similar to the ordination of a pastor. It was an act that could supersede public opinion about the "proper sphere" for women. For Charlotte and for other women, appointment meant calling things by their right names.

Charlotte's story deserves to be told.

CHARLOTTE ATLEE WHITE ROWE

# PART 1

⤝

# AMERICA—THE MAKING OF A MISSIONARY

"*God is with us!* The best ship in the harbor of Philadelphia is at the service of brother Hough and yourself. The passage *without money*."[1] Charlotte was thrilled. Those words opened a door for her that some influential men were trying to keep shut—and locked! After all, she was thirty-three. A proper widow would by now be remarried, raising children, and making her husband successful.

But Charlotte Hazen Atlee White would not give up. She had overcome too much to meekly curtsy to standing tradition. She was an *Atlee* and embodied her family's tenacious spirit perhaps more fully than any of her older siblings.

She would need that spirit to survive. To follow her call.

*Chapter 1*

# PERSONAL AND NATIONAL REVOLUTION

Some said that Charlotte's family descended from Sir Richard-at-the-Lee, the English knight who protected Robin Hood from the Sheriff of Nottingham. Hence the family name, Atlee.[1] Charlotte's grandfather, William Atlee, braved the Atlantic by sailing from England to Barbados in 1733. There he served as personal secretary to Lord Howe, the colony's new governor. The ocean's breadth created a safe space that enabled her grandfather to marry the woman he loved, for a life with Jane Alcock was otherwise unattainable. Jane was a clergyman's daughter and the Earl of Chatham's cousin. She was also a maid of honor to the queen. King George III and Queen Charlotte wanted Jane to marry into the royal family, but Jane's love for William overcame her fear of royal displeasure or the dangers of the sea. Bolstering her love with courage, she ran away and followed William to Barbados where they married "according to the Canons and Constitution of the Church of England" in 1734.[2]

William and Jane Atlee's adventures did not end there. Several days after their wedding, they sailed from Barbados and arrived three weeks later in the New World's largest city, Philadelphia. Charlotte's grandparents had become the first Atlees to reach America. A year later in a house on Market Street, Charlotte's father, William Augustus Atlee, was born. William, Jane, and baby William Augustus moved to Trenton, New Jersey, where William became "a contractor for transporting the mails through the adjacent region" and where three more children were born.[3]

The Atlees returned to Philadelphia, but in 1744 William died. This devastated the family and began Jane's thirty-three years of widowhood. Eight-year-old William Augustus Atlee was now fatherless. By age fourteen he was supporting his mother, his two younger brothers, and younger sister by working in Lancaster, Pennsylvania, as a clerk in the recorder's office.

The next decade seemed to promise Charlotte's father a more settled life than that of his parents. William Augustus Atlee studied law with a local judge and was admitted to the Lancaster bar. He married Esther Bowes Sayre in Philadelphia in 1763 and started what would become a large family. He and Esther had six children by 1773 when colonists masquerading as Native Americans boarded three British ships in Boston harbor and dumped tea overboard to protest unfair taxes. Stirrings of political revolution now began to shake the Atlee's settled colonial life.

Six months after William Augustus and Esther welcomed their seventh child, the First Continental Congress began meeting at Carpenters' Hall in Philadelphia, several blocks from William Augustus's birthplace. The Congress petitioned King George III for redress of their grievances. Their petition went unanswered.

"Brown Bess" muskets had fired the first shots of the revolution at Lexington and Concord in Massachusetts before the Atlee's eighth child was born in Lancaster. By now the Americans had declared their independence from England. William Augustus Atlee was among the ardent patriots.[4] His younger brother, Samuel, had already fought in the battle of Long Island and been captured.

In the following year, 1777, William Augustus Atlee's distinguished legal skills led to his appointment as the first associate justice of the Pennsylvania Supreme Court. That year, British troops occupied Philadelphia. The Continental Congress fled to the Lancaster Court House before moving on to York, Pennsylvania, the following day. With the revolutionary war fully underway, William was appointed chairman of the Lancaster County Council of Safety as well as commissary and superintendent of the arsenal, barracks, and British prisoners of war being held at Lancaster. His robust exercise of his role led a Tory poet to write: "Should Atlee summon to his savage bar / to tremble at his rod, be from us far."[5]

Samuel Atlee's ongoing imprisonment was harsh. He and other prisoners of war were ill fed and for two weeks lived on chestnuts.[6] For a time, he was held aboard a British prison ship. Despite the difficulties of his incarceration, Samuel was able to write to his older brother, expressing hope of being freed in a prisoner exchange.[7]

In 1778 Esther bore her ninth child. That year, after eighteen months as a prisoner of war, Samuel was freed in a prisoner exchange. A month later Samuel was elected a delegate to the Second Continental Congress.

A tenth Atlee child was born in 1780. General Cornwallis surrendered to George Washington at Yorktown in 1781. British soldiers and colonists loyal to the king began to leave, and the new nation was born.

The Atlee's eleventh and last child was born in Lancaster, Pennsylvania, on July 13, 1782. They christened their new baby "Charlotte Hazen Atlee" only four and a half months after the victorious colonists christened their new nation "The United States of America." Charlotte's name derived from new friends her parents had made during the revolution. In 1777 the British and Hessian prisoners of war being held in Lancaster had threatened to set the town ablaze, and several years later they plotted an escape. Congress responded by strengthening the military guard in the city and placing Brigadier General Moses Hazen from Haverhill, Massachusetts, in charge.[8] The general was stationed in Lancaster for eleven months and was accompanied by his wife, Charlotte de la Saussaye Hazen.[9] The Hazens and Atlees became such close friends that the Atlees named their baby after Mrs. Charlotte Hazen, who was present as a sponsor when her namesake was baptized.[10]

## Charlotte's Formative Years 1782–1815

Charlotte's early childhood as the youngest in a family of many siblings was pleasant and stimulating. Her father now held an even more influential position as the president judge of Pennsylvania's First District Court, a circuit of four southeastern Pennsylvania counties. Charlotte was growing up in a home described as "the resort of the beauty and intelligence of the surrounding country."[11]

Then two grievous events shattered her world. One week before Charlotte's eighth birthday, her forty-two-year-old mother died. Three years later, Caribbean refugees fleeing political turmoil in Santo Domingo poured into Philadelphia. With them came a deadly fever. Philadelphia's newly built City Hall was providing space in which the Pennsylvania Supreme Court and the U.S. Supreme Court took turns meeting. Ominously, by the time Charlotte's father arrived in the city for court duties in 1793, City Hall had also become the gathering place for volunteers frantically struggling to come to grips with a full-blown epidemic in the city. Dr. Benjamin Rush had identified the malady as "bilious remitting yellow fever" and urged anyone who could flee to do so.[12] President Washington and Congress had relocated north to Germantown while rich and poor alike succumbed to the scourge. The city's *Independent Gazetteer* commented on the yellow fever epidemic: "Philadelphia, the boast of America, has been deserted by near half its inhabitants! who have fled in all directions for the preservation of their lives, — In consequence whereof very little business is at present transacted here."[13]

For Charlotte's father, however, such information was too late. William Augustus Atlee contracted yellow fever and died on September 9, 1793. Eleven-year-old Charlotte was now an orphan.

As though disappearing in a thick morning fog, the next decade of Charlotte's life became a mystery. She most likely went to Rutland in the very center of Massachusetts to live with her oldest sister, Elizabeth, and her husband, Maj. Moses White, who had been Gen. Hazen's paymaster and aid.[14] Elizabeth was seventeen years older than Charlotte and had been the other female sponsor at Charlotte's baptism. Elizabeth and Moses would have taken Charlotte into a family that already had four children and would have six more. By contrast, it is unlikely that young Charlotte Atlee could have gone to live with her other baptismal sponsor and namesake, Mrs. Charlotte de la Saussaye Hazen. The Hazens were living in Troy, New York, when Charlotte became an orphan and were struggling with ill health and poverty. Gen. Hazen was partially paralyzed from a stroke and had been largely bedridden for seven years. Mrs. Hazen had been forced to sell her silver spoons to buy food and had written to George Washington that she had been "frequently without a shilling to procure dinner for my family."[15]

Charlotte's education is also part of the mystery. As children of a prominent Pennsylvania judge, it is likely that Charlotte and her siblings received formal schooling in Lancaster. Charlotte's later life as a teacher, school administrator, and linguist gave ample evidence of a good education. But it is unclear where in Lancaster Charlotte was taught or how her education continued following her parents' deaths. Educational opportunities were few for most girls in the new republic. In Charlotte's birth year, 1782, the Rev. John Eliot of Boston wrote to a fellow clergyman,

We don't pretend to teach the female part of the town anything more than dancing or a little music perhaps (and these accomplishments must necessarily be confined to a very few) except the private schools for writing, which enables them to write a copy, sign their name, etc., which they might not be able to do without such a privilege, and with it I venture to say that a lady is a rarity among us who can write a page of commonplace sentiment, the words being spelt, and the style and language kept up with purity and elegance.[16]

Marriage and motherhood were the expected roles for daughters. If Charlotte lived her adolescence and young adulthood with Moses and Elizabeth White in Rutland, she would have had natural occasions to meet Moses White's half-brother, Nathaniel Hazen White, who was eighteen years younger than Moses. Nathaniel was born in Methuen, nine miles southwest of Haverhill, Massachusetts, but had moved to Rutland where he was a merchant. Like most people, Nathaniel worshiped at Rutland's Congregational Church, which was owned by the town.[17] On October 28, 1803, Nathaniel presented himself to the church clerk and "entered his intentions of marriage with Charlotte H. Atlee." Both were stated to be from Rutland.[18] Three weeks later in Rutland on Thursday, November 17, 1803, Charlotte and Nathaniel were married by the pastor, Hezekiah Goodrich.[19]

Nathaniel was twenty-nine and Charlotte was twenty-one when they married and began building their life together. The following year Charlotte and Nathaniel welcomed the birth of a son. They gave the baby his father's name, Nathaniel Hazen White. Their little family was putting down roots.

Charlotte's joy as a new wife and mother, however, was tragically short-lived. Once again, two grievous deaths shattered her world. On Christmas Day 1804, her husband died. He was only thirty years old. Charlotte's grief over Nathaniel's death intensified five months later when their nine-month-old baby died.[20]

Amidst this dual trauma, Charlotte moved to Haverhill, Massachusetts, the Whites' ancestral home sixty miles northeast of Rutland. Nathaniel had sixteen siblings, and Charlotte may have moved to be closer to members of his extended family. With more than 2,700 inhabitants, Haverhill was twice the size of Rutland and may have offered more opportunities by which a widow could support herself.

Most Haverhill families belonged to the Congregational Church, the "standing order" throughout New England. Charlotte had worshipped in her parents' Episcopal church at Lancaster and in her husband's Congregational church at Rutland. But she had also been exposed to the Baptists. Nathaniel's parents in Methuen were "New Light" followers of George Whitfield who had become Baptists. They had taught their children that one needed a change of heart that could only be brought about by an individual's response of faith to God's grace.[21] The elder Whites were close friends with Rev. Hezekiah Smith, founder of the Haverhill Baptist Church and its pastor for four decades.

Following Smith's death, Rev. William Batchelder was invited to preach in Haverhill. Batchelder was known for his leading role in a spiritual revival in York, Maine. There he had preached to huge crowds that "met in fields, orchards, and forests when churches would not hold the crowds." Some 1,400 people attended one four-hour meeting that ended in the evening with Batchelder baptizing new believers at the seashore.[22]

On December 4, 1805, seven months after Charlotte's infant son died in Rutland, Rev. Batchelder became the new pastor of the Baptist church in Haverhill. Batchelder's fervent preaching was called "experimental or evangelical."[23] His active outreach throughout Haverhill at the start of his ministry led many people to experience profound spiritual awakenings that changed their lives. Twenty-four-year-old Charlotte Hazen Atlee White was one of those people. She called it her conversion and wrote, "I was led to search the Scriptures in order to find assurance that Jesus Christ is the son of God; in doing which, I was blessed with a desire to be converted from darkness to light; the Holy Spirit rousing me to repent, and enabling me to confess Christ as my Lord and Saviour."[24]

Charlotte's testimony revealed that her spiritual awakening was not a momentary emotionalism but an experience that engaged her intellect, spirit, and will. Batchelder's winsome witness had spurred her "to search the Scriptures." In so doing, she gained "a desire to be converted." The exercise of her mind was coupled with the Holy Spirit's prompting of her spirit, "rousing me to repent." God's work in her mind and spirit led her to take an act of the will "to confess Christ as my Lord and Saviour." The character of her conversion would influence Charlotte's work as a missionary in the years ahead.

The new believers in Haverhill gave public witness to God's work in their lives by being baptized in the Merrimack River that separated the communities of Haverhill on the north from Bradford on the south.

8

Batchelder would eventually baptize 208 people as the Haverhill Baptist Church continued to grow.[25]

Some Congregationalists considered the Baptists a "sect." Leverett Saltonstall held that opinion. He was a close friend of Charlotte's brother-in-law Daniel Appleton White and had begun a law practice in Haverhill near the Haverhill Bridge. Saltonstall was nevertheless open-minded enough to occasionally attend Baptist worship services, especially in 1806 when the Congregationalist Church lacked a permanent pastor. He was also curious enough to join others at the riverside to watch people being baptized, or "plunged" as he termed it.

Saltonstall's journal noted that Rev. Batchelder baptized seventeen new believers on Sunday, May 18, 1806. The next month, Saltonstall described Sunday, June 29, 1806, as a "very pleasant" day. That day he watched two women being baptized in the Merrimack. One of them was his good friend's sister-in-law, "Mrs. White, widow of Natl. White late of Rutland, formerly Charlotte Atlee." Although Saltonstall had witnessed "plungings" before, Charlotte's baptism caught him by surprise. As she waded into the water to be baptized, Charlotte began to sing. As Saltonstall described it, "Mrs. W. just before she was plunged struck up a verse to the tune of Amherst."

A proper Congregationalist, Saltonstall was taken aback by Charlotte's spontaneous singing. He wrote, "I was sorry for it—it was unusual and unnecessary and however sincere she might have been, it seemed very like ostentation." Not infrequently, identical actions by men and women are judged differently. Rather than hearing Charlotte's singing as an extemporaneous expression of sincere spirituality, Saltonstall credited it to Charlotte's personality. "She had a very romantic disposition," he wrote, "which I presume is not changed but only directed to religion."[26]

Interestingly, Saltonstall had recognized the tune. AMHERST was composed in 1770 by William Billings, a Massachusetts composer whose music was widely sung by New England congregations in the late 1700s. Billings consciously refused to bow to established custom as he composed tunes that breathed life and energy into the region's sacred music. He was described as a "brilliant, if headstrong and lovable wanderer from the straight and narrow way."[27] Billings acknowledged, "for my own part...I don't think myself confined to any Rules for Composition laid down by any that went before me...I think it best for every Composer to be his own Carver."[28]

9

Charlotte never knew Billings but must have sensed power to freely praise God in his tune's disregard of musical convention. Charlotte White would need that tenacious convention-breaking power in the years ahead. As one who would compose her own role in the emerging world mission movement, Charlotte would be her own carver.

*Chapter 2*

# CHARLOTTE'S WORLD:
# HANNAH, MARY, HARRIET, AND ANN

It is difficult to identify the precise beginning of movements, including the part of the global mission movement that originated in America. Whatever else is certain about it, Christian mission in colonial America was not an exclusively male endeavor. As can be seen among the Moravians, women actively and effectively participated in mission. In 1742 in Bethlehem, Pennsylvania, Count Nicolaus Ludwig von Zinzendorf conducted a wedding for Janettje Rauh and Gottlob Büttner. It was a double wedding that also joined Margarethe Bechtel and Martin Mack. The men were Moravian missionaries about to join the mission that Christian Rauch had begun two years earlier at the Mahican village of Shekomeko in southeastern New York. Janettje Rauh and Margarethe Bechtel were chosen by lot and consented to marry Büttner and Mack and become part of the missionary team. Both women were excellent linguists and worked among men as well as women as Shekomeko became the first Native American Christian congregation formed by the Moravians.[1] Janettje and Margarethe are considered possibly two of the first Protestant women missionaries in colonial North America.[2]

Women and men also partnered in the mission movement from the earliest days of the new Republic. The American Revolution did more than transform colonists into Americans and Anglicans into Episcopalians. Though little noticed at the time, the revolution also launched the new nation's first foreign missionary couple, Hannah and George Liele.

## Hannah Hunt Liele:
## First Woman Missionary from the United States

Several months after Charlotte Hazen Atlee's birth, former slaves Hannah Liele, her husband, George, their three sons and one daughter boarded a ship bound for Jamaica. So little is known about Hannah that George alone has typically been honored as the first missionary from the United States. Like the women disciples who accompanied Jesus and supported him out of their personal resources, Hannah has been seldom named and scarcely acknowledged.

To be sure, Hannah's husband was a heroic figure. George Liele was born into slavery in Virginia about 1751. In that year colonial Georgia legalized slavery within its borders after prohibiting it for fifteen years. As a young man, George Liele was taken into Georgia and sold to Henry Sharpe, a plantation owner and Baptist deacon. By contrast, Hannah Hunt's birthplace is unrecorded. Her surname is known only because it is found in George Liele's will.[3] George supposed that she was about his own age and had been born about 1751 but acknowledged, "I cannot justly tell what is my age, as I have no account of the time of my birth, but I suppose I am about forty years old." Hannah and George may have married about 1771 since twenty years later George wrote that their oldest child was then nineteen.[4] George expressed what was presumably a mutual compatibility in their marriage, writing, "I have every satisfaction in life from her."[5]

In 1773, while in his early twenties, George Liele (also spelled Lisle) became a Christian. Almost immediately he began sharing his faith and preaching to fellow slaves. Deacon Sharpe approved and freed George to carry out this preaching ministry on plantations along the Savannah River. If Sharpe also owned Hannah, no mention is made of him freeing her. In 1775 George Liele became the first African American to be formally ordained as a Baptist pastor. In addition to the nearby plantations, he preached for about three years at Brunton Land in Savannah as well as nearby Yamacraw. Hannah came to faith through George's preaching, and he baptized her at Brunton Land.[6]

At the outbreak of the Revolutionary War, the British sought to weaken the economy of the slaveholding colonies by offering freedom to slaves who would run away and seek refuge behind their lines. When

British troops entered Georgia and captured the city of Savannah, most of Liele's church and many other slaves fled to the city. Although George was already free, he and his family moved into Savannah. In the British-occupied city, Hannah and the children now likewise became free. George continued his ministry throughout the 1779–1782 occupation of Savannah.

When Lord Cornwallis surrendered to George Washington at Yorktown, the former slaves became at risk; the returning planters would surely re-enslave them. Hannah and the Liele children faced that danger. George was threatened in another way. Deacon Sharpe was now dead, and his heirs were laying plans to strip George of the freedom their father had granted him. As the British followed orders to withdraw, thousands of former slaves preserved their freedom by following the troops into Canada. George Liele, however, turned south. He indentured himself to British colonel Moses Kirkland, bought passage on a sailing ship, and late in 1782 departed to Jamaica with Hannah and their four children. By forfeiting George's freedom until the debt could be repaid, Hannah and George Liele followed their call to share the good news of Jesus among enslaved people. Upon arriving in Jamaica in early 1783, George presented himself and his papers to the governor. In return, the governor issued papers certifying that George, Hannah, and their four children were free British subjects.

Hannah and George worked as self-supporting missionaries. She along with George and two others formed the first Baptist church, birthing the Jamaican Baptist movement. The available records focus on George while Hannah is mentioned almost incidentally. Yet she, too, must have experienced both the satisfaction and heartaches of their work. She must have recoiled when the drunken white planter rode his horse into the Baptist church during the Lord's Supper and demanded that her husband serve communion to his horse. Like Adoniram Judson, who was imprisoned in Burma several decades later, George Liele was jailed for three and a half years in Jamaica. And like Ann Judson after her, Hannah attempted to visit her imprisoned husband, but unlike Ann, Hannah was prevented from seeing her husband or attending to his needs.[7]

Hannah's life and ministry are shrouded in silence. Was she literate? That George named her in his will as an executor of his estate suggests that she was.[8] How did she participate in evangelism or training new believers? The covenant of the Lieles' church spoke of "brothers and sisters" rather than "brothers" or "brethren," wording that specifically included both men and women. The church also had twelve male elders and twelve female elders.[9] Did these expressions of gender equality suggest Hannah's influence? After forty years in Jamaica, George Liele was invited to England where from 1822–1826 he ministered to people of color in London, after which he returned to Jamaica. Did Hannah accompany him? These and other questions about this self-supporting first woman missionary from the United States remain unanswered. The fruit of Hannah and George's ministry, however, was evident. When the first English Baptist missionaries came to Jamaica in 1814 to assist the mission, the movement that she and her husband had birthed already numbered more than 8,000 believers. By the 1840s the movement's vitality led Jamaican Baptists to form their own mission society and send Jamaican missionaries to Cameroon in central Africa.

The Lieles were serving in Jamaica when Charlotte discerned her call to missionary service in Asia. Hannah and George Liele exerted initiative and ingenuity to pursue their mission. Charlotte would need the same qualities to follow her call.

## Discerning Her Call to Mission

Charlotte's family had received ministry from missionaries before her birth. The Atlee family belonged to St. James Church in Lancaster, a church founded in 1744 by missionaries from the Society for the Propagation of the Gospel in Foreign Parts (SPG). The archbishop of Canterbury had overseen the SPG's formation at Lambeth Palace in 1701. The society enabled the Church of England to do mission in the New World among Indigenous Americans, Africans, and colonists in areas that otherwise lacked Anglican spiritual care.

The pastors at St. James were all SPG missionaries until the start of the American Revolution. Charlotte's father, a warden at St. James for three decades, had intimate knowledge of missionary service. He recognized the missionaries' difficulty in maintaining communication with society leadership an ocean away. He walked alongside the missionaries in their ongoing struggle to secure adequate financial support for themselves and their families. He saw the missionaries' care for the spiritual formation of those they served. Charlotte and her siblings may have read from *The Family Prayer-Book Containing Morning and Evening Prayers*, a book that

Rev. Thomas Barton, St. James's last missionary priest, adapted from the *Book of Common Prayer*. Rev. Barton had the book printed in 1767 by the Seventh Day Baptist monks at Ephrata, Pennsylvania for use in the three churches he served.[10]

And finally, Atlee observed how missionaries must constantly balance their commitment to the people they serve against the missionaries' loyalty to their home country. As the revolution grew near, Rev. Barton continued reading the liturgical prayer for King George III and was faithful to his ordination vow that pledged loyalty to the British sovereign as head of the Church of England. At the same time, he carefully refused to preach against the colonial cause. Writing to the SPG secretary, Barton explained, "In the present unhappy and unnatural dispute between the parent kingdom & these colonies, I foresaw that my taking an active part could do no service, but would rather injure the cause I wish to support, I mean that of Religion;—I therefore consulted the interest of the Church, & my own peace & quiet—Would to God, a happy reconciliation could soon take place!"[11]

During the revolution, worship services at St. James were suspended. The church building was boarded up and remained so for five years while Rev. Barton continued to meet with parishioners in their homes. When Barton refused to pledge allegiance to the patriot cause, he was confined to Lancaster County. This made it impossible for him to visit the many church members that lived outside the county. It also became increasingly difficult for Barton to care for his wife and family. Finally, at his own request, in 1778 he was exiled to British controlled New York. Charlotte's mother wrote to her husband describing their missionary's departure.

> Our late parson (Mr. Barton) set off yesterday with his lady; they have taken leave of us altogether. I can assure you that it affected me much when they called to bid me adieu. I could not help looking back upon many happy opportunities of doing my duty under his office; but I hope we shall find someone or other to tell us our duty again, and who will show us the way to heaven as well as tell us that there is such a place.[12]

Two years later he died, still exiled in New York.

Rev. Barton's missionary experience may have been both instructive and inspirational for Charlotte. However, since Charlotte was born two years after Barton's death, her knowledge of him was limited to information that others passed on to her. Having been orphaned at eleven, Charlotte was deprived of her parents who could have shared the most extensive insights from Rev. Barton's ministry. Charlotte's four oldest siblings, Elizabeth, Mary, Jane, and William, remembered Rev. Barton, having been thirteen, twelve, nine, and six respectively when he was exiled to New York. Nevertheless, Charlotte left no record of the things she may have learned from her family's involvement with their missionary priest. Nor did she indicate the potential influence of her uncle, the Rev. John Sayre, an SPG missionary priest in New York, who also died two years before her birth.

Charlotte discerned her call to mission while living in Haverhill. She wrote of this in her letter to the Baptist Board applying for missionary appointment: "Since the date of my conversion, I humbly hope my desire has been to do good, and glorify my Redeemer; and especially since missionary endeavours have come within my knowledge I have felt myself deeply interested in them; and their success has been the constant subject of my prayers."[13]

## Haverhill—A Rich Mission Environment

Haverhill was an especially fruitful place to become knowledgeable about mission and about women's participation in those endeavors. When Charlotte arrived, Baptists in and near Haverhill were already active in foreign mission and women were among the leaders. Forty miles south of Haverhill, Mary Webb had formed the first women's missionary society in America. Mary, a member of the Second Baptist Church of Boston, was a most unlikely leader. She was a young woman in a culture that gave preference to men over women and to age over youth. Mary's father was dead. She was single. She had no brothers. All this at a time when a woman's security, social status, and ability to establish legal contracts were determined by a man in her life such as a father, husband, or brother. Furthermore, Mary used a wheelchair, having lost the ability to walk or stand due to a severe illness at the age of five. Yet Mary Webb had remarkable organizational skills. On October 9, 1800, twenty-one-year-old Mary Webb formed the Boston Female Society for Missionary Purposes. The work of British Baptist missionary William Carey and his colleagues in India was widely known and fired the imagination of evangelicals in the United States. Mary Webb's society organized Baptist and Congregationalist women to pray for and support the British Baptist mission in India as well as outreach among the Native American nations.[14]

Two years later, on May 26, 1802, Baptists in Boston formed the Massachusetts Baptist Missionary Society "to furnish occasional preaching, and to promote the knowledge of evangelistic truth in the new settlements within these United States; or further if circumstances should render it proper."[15] Haverhill's Baptist pastor, Rev. Hezekiah Smith, moderated the meeting while Dr. Thomas Baldwin of Boston and Dr. Lucius Bolles of Salem played leading roles.

Baldwin and Bolles became close associates of Rev. William Batchelder and participated in his 1805 installation as pastor at the Haverhill Baptist Church following Hezekiah Smith's long pastorate. Batchelder, Baldwin, and Bolles were all trustees of the Massachusetts Baptist Missionary Society when it was incorporated in 1808.[16] Batchelder continued to serve as a trustee throughout Charlotte's time in Haverhill. He also served locally as president of the India and Foreign Missionary Society of Haverhill and Vicinity, which became an auxiliary society to the Baptist Board of Foreign Missions.[17] While the India Society had an all-male leadership of four officers and seven trustees,[18] the Haverhill Baptist Church had a Female Mite Society that also supported missions.[19] Through her pastor and church, Charlotte had excellent access to information about missionaries serving in Maine, Vermont, Canada, Haiti, the Tuscarora nation, and India.

Charlotte could also read ongoing news of the British Baptist mission in India in *The Massachusetts Baptist Missionary Magazine*. Both the Baptist periodical and the Congregationalist *Massachusetts Missionary Magazine* made the name of William Staughton known in Massachusetts by reprinting his correspondence with William Carey. Their letters continued the relationship that had begun between the two men in 1792 in England. Charlotte would soon meet William and Maria Staughton, both of whom would recognize and resolutely support her call to mission.

## Visits from British Baptist Missionaries

Baptists in the region also received valuable first-hand mission information from British Baptists who sailed between England and India via the United States. This circuitous route was caused by the East India Company.

At its start, the company was the private commercial enterprise of a small group of English merchants. Their stunning early success came from bringing nutmeg from Indonesia to England where the nutmeg's subsequent London street-price fetched a phenomenal 3200 percent profit. Speculators quickly wanted part of the wealth and in 1600 formed themselves into "The Company of Merchants of London Trading into the East Indies."[20] The company soon diversified into anything that would yield a profit for its stockholders, including cotton, tea, saltpeter, silk, salt, coffee, and eventually, opium. Queen Elizabeth I gave the company a fifteen-year monopoly on Eastern trade. Her successor, King James I, made the monopoly indefinite.[21] Its growing wealth and influence led the company to style itself as "the Grandest Society of Merchants in the Universe." It grew to have its own army and navy, coined its own currency, created its own laws, established its presence in India either with consent or conquest of local rulers, and administered colonial rule on behalf of the Crown. The East India Company built Bombay and constructed forts at Madras (1644) and Calcutta (1696), creating three great administrative areas known as "Presidencies" that constituted British India.[22]

The East India Company, invariably referred to as "the Honorable Company," feared that evangelical missionaries might disturb the local populace and imperil its profits. Therefore, apart from Anglican chaplains serving the Crown's subjects abroad, the company refused to grant travel licenses to missionaries departing for India on any of its ships. Given the East India Company's monopoly on trade with the East, the travel ban posed a significant obstacle for British missionaries. If they could not secure passage on other nations' ships passing through British ports en route to India, they were forced to travel to an intermediate country, then re-embark to India. British Baptists were among the missionaries who sailed first to the United States and then proceeded to India on U.S.-flagged vessels. Although this detour more than doubled the length of their journey, the stop in America circumvented the Honourable Company's travel ban and gave missionaries an opportunity to raise support for their work in India.

The first Baptist missionaries who were sent from England on this circuitous journey were John and Hannah Chamberlain. The couple arrived in New York in July 1802. There, through the hands of New York Baptist pastor William Williams, they received an invitation from William and Maria Staughton to stay at their Burlington, New Jersey, home, where "for the reception of Baptist Missionaries, the doors stand ever open." Staughton asked Williams to "tell Mr. and Mrs. C. I can increase their relish for Calcutta (or rather Serampore) by shewing them vegetables &c. in my garden, the seeds of which were transplanted from the garden of the Mission house Bengal."[23] William Staughton, one of the founders of the Baptist Missionary Society, was already attempting to start a foreign mission society in the United States. Chamberlain wrote of Staughton,

> He interests himself much in the prosperity of Zion, partakes of a missionary spirit, and stands as a witness against the negligence of many in their country who profess Christianity. At several Associations, he has proposed that something should be done for the spread of the gospel among the heathen: and though it has been hitherto in vain, yet he renews his applications every year, and I hope he will finally succeed. His object is to establish a Society in this place, to co-operate with the Baptist Missionary Society in England, or to send missionaries among the heathen from hence.[24]

The Chamberlains remained in the United States for more than a year until they found an American ship sailing to India.

The next visits by British Baptists to America had unforeseen implications for Charlotte. On Friday afternoon, April 20, 1804, a "fine, fair wind" brought four newly appointed Baptist missionaries and their wives into New York City en route to India.[25] Onboard the brig *Hannah* were John and Hannah Biss with their daughter Mary, Richard and Rhoda Mardon, William and Eleanore Moore, and Joshua and Elizabeth Rowe.[26] Rev. Rowe would dramatically enter Charlotte's life thirteen years later.

In 1806 Joseph Maylin and John Fernandez came to Philadelphia from Serampore, India, on their way to England.[27] Maria and William Staughton hosted them in their home during their Philadelphia stop and introduced them to others with whom they shared information about the Baptist mission in India.[28] Maylin did not continue on to England. Instead, he remained in Philadelphia where in 1807 he married Elizabeth M'Cutchen, joined Dr. Staughton's church, and eventually became an ordained pastor.[29] Eight years later, Maylin would become a valuable informant for Charlotte.

In 1810 two more Baptist missionary couples arrived in Philadelphia en route to India, Dr. William and Ann Johns and John and Frances Lawson. While in the area they raised funds for William Carey's Bible translation work. Like Rowe and Maylin, Dr. Johns would be a third Englishman shaping the context in which Charlotte would discern and follow her call.

## Harriet Atwood and Ann Hasseltine

Baptists were not the only people through whom God may have worked to call Charlotte into mission. Two Congregationalist women in and near Haverhill fired the imaginations of those who knew or heard about them. In 1806, the summer of Charlotte's baptism in Haverhill, Harriet Atwood, the thirteen-year-old daughter of Haverhill merchant Moses Atwood, began attending Bradford Academy a half mile away. A spiritual revival had begun in May 1805 in the Haverhill Baptist Church. By the winter it had spread into Bradford where it influenced Harriet and other students at the Academy.[30] "I have found Christ," Harriet wrote. "I felt assured that, if I sought him with my whole heart I should find him; and I *have* found him."[31]

At Bradford Academy, Harriet became friends with Ann (Nancy) Hasseltine, who had come to faith through the revival some months earlier.[32] Harriet had not previously known Ann, who was four years older, though she had lived in sight of Ann's home, which stood a mile from hers but on the Bradford side of the Merrimack River.[33]

Although Ann Hasseltine and Harriet Atwood never met Charlotte face to face, Ann later wrote that she was "well acquainted with [Charlotte's] family connections, who most of them live in Haverhill."[34] Despite her lack of personal contact with either woman, Charlotte could not have missed the stir they caused. People in Haverhill and Bradford had never witnessed such things. Harriet and Ann had accepted marriage proposals. This in itself was not unusual. The startling revelation was both women's declaration that God was calling them to leave America to serve as foreign missionaries with their future husbands.

Their discernment of that call had not come quickly. Neither Ann nor Harriet experienced any miraculously unmistakable knock-you-off-your-horse event as that of the apostle Paul (Acts 9:3-9). They had not had vivid spiritual encounters like that of Patrick (c. 387–461), the British missionary who was called to the Irish while seeing a vision and hearing a voice, or Cyril (826–869), the Greek missionary who was called to the Slavs while struggling to read Gregory of Nazianzus and discovering the power of translation to convey God's Word. Discernment did not come to them in a single moment of clarity as experienced more than a century later by Mother Theresa (1910–1997), the Albanian nun who was called to the poor of Calcutta while riding a train and sensing an awareness so clear that she could say, "It was an order."

Nor did Ann and Harriet recognize God's will through instantaneous, private events. Instead, like many other missionaries, the two women discerned God's call through a gradual process that involved other people.

Ann Hasseltine's call grew from her simple desire "to be useful." Although she initially lacked a clear sense of God's will, she realized that her education could be useful, so she began teaching several children. Ann continued seeking guidance. While reading Jonathan Edwards's biography of David Brainerd, missionary to Native Americans, she began thinking of people around the world who had yet to experience the fullness of God's love through Jesus Christ.

Then she met Adoniram Judson.

The young seminarian had come to Bradford where the Massachusetts Congregationalist leaders were holding their 1810 General Association meeting. After urging them to form a mission society, Judson was invited to dine at the Hasseltine home, where he met their daughter Ann. When Judson asked Ann to marry him and to share life together as missionaries in Asia, her process of discerning God's call continued. On August 8, 1810, she wrote in her journal,

> Endeavoured to commit myself entirely to God, to be disposed of according to his pleasure... I do feel that his service is my delight. Might I but be the means of converting a single soul, it would be worth spending all my days to accomplish. Yes, I feel willing to be placed in that situation, in which I can do the most good, *though it were to carry the Gospel to the distant, benighted heathen.*[35]

Ann struggled as she sought clarity about God's will. After several months she was closer to a resolution about the Spirit's leading. On the morning of October 10, she visited Harriet, who wrote in her diary, "She informed me of her determination to quit her native land, to endure the sufferings of a Christian amongst heathen nations—to spend her days in India's sultry clime." That conversation with Ann spurred the process of discernment within Harriet. She continued,

> How did this affect my heart! Is she willing to do all this for God; and shall I refuse to lend my little aid, in a land where divine revelation has shed its clearest rays? I have *felt* more for the salvation of the heathen, this day, than I recollect to have felt through my whole past life.... What can *I* do, that the light of the Gospel may shine upon them? They are perishing for lack of knowledge, while I enjoy the glorious privileges of a Christian land! Great God, direct me! O make me in *some* way beneficial to immortal souls.[36]

Like Ann's, Harriet's recognition of God's call to missionary service was not an immediate insight, but a process prompted by an introduction. She recorded it in her diary: "Oct 23, Mr M introduced Mr Newell to our family. He appears to be an engaged Christian. Expects to spend his life in preaching a Savior to the benighted pagans."[37]

Meanwhile, the process continued for Ann Hasseltine. Her journal entry for October 28 noted, "no female has to my knowledge ever left the shores of America, to spend her life among the heathen; nor do I yet know that I shall have a single female companion."[38]

On April 17, 1811, Harriet received a letter from Samuel Newell proposing marriage. Though Newell requested an immediate answer, Harriet sought counsel from others. A widening circle of Haverhill people came to know about the proposal and its implications. Harriet noted, "*All* my friends with whom I have conversed since my return to Haverhill, advise me to go. Some Christians who were formerly opposed, after obtaining a more extensive knowledge of the subject, think females would be useful." Most importantly, her father having died three years earlier, Harriet sought advice and consent from her mother. With tears in her eyes, Mrs. Atwood gave her daughter counsel that was both wise and compassionate: "If a conviction of duty, and love to the souls of the perishing heathen, lead you to India, as much as I love you, Harriet, I can only say, *'Go.'*[39]

By June 1811, Harriet had answered God and Samuel Newell in the affirmative. Meanwhile, Ann's prayerful consideration of God's call increasingly brought a settled serenity to her mind. Her journal entry of November 23, 1811, stated her resolution on the matter:

> Felt an ardent desire to be instrumental of spreading the knowledge of the Redeemer's name, in a heathen land. Felt it a great, and undeserved privilege, to have an opportunity of going. Yes, I think I

would rather go to India, among the heathen, notwithstanding the almost insurmountable difficulties in the way, than to stay at home and enjoy the comforts and luxuries of life. Faith in Christ will enable me to bear trials, however severe. My hope in his powerful protection animates me to persevere in my purpose. O, if he will condescend to make me useful in promoting his kingdom, I care not where I perform his work, nor how hard it be. *Behold the handmaid of the Lord; be it unto me according to thy word.*[40]

Charlotte White didn't elaborate on how the Holy Spirit used these people and events to help her recognize that God was calling her to mission. But responding to that call, Charlotte moved from Haverhill to Philadelphia.

*Chapter 3*

# WOMEN MISSIONARIES

Philadelphia offered several Baptist churches that Charlotte could join. She chose the newly formed Baptist Church on Sansom Street.

The church's building itself would have drawn her attention. Though just two years old, the church's rapid growth had created the need for a new house of worship. The meetinghouse they built had very distinctive architecture. It was circular in form with 300 pews and a round baptistery in the center. The distinctive style may have been suggested by the equally eye-catching round building on Sansom Street standing immediately beside the new church. The pre-existing round building was an amphitheater, the interior of which depicted a panorama of the Holy Land.[1] Together, the two round buildings attracted the attention of citizens and visitors alike. When the new church building was dedicated with three worship services on August 16, 1812, the first service alone attracted more than three thousand people.[2]

Sansom Street was a very mission-active church. Its commitment to mission was symbolized by the presence of Elder Edmund J. Reis, who opened the afternoon dedication service with prayer. Ries was from Paris and had become a Christian in 1807 in Nova Scotia. Informally supported as a missionary by the Massachusetts Baptist Missionary Society,[3] he passed through Philadelphia en route to New Orleans, where he would be the first Baptist missionary in New Orleans and the first French-speaking Baptist pastor in all of Louisiana.[4] Reis "drew thousands after him, so novel was the sight of an evangelical French Baptist minister."[5] In

Philadelphia he drew much attention by delivering a discourse in French in the newly built Sansom Street church. It was fitting that the French missionary should pray at the church's dedication.

## William and Maria Staughton—Charlotte's Advocates

Even better known than the church's architecture or any of its dedication day participants was the church's pastor, the Rev. Dr. William Staughton. Born in England in 1770, Staughton would help lead Baptists in the United States to unite nationwide around foreign mission as he had in England.

In 1792, while still a student at Bristol College, William Staughton had been drawn to the mission passion and logical reasoning of the cobbler William Carey who was also a Baptist pastor. Carey had written *An Enquiry into the Obligations of Christians to use Means for the Conversion of the Heathens.* In it he argued that Jesus' command to make disciples of all nations was not limited to the twelve apostles but was an enduring command for all Christians in every age. The *Enquiry* proposed that Baptists form a voluntary society for the purpose of sending and supporting missionaries. On October 2, 1792, in Kettering, England, Staughton and eleven pastors founded the Baptist Missionary Society (BMS). Since the young Staughton was not yet an ordained minister, he did not sign the society's founding document.[6] He nevertheless demonstrated his wholehearted commitment to the cause by emptying his pockets to give all that he had—a borrowed half-guinea.[7]

Though he was but a twenty-two-year-old seminarian, Staughton was elected to the society's executive committee. He subsequently helped select and appoint William Carey and Dr. John Thomas as the society's first missionaries and was on the wharf in March 1793 to pray with Carey and Thomas when they departed for India.

That autumn, Staughton, having been recruited by Richard Furman to organize a new Baptist church in South Carolina, moved to America. Sailing with William Staughton was Maria Martin Hanson, the woman to whom he was engaged. They married soon after their arrival in South Carolina. Then they moved from Charleston to Georgetown where they organized that city's first Baptist church.

William and Maria abhorred the slavery surrounding them in South Carolina and after two years resolved to move. In 1795 they sailed north from Charleston to New York. After seven days of pleasant winds and success in avoiding privateers, the Staughtons' ship arrived in New York City. William wrote appreciatively, "The climate is pleasant, and the city very strongly resembles an English seaport." Meanwhile, the yellow fever that two years earlier had taken the lives of 10 percent of Philadelphia's population and made Charlotte an orphan, had spread elsewhere. New York tried to keep the epidemic at bay by placing boats from Philadelphia under quarantine. Those efforts succeeded—for a while.

As the Staughtons arrived in New York, they did not know that yellow fever was already in the city.[8] Several weeks after their arrival, William contracted the fever. Maria worked "with incessant watching and toil" and, despite her own illness, slowly nursed him back from "almost to the grave."[9] William owed his life to Maria.

Maria's father was a medical doctor and had provided her with formal education. Years later at her deathbed, William Staughton would recite lines of Latin poetry to her, knowing that she understood.[10] Maria's education had enabled her to teach in Europe, and she had continued her profession while in South Carolina by "keeping a boarding school for young ladies."[11] In New York, William Staughton advertised for students, and Maria "was known to have opened a girls' school that year."[12] As soon as they were able, the Staughtons moved to a healthier location and assumed operation of an academy in Bordentown, New Jersey, where William also preached and was ordained.[13] Later they moved to Burlington, New Jersey, to run a boarding school academy. There, William became pastor of the Baptist church and expanded his ministry. In all those endeavors Maria proved to be a full and effective partner.

In 1805, after preaching numerous times in Philadelphia as a visiting minister, William Staughton was given a one-year call to the First Baptist Church. Maria and their children continued to live in Burlington when William began that ministry. The next year William became the church's permanent pastor. The congregation was "one of the smallest in the city," but in the next five years under Staughton's leadership it added more than four hundred more members.[14]

William Staughton would later say that one of the greatest achievements of his life was helping to organize the Baptist Missionary Society and send William Carey to India. His commitment to mission that first expressed itself in Kettering, England, continued to grow in Philadelphia. Staughton maintained trans-oceanic correspondence with William Carey, sharing encouraging thoughts about mission and even sending North American plant specimens to Carey. His correspondents in Serampore, India, expanded to include William Ward, Joshua Marshman, and others. By 1811 Staughton's extensive contacts had enabled him to write *The Baptist Mission in India*, a 312-page narrative of the British Baptist mission effort in India. Joseph Maylin, the Staughtons' guest from Serampore, once remarked to William, "The arrival of a vessel from Philadelphia, without letters from you, will pain the friends of the Mission House."[15] Maria Staughton seems to have known Carey from England as well, as she also sent messages to him and his associates.

As a mission theorist, William Staughton recognized the power of collective effort. He was willing to work both ecumenically and among the Baptists to accomplish mission objectives. In May 1798 he delivered a discourse titled *Missionary-Encouragement* to the Philadelphia Missionary Society and the congregation of Baptist Meeting House in Philadelphia. The ecumenical society comprised mostly Presbyterians, Baptists, and Congregationalists working together to promote mission in new settlements on the U.S. frontier and within the Native American nations. In 1804 the Baptists formed the Philadelphia Baptist Missionary Society for similar purposes. And by 1813 they organized the Philadelphia Baptist Foreign Mission Society to take initiative in mission in foreign nations. Staughton was a leading and motivating force in all these settings.

The First Baptist Church had twice released groups of its members to form the nuclei of new Baptist congregations in northern and southern parts of Philadelphia. By 1811 the church had again "grown to a size too unwieldly [*sic*] for its comfort."[16] Some members of First Baptist were also uncomfortable because they felt Dr. Staughton was tending to make the church "too British." This, at the very time that political tensions were growing between the United States and Britain, tensions that would lead President James Madison to declare war on England and start the War of 1812.

In a move that eased both the mounting physical and relational pressure, a group of members requested dismissal from First Baptist to form a church on the city's west side. There they organized the Fifth Baptist Church, commonly called Sansom Street Baptist Church, and invited Dr. Staughton to be their first pastor.

As had been the case at First Baptist, the Sansom Street church grew rapidly under Staughton's pastoral leadership. Many of the new members were people that came to faith under Staughton's ministry and joined the church by baptism. Others joined by transferring their membership from other churches. This was the church that Charlotte White chose to join—a two-year-old church with a one-year-old building and a mission activist pastor.

Following worship on September 3, 1813, the congregation convened a meeting to read a letter from the Baptist Church at Haverhill, Massachusetts, dismissing Charlotte H. White from their membership so she could join the Sansom Street church. The church unanimously received Charlotte into membership and then adjourned the meeting.

They had no idea what their newest member would become.

## Women as "Assistant Missionaries"

But what had Harriet and Ann become? On Wednesday, February 5, 1812, Rev. Jonathan Allen stood in Haverhill's Congregational church and preached his *Sermon on the Occasion of two Young Ladies being about to embark as the wives of Rev. Messieurs Judson and Newell, going Missionaries to India.* The expectation that both missionary couples would be present was frustrated. Earlier that morning Rev. Allen had conducted the wedding ceremony for Adoniram and Ann in the Hasseltine home in Bradford. Now in the afternoon, the Judsons as well as Samuel Newell had been "providentially called away." Rev. Allen accordingly abridged his sermon, but later published and circulated it in its full form. Rev. Allen directed a portion of his sermon personally to Harriet and Ann:

> You are now engaged in the best of causes. It is that cause for which Jesus the Son of God came into the world suffered and died. You literally forsake father and mother, brothers and sisters, for the sake of Christ, and the promotion of his kingdom. In this employment, you, probably, have an arduous work before you—A work, that will occupy all your talents and much of your time.[17]

Rev. Allen expressed his firm belief that Harriet and Ann would minister among women in India to whom their husbands could have little or no access. They would have the privilege of enlightening women's minds and affirming their dignity.

> Teach them to realize that they are not an inferior race of creatures, but stand upon a par with men. Teach them that they have

immortal souls, and are no longer to burn themselves, in the same fire, with the bodies of their departed husbands. Go, bring them from their cloisters into the assemblies of the saints. Teach them to accept of Christ as their Savior, and to enjoy the privileges of the children of God.

Should you be able, in any measure, to raise the female character in the east, and bring but a small proportion of them to know their Savior, it will, undoubtedly, afford you great satisfaction.... May you live to see the fruit of your labors, in the conversion of thousands of your sisters in the east, and find that they, with their husbands and others, have turned from their Idols, to serve the only living and true God. And may the Lord himself be with you, and support and comfort you, and be your portion forever.[18]

Despite having delivered such inspiring words, Rev. Allen's sermon characterized the women as wives who would assist their husbands. Rev. Allen assured Harriet's and Ann's parents that their daughters were departing not because they wanted to leave their families but "because they have a desire to aid those, who are going to carry the glad tidings of the gospel to the heathen."[19] As if to reinforce this concept, the congregation sang a hymn composed for the occasion that proclaimed in its first two verses:

Go, ye heralds of salvation;

> Go, and preach in heathen lands;
Publish loud to every nation,
> What the LORD of life commands.

Go, ye sisters their companions,
> Sooth [sic] their cares, and wipe their tears;
Angels shall in bright battalions
> Guide your steps, and guard your fears.[20]

The message was subliminal but nevertheless clear. Samuel and Adoniram were the heralds of salvation. Harriet and Ann were their assisting companions.

The next day in Salem, Harriet Atwood and Ann Hasseltine Judson joined the assembled congregation while their husbands and their colleagues Samuel Nott, Gordon Hall, and Luther Rice, were ordained as clergy and commissioned as missionaries. At the culmination of the service, Ann Judson was moved to rise from her seat, step into the aisle, and kneel at the end of the pew alongside the men. The hands of the clergy, however, were laid only upon the men, commissioning them as missionaries.[21] Ann, Harriet, and Samuel Nott's future wife, Roxana Peck,[22] were indeed being sent, but as wives and assistants without appointment.

Both secular and religious media reported the unprecedented event of five American men being sent as missionaries to Asia. The *Philadelphia Gazette* covered the February 18 departure from Philadelphia of the two single men Hall and Rice as well as the four married men William Johns, John Lawson, Robert May, and Samuel Nott, each accompanied by "and lady."[23] The *Massachusetts Baptist Missionary Magazine* reprinted the *Gazette* article and reported the men's February 6 ordination in Salem as well as the February 19 departure from Salem of Newell and Judson "with their wives."[24] The women had no appointments and, apparently, no names.

Ann and Adoniram Judson departed from Salem in the brig *Caravan* with Harriet and Samuel Newell. A week later, Roxana and Samuel Nott sailed from Philadelphia in the ship *Harmony* with Gordon Hall and Luther Rice. The decision to divide the missionaries into two parties and send them aboard two separate vessels was undoubtedly a security measure. If one of the ships encountered mortal danger on the journey, there could be hope that the other party might survive. And indeed there were dangers to encounter. About one week out from Salem, the *Caravan* sprang a leak that almost sent the Newells and Judsons to the ocean bottom. Meanwhile, England and France were at war and neither nation was honoring the neutrality of American vessels. Britain worked to keep its naval power at full strength by stopping American vessels, removing sailors, and impressing them into the British navy. And as always, ship-destroying storms and mercenary pirates were continual threats. There were good reasons to send the missionaries forth with prayer and in two separate parties.

## Willing, Unwilling, Coerced, and Circumstantial

Judson, Newell, and Nott were fortunate to be accompanied by spouses who were eager to serve as missionaries. Twenty years earlier, the first two British Baptist missionary couples struggled with whether both spouses discerned the same call to mission. Dr. John Thomas had sailed twice to India as a surgeon for the East India Company, leaving his wife and family behind in England for more than six years. When the newly constituted Baptist Missionary Society chose to send John Thomas and William Carey as missionaries to India, Mrs. Thomas consented to go. Dorothy Carey, however, "never shared her husband's aspirations." She refused to go.

William Carey took the Careys' eight-year-old son Felix with him to India. Felix and his father boarded the *Earl of Oxford* to depart from London along with Dr. and Mrs. Thomas and the Thomases' young daughter. The *Oxford* started down the River Thames but was halted when the East India Company claimed that the captain had taken on an unspecified, unlicensed passenger. John Thomas, William Carey, and young Felix disembarked to sort things out while, amazingly, Mrs. Thomas and her daughter continued on to Calcutta without them, "in hopes that the rest would find means to follow."[25]

Back on shore, William Carey again tried to convince his wife to change her mind, but to no avail. John Thomas then insisted on visiting Dorothy. Thomas later described how he argued Dorothy Carey into coming.

> I went back, and told Mrs. Carey her going out with us was a matter of such importance, I could not leave her so—her family would be dispersed and divided for ever—*she would repent of it as long as she lived.* As she tells me since, this last saying frequently repeated, had such an effect upon her, that she was afraid to stay at home; and afterward, in a few minutes, determined to go, trusting in the Lord; but this should be on condition of her sister going with her. This was agreed to.[26]

Dorothy Carey left England under duress. Fear of losing her children and dire warnings of future remorse were powerful motivators. It is unknown whether this caused or only intensified Dorothy's ensuing mental illness in India.

In the United States as well, it was not a foregone conclusion that a woman would marry a man intent on service as a missionary. The appointment of missionaries was novel. The thought of being a missionary was daunting. Accepting a marriage proposal was disquieting if it meant never again seeing one's family for the sake of mission in a distant land. Luther Rice courted Rebecca Eaton in Massachusetts. Rebecca gave every indication that she felt drawn to Luther, but to his deep regret Rebecca did not share his call to mission, and the relationship ended.[27] Luther remained single.

Gordon Hall did not find a bride until he arrived in India. There he met and married Margaret Lewis, an English woman already residing in Bombay. Margaret's fluency in Marathi equipped her to partner effectively with him in what came to be called the American Marathi Mission.[28]

## Sarah Farquhar Loveless

Gordon Hall was not the first American to find a missionary spouse in Asia. That precedent was set ten years earlier by an American Presbyterian woman, Sarah Farquhar (also Farquharson). Like Margaret Lewis, Sarah had moved to India for reasons other than mission. A native of Long Island, Sarah received formal education in New York at the prestigious school for girls run by Scottish American educator Isabella Graham. Sarah's intellect and management skills made her Graham's assistant. When Isabella Graham retired, she asked her student and friend Sarah to lead the school, but Sarah declined.[29]

Meanwhile, the yellow fever that had nearly taken William Staughton's life in 1795 re-emerged in New York in 1798, 1802, 1804, and 1805. Sarah survived the 1804 epidemic but in a greatly weakened state. Her doctor urged her to move to a warmer climate to save her life. Providentially, her beloved teacher's merchant son-in-law was sailing to Madras and Calcutta via London and accepted Sarah as a passenger. Their ship, the *Alleghany,* crossed the Atlantic and arrived in London in late 1804.

Before the *Alleghany* departed London for India, John Taylor and William C. Loveless boarded the ship. The two Englishmen were missionaries whom the London Missionary Society was sending to Surat in northwest India. After the East India Company denied them permission to travel on its ships, they were eager to circumvent the travel ban by sailing on an American vessel. During the voyage, a romance ensued between Loveless and Farquhar that led to their marriage at the Fort Church in Madras in May 1806. Getting to India was just the first challenge. Now the couple had to evade the threat of being expelled by the East India Company for lack of a company license to live in India. To do so, Loveless became superintendent of the Military Orphan Male Asylum where he and Sarah cared for 350 boys.

An early biographer who was unaware of Hannah Liele claimed that Sarah Farquhar was "the first American female who engaged in foreign missions."[30] Others who have also been unaware of Hannah Liele have repeated that mistaken claim although Sarah followed Hannah by twenty-four years.

Like Hannah, Sarah engaged in effective mission. Sarah and William Loveless found a measure of distance from the East India Company's influence by building "Loveless Chapel" in Black Town outside the Madras fort in the midst of Hindu temples. They started schools for boys and girls without regard to their religious backgrounds. After William left his role as superintendent of the Military Asylum in 1812, he and Sarah supported themselves by starting a boarding school. They had up to thirty boarders in addition to day students. Some of their students were girls. The business skills Sarah had learned under Isabella Graham's tutelage in New York made these endeavors highly successful. William acknowledged that, "through the blessing of God on (Sarah's) agency, in advice and management, I owe chiefly my temporal prosperity in India, and the enjoyment of it in England."[31]

Sarah recognized that a good education had opened opportunities for her and that schooling could also have positive impact in the lives of women and girls in India. Despite the schools that she and William had already begun, Sarah saw that a huge need still existed. Girls were either the last to be offered spaces in schools or were ignored altogether. Many locals lacked any real concern and simply said, "It is not the Malabar custom to teach women to read."[32] Whereas other avenues may have been closed to Sarah, Loveless Chapel was a setting in which she could introduce change. Sarah therefore started a Free School for girls in connection with the chapel.

Even a free school, however, required financial resources. Because the East India Company had developed Madras into their chief seaport on India's east coast, the fortified city had become "the Presidency," the seat of colonial government for the area. A growing number of Europeans had settled in Madras to attend to its commercial, governmental, and military needs. Using her diplomatic skills, Sarah built relationships with enough Europeans residing within the Madras Presidency to secure the financial support needed for the school. This was a major achievement because the officials of the East India Company resisted the work of evangelical missionaries among the local people and specifically opposed education for the local populace because they feared it would imperil colonial rule. In 1792 William Wilberforce had sought to introduce clauses into the East

India Company's Charter Act to promote education in India. It was the first time that the company's court of directors had been obliged to publicly address the topic. During the debate in Parliament, one of the directors advanced the view that England had lost the American colonies due in part to the folly of having allowed schools and colleges to be established in America. The director warned against repeating that folly in India.[33] Opposition to Wilberforce's clauses was so great that they were withdrawn.

Sarah's networking among the expatriate community was remarkable also because Sarah was an introvert. Her biographer wrote that she

> was of a most retiring disposition, and could speak but little, from natural diffidence; yet, when in the presence of friends, and especially when among the poor of her own sex, and among children, then her embarrassment was removed, and she would reprove any tendency to sin, and direct them to Christ as the only Saviour, with peculiar tenderness and becoming faithfulness.[34]

Even while deeply involved in educational ministry, Sarah exercised a robust gift of hospitality. The Loveless home became a veritable inn where Sarah hosted a continuing stream of missionaries entering and departing India through Madras. This included Ann and Adoniram Judson.

In 1813 the East India Company, regarding them as unwanted evangelicals who had arrived without permission, ordered the Judsons to leave India. Before the company could remove them to England, the Judsons left Calcutta seeking somewhere else to settle into mission work. They sailed to the Isle of France (Mauritius), then tried to find passage to Penang, Malaysia, and finally sailed to Madras. Sarah and William Loveless cared for them in Madras until they found a small Portuguese vessel that took them to Rangoon.[35]

In 1815 ill health forced Ann Judson to sail to Madras to seek medical help that was not available in Rangoon. Ann again stayed in the Loveless home in Madras where for three months "every kind attention was paid to her."[36]

Two years later Adoniram Judson unexpectedly found himself again dependent upon Sarah and William Loveless. Judson had attempted to sail from Rangoon to Chittagong in 1817 to recruit assistance for the American mission in Burma. Contrary winds and the unmanageable nature of the vessel caused Judson's ship to be diverted to Madras. Stranded and sick, Judson survived because of Sarah and William's care. Eventually a ship arrived that could return him to Rangoon. Adoniram had expected to be away from Ann for three months. His ordeal lasted eight months.[37]

Through the years, Sarah bore four children to William. Heartache comingled with joy as one by one, the first three children died. When their fourth child became seriously ill, William and Sarah decided to send the child to England to save his life.[38] Finally in 1824, fifty-year-old Sarah's health had become so weakened that she and William moved permanently to England where they were reunited with their son. Thirteen years later, on September 20, 1837, Sarah died just three days before her sixty-third birthday.

*Chapter 4*

## CLOSER TO APPOINTMENT

Charlotte White's precise location in February 1812 is uncertain. If still in Haverhill, she would have been near four much talked about events: the Newell-Atwood and Judson-Hasseltine weddings, the missionary ordination service, and the couples' departure from Salem. If already in Philadelphia, she would have been near three memorable events occurring on three consecutive days: On Sunday, February 16, several Philadelphia churches collected offerings to support the Congregationalist missionaries Hall, Rice, and the Notts.[1] On Monday night, February 17, a large interdenominational crowd filled the independent Tabernacle church to pray for and bid farewell to the India-bound missionaries. Charlotte may have been in attendance that night. Most of the Baptist pastors were present, and her new pastor, William Staughton, was among the Baptist, Presbyterian, and Independent pastors who lead the ecumenical prayer service. On Tuesday, February 18, a large crowd assembled to watch the missionaries depart Philadelphia and move in a small packet boat down the Delaware River. At New Castle, Delaware, they boarded the *Harmony* and continued on to Port Penn until, on February 24, a strong wind moved them out to sea.

The *Harmony* carried thirty-nine passengers, twelve of whom constituted the party of missionaries. On board with the Congregationalists Notts, Hall, and Rice were three other missionary couples and two single women from England. The two British Baptist couples were the aforementioned William and Ann Johns and child as well as John and Frances

Lawson and child. The London Missionary Society had sent the third couple, Robert May, his wife, and child. The single women were Miss Green and Miss Chaffin.[2]

The perceived role of the two single women would have relevance to the sending of Charlotte White several years later. Miss Green from the London Missionary Society may have been sent to assist the May family as a nurse or housekeeper.[3] The other single woman was Miss Ann Chaffin. Luther Rice's February 19, 1812, journal entry identified her as among the British Baptist passengers: "Mr. Johns & his wife and child, Mr. Lawson, & his wife and child, & Miss Chaffin their nurse, baptist missionaries."[4]

The implication was that Miss Chaffin was sent to assist one or both families with childcare rather than with direct missionary service. Nevertheless, Ann Chaffin served in Serampore with Dr. Johns and was reputedly the first woman missionary nurse in India.[5] Neither Green nor Chaffin had been appointed by their respective mission societies. Their presence was hardly noted. Gordon Hall wrote from the *Harmony* listing the Baptists on board as the Johns, Lawsons, two children, "and an unmarried female."[6] Their role as missionaries was largely unacknowledged in both the secular and religious press.

The English missionaries had sailed late in 1810, first going to America like others before them to evade East India Company travel ban.[7] Following a short stay, they departed for India in the *Daphne*. A fierce storm nearly sank their ship, and they struggled back to shore. It would be a year before new arrangements could be made for them to continue their journey to India on the *Harmony*, a ship they regarded as more seaworthy than the repaired *Daphne*.[8] While in the States, the Lawsons lived for a time with the Staughtons. Rev. Lawson preached at Sansom Street Baptist Church and was well regarded as a particularly effective preacher to children. The Rev. Dr. Johns preached and collected funds in Boston, Salem, and Philadelphia for Carey's Indian Bible translation work. Little did Staughton or anyone else imagine that Johns would be the catalyst leading Rice to become a Baptist.

The long journey to Calcutta was particularly trying for Luther Rice. He was seasick much of the time. Added to this was the other persistent annoyance, the Rev. Dr. Johns. Throughout the voyage, Johns challenged Rice's view that infant baptism was scriptural. Rice must have expected discussion about baptism to arise with the British Baptists in India, for he had brought with him Alexander Pirie's 1786 book, *A Dissertation on Baptism Intended to Illustrate the Origin, History, Design, Mode and Subjects of the Institution, Wherein the Mistakes of the Quakers and Baptists on that subject are Pointed Out and their Objections Refuted.*[9] During the journey he studied the book to build his defense against Rev. Johns. He continued examining the subject once he arrived in India and, to his surprise, found that he and the Judsons had come to similar understandings about baptism. On September 6, 1812, Ann and Adoniram Judson were baptized by immersion in Calcutta by British Baptist missionary William Ward. Two months later, on November 1, 1812, in the same Lall Bazar Baptist Church, William Ward also baptized Luther Rice.[10]

By 1813 Charlotte White had joined the Sansom Street Baptist Church. When the Judsons and Rice became Baptists in India, Carey and his co-worker William Ward sent the surprising news to William Staughton. Carey pressed Staughton to help Baptists form a mission society in America, either as an auxiliary to the British society or as an independent, sister society. Carey and his colleagues would help the Americans as they were able but could not appropriate funds without London's consent. The need for Baptists in America to organize was urgent. "Do stir in this business," Carey wrote Staughton.[11] Ward, who had baptized the Americans, was equally emphatic, saying, "Put your shoulder to this, my dear Staughton."[12] The Americans needed a base of support in the United States that could last beyond initial enthusiasm and occasional generosity; they needed an agency that could call, prepare, care for, and ensure accountability of missionaries.

William Staughton had been promoting the formation of an American Baptist foreign mission agency as early as 1802. Now Charlotte's pastor and his new church were able to become deeply involved in building that kind of agency.

## Organizing Nationally for Mission

A growing sense of mission had already led Baptists to begin organizing local missionary societies. Those scattered societies knew, however, that they could not achieve the coordination, financial support, and continuity necessary for long-term sustainability. Luther Rice returned from India and traveled tirelessly, repeating the call from Staughton and others for a national organization. Finally, in May 1814, delegates from eleven states and the District of Columbia gathered for eight days at Philadelphia's First Baptist Church. On May 21 they formed the "General Missionary Convention of the Baptist Denomination in the United States of America for Foreign Mission."

Because the convention would meet every three years, it quickly became dubbed the "Triennial Convention" and formed a "Baptist Board of Foreign Missions" to conduct the ongoing work of missionary appointment, instruction, and oversight.[13] William Staughton was chosen to be the founding corresponding secretary. The Board knew that the new Baptists, Adoniram and Ann Judson, were already serving in Burma and immediately appointed Adoniram as its first missionary. Like the Congregationalist board before it, the Baptist Board did not appoint Ann.

## Sansom Street Baptist Women Organize

The presence of Charlotte White, Maria Staughton, or any other women during the eight days of deliberation cannot be documented since only the names of the delegates were listed, and the official delegates were all men. Donations to the Triennial Convention, however, were noted, and the first recorded contribution was fifty dollars given by a woman.[14] Five weeks later, Charlotte and other women from the Sansom Street Baptist Church met at Maria and William Staughton's home. Luther Rice, also a Sansom Street church member, was the only man other than William Staughton whose presence at this meeting was recorded. Luther was asked to record minutes of the meeting.[15]

William Staughton opened the meeting on that Monday morning, June 27, by reading from Isaiah 52. Given the purpose of the gathering, he undoubtedly focused on the seventh verse that extolls messengers who announce peace, good news, salvation, and God's reign.

Maria, Charlotte, and the rest of the women were committed to sending and supporting missionaries to share that good news. They knew about the Philadelphia Baptist Society for Foreign Missions, the citywide body that William Staughton had helped to organize the previous December.[16] But the women believed it would be more effective to have a number of local mission societies throughout Philadelphia since one general society for the whole city "might become too unwieldy for convenience." Left unsaid was the fact that the citywide organization was male dominated. The women proceeded to organize their own Sansom Street Baptist Female

Society for Promoting Evangelical Missions. Although theirs was an autonomous body, the women did not have a separatist attitude. Instead they committed "to assist the Philadelphia Baptist Society for Foreign Missions or the General Convention that has assembled in Philadelphia."[17]

The women elected twenty from among their group to serve as managers, one less than the number of men serving on the Baptist Board of Foreign Missions. Charlotte White was one of the twenty. Listed in alphabetical order the women were:

| | |
|---|---|
| Mrs. Anderson | Mrs. Norman |
| Mrs. Earp | Mrs. Owen |
| Mrs. Gregory | Miss Ought |
| Mrs. Howe | Miss Randall |
| Miss Lockhart | Mrs. Staughton |
| Mrs. Maylin | Mrs. Smith |
| Mrs. Morris | Mrs. Simes |
| Miss Miles | Mrs. Welsh |
| Miss Musser | Mrs. White |
| Miss Nicholson | Mrs. Wythe |

The women then elected Maria Staughton as "First Directress" and Charlotte White as one of four "vice-directresses." A total of eight women served together as the full slate of officers:

| | |
|---|---|
| First Directress | Mrs. Staughton |
| Vice-Directresses | Mrs. Maylin |
| | Mrs. Nicholson |
| | Mrs. Norman |
| | Mrs. White |
| Treasurer | Mrs. Smith |
| Corresponding Secretary | Miss Randall |
| Recording Secretary | Miss Miles |

Notable also was the selection of Mrs. Maylin as a vice-directress. Except for Luther Rice, who had been there briefly, Mrs. Maylin's husband was the only person in the Sansom Street congregation, indeed in all of Philadelphia, who had lived in Serampore and had seen the British Baptist mission in operation firsthand. The Maylins' knowledge and perspective were of great value to the women's society in general and to Charlotte

White in particular.

The women knew that a sustainable organization needed a clear process for leadership succession. To that end they agreed that when needed, a new vice-directress would be chosen based on the person's age, length of service in the society, or by the mutual agreement of the managers.

They decided to hold the society's annual meeting on the first Monday of each July and to meet bi-monthly in August, October, December, February, April, and June. They further agreed that members would pledge to contribute at least $1 per year. Any woman contributing $25 would be named a life member.

Luther Rice told the group that the Sansom Street society was the first woman's society in the United States "after your sisters in New York, whose express object is to extend the knowledge of salvation to those benighted souls, who ignorant of the precious name of Jesus, are *perishing for lack of vision.*"

While Rice appropriately recognized the New-York Baptist Female Society for Promoting Foreign Missions, he erred in saying it was the only other woman's society in existence. Mary Webb had organized the Boston Female Society for Missionary Purposes fourteen years earlier. Luther Rice may have been unaware of the Boston society, or he may have intended to only cite *Baptist* societies, knowing that Mary Webb's was ecumenical and included both Baptist and Congregationalist women.

Nevertheless, Rice underscored the potential outcomes in India of the women's efforts. Their endeavors could result in saving infants from being drowned in the Ganges and widows from being burned on funeral pyres.

Luther Rice's minutes did not identify the author of the society's constitution. If written by a woman, the author was most likely Maria Staughton. While source materials on Maria are rare, those available paint a picture of a remarkable individual. People who knew her all testified to her character and abilities.

Richard Furman, the prominent South Carolina Baptist clergyman who recruited William Staughton to move to the United States and conducted William and Maria's wedding, had observed Maria's work as an educator when the Staughtons lived in South Carolina. Furman said Maria was "eminently qualified" and had "taught with reputation in this country as well as in Europe."[18]

James D. Knowles had known Maria when he was a student at Columbian College during William Staughton's presidency of the college.

Following Maria's death, Knowles wrote to Staughton on behalf of a committee of students. Betraying a cultural prejudice that expected to find strong intelligence only among men, Knowles praised Maria Staughton for "her masculine intellect." In his appreciative reply, William Staughton acknowledged that Maria "was not less a friend of science than a disciple of Jesus."[19]

The third and perhaps most distinctive tribute to Maria came from Josiah Randall, a close associate of the Staughtons. Josiah's father, Matthew, was a merchant who had emigrated from London and settled in Philadelphia in 1783. Matthew's wife, Mary, their son Josiah, and his five sisters moved to Philadelphia the following year. When a reversal in business eight years later forced Matthew to work temporarily at sea, Mary Randall, Josiah (then eleven or twelve years old) and his sisters moved to Burlington, New Jersey. The Randalls stayed in Burlington for three years. There they met the Staughtons. Maria and William were operating their academy, and William was pastor of the local Baptist church. The Staughtons and Randalls developed a close relationship. William Staughton baptized Matthew Randall in 1801, and the family joined the Baptist church. Josiah lived in the Staughton home and completed his education under Maria and William's tutelage. When Matthew Randall's finances stabilized, he moved his family back to Philadelphia but retained his membership in the Burlington church for the rest of his life. In May 1814, when the Baptist delegates gathered for eight days in Philadelphia to organize for mission, the Randall home served as a meeting place for various committees. Matthew, representing New Jersey, was among the delegates who founded the Convention.

Josiah Randall subsequently became a prominent lawyer and member of the Pennsylvania state legislature (1819–1820). In 1864 when the American Baptist Missionary Union (as the convention was then called) met to celebrate its fiftieth-year jubilee, Josiah Randall rose to give tribute to William Staughton. While describing his friend, Josiah Randall astutely observed that Staughton "was influenced by his wife, a Goliath in intellect."[20]

Intellect and theological perception were both evident in the language of the Sansom Street Society's constitution. The document presented a theological basis for the society, stating that "the obligations of Christians to diffuse the savour of the Lord Jesus remain unquestionable and strong" and that "God places it in the power of those who profess his name to employ their substance and consultations" for the salvation of others.

Those phrases echoed the language and theology embodied in William Carey's *Enquiry into the Obligation of Christians to use Means for the Conversion of the Heathen.* The assertion that Christians have an obligation to work proactively in global mission signified a shift from rigid Calvinism to a theology that balanced God's sovereignty with humanity's responsibility.

Maria Staughton, like her husband, had been corresponding with the British Baptist missionaries in India and may have known William Carey personally. She certainly knew his writing and affirmed his missiology. Based on its echo of William Carey, either William or Maria Staughton could have authored the Sansom Street Society's constitution.

But one remaining factor may favor Maria Staughton as the author: gender egalitarianism.

William Carey's *Enquiry* bore the subliminal gender bias of its time. Carey had written, "The missionaries must be *men* of great piety, prudence, courage and forbearance." Carey urged people to form themselves into a society to send and support missionaries. Such people "must consist of persons whose whole hearts are in the work, *men* of serious religion and possessing a spirit of perseverance."[21]

The Sansom Street Society's constitution went beyond Carey's pro-mission theology to advance a tightly constructed, four-fold rationale for *women's* engagement in mission.

First, women had a personal stake. The constitution's author wrote,

> Do any ask—why should females engage in this service? It is answered—their important interests are involved. Where the gospel is not, the female character is degraded: where it spreads, woman is happy in domestic life, & happy in realizing its blessed power in the purifying consolation of grace & the reviving prospects of eternal glory. May not a female weep over the desolation of sin & humbly extend her hand for their removal?

Second, there was scriptural precedent. The author asked, "Did Jesus accept the cheerful offers of benevolence from females when on earth, & will he reject them now he is filling his throne in heaven?" Jesus' friendship with Lazarus, Mary, and Martha and his reception of hospitality at their home were well known (Luke 10:38-42). But here the constitution's author may have been carefully noting another Gospel narrative that seems often ignored by men—that women were part of Jesus' traveling company and supported Jesus and the twelve out of their own resources (Luke 8:1-2).

Third, anticipation of the Lord's imminent return pointed to the timeliness of the mission task. But for the author, this eschatology underscored the urgency for women and men to exert themselves equally in mission. "Do not the present times call for the exertion of each of the sexes, when intimations numerous & animating, are given that the glory of the latter days is at hand?"

Finally, the author advanced reasoned pragmatism. Women's societies for other purposes had already been proven successful. It was reasonable to believe that the Sansom Street women's society would be just as successful and useful in pursuit of its purpose, the promotion of evangelical missions. "Have not female associations for the honour of God already been blessed—& may not female example in humble spheres be useful?"

By advancing this four-fold argument in the form of hortatory questions, the author skillfully invited the progressive assent of the readers.

Under Maria Staughton's leadership, the Sansom Street Society provided not only financial resources for mission but also a missionary candidate. After serving for a year as one of the society's four vice-directresses, Charlotte White applied for missionary appointment to Burma. If approved, Charlotte would be the first woman missionary, single or married, to be appointed by the Baptist Board or by any mission agency in America.

## Applying for Appointment

Nine years had passed since Charlotte White's conversion and her discernment in Haverhill that God was calling her to be a missionary. Now, events in Burma stimulated her to apply to the Baptist Board for appointment. Adoniram and Ann Judson, both gifted linguists, had been translating Scripture and writing religious tracts in Burmese. Needing a means to circulate their writings to the Burmese people, the Judsons had asked the board to appoint a missionary with the skills of a printer. The provision for that need came from New England.

George Hough, a native of Windsor, Vermont, had trained as a printer before he was ordained. Hough was the first pastor of the Baptist church in New Bedford, New Hampshire.[22] While there he helped David Benedict produce a history of Baptists in America through "the whole laborious task" of transcribing Benedict's two-volume work for the press.[23] In so doing, his printing expertise served Baptist interests throughout the United States.

Hough's "disposition of mind towards a missionary life" had begun at the time of his conversion. His letter of application to the Baptist Board stated, "For about one year past, my impressions of duty relative to engaging in the India mission have been increasing." Hough's skills now appeared to coincide with the mission's need. He wrote,

> Having spent my early years in acquiring the art of printing, and it having been intimated that a new station would be sought by the American missionaries, where a printing establishment would be eminently useful towards accomplishing the object of the mission, I felt upon my mind a kind of double obligation to offer myself to the respected Board of Foreign Missions for their patronage and assistance; that they would allow me the happiness of making the sacrifices, encountering the trials, enduring the fatigues, and dying the death of a missionary.[24]

In 1815 George Hough and his wife, Phebe, came to Philadelphia to be considered for that work. At the board's request, Hough provided "a written address" discussing his anticipated missionary service. Phebe Hough provided a letter she had written to her parents. Phebe's letter requested her parents' permission to accompany her husband to Burma. At this, the board's "pleasure was greatly heightened." Noting the evidence that the Houghs were "breathing an ardent Missionary spirit," the board appointed George Hough as a missionary on April 11, 1815. The vote was taken "without one dissenting voice."[25]

On Thursday, May 25, 1815, a commissioning service for George Hough was held at Sansom Street Baptist Church. Five Baptist pastors took part in "the imposition of hands." They were William Staughton, Henry Holcombe, William White, Jacob Grigg, and Luther Rice. Staughton prayed as the five clergy laid their hands on George Hough's head and shoulders. Holcombe issued a charge of sacred duties to Hough, and Staughton addressed the assembly. Since Sansom Street was Charlotte White's home church, she was most likely present on that solemn occasion.[26]

During conversations with George and Phebe, Charlotte expressed the desire to travel with them to India. George advised her to apply for appointment by writing to the Baptist Board as he had done. Two months after George Hough's appointment, the board received Charlotte White's letter dated June 13, 1815. Charlotte explained to the board that, "On the coming of Mr. and Mrs. Hough to this city, and my being made acquainted with them and their missionary views, my ardour has been revived, and a desire produced to accompany them to India."[27]

Now the controversy began.

*Chapter 5*

# THE SCANDAL

Charlotte had caused a scandal in the eyes of some members of the Baptist Board of Foreign Missions as well as society at large. By daring to apply for missionary appointment, Charlotte had radically departed from assumptions about a woman's proper role and challenged firmly held views about gender. Since Charlotte was neither male nor ordained, did she qualify to be appointed as a missionary? Those for whom this was a dilemma apparently saw a solution in the fact that the Houghs had two small children. Could not the widowed Mrs. White accompany the Houghs to help care for the children? British mission societies had set this precedent by sending Miss Green, and possibly Miss Chaffin, to assist their missionary couples with children.

Charlotte was apparently aware of that thinking, for she told the board, "My wishes are to reside in [the Hough's] family" but with the crucial qualifier, "in the character of a sister to Mrs. Hough and a sister in the Lord."

Charlotte understood that God was calling her to something other than childcare. She wanted to travel to Burma with the Houghs "to pursue such studies as are requisite to the discharge of missionary duties." Lest the men of the board misunderstand, Charlotte wrote that she expected "to apply what talents I possess wholly to the service of the mission, either in the management of a school, or to hold private meetings, should there be opportunity, with native females, to instruct them in the principles of the gospel, hoping, by the blessing of God, that some of them will be raised from their degraded and miserable condition to participate in the riches of salvation."[1]

Charlotte explained that she had previously "been excluded from rendering any service to the mission, but I now rejoice that God has opened a way." She had no family obligations. She had the Staughtons' support. She was an experienced educator. And she could sail safely to Asia in the company of the Hough family.

The Board considered her application, and on June 14, 1815, voted its approval. Charlotte Hazen Atlee White had become the first American woman to receive official appointment by any sending body to serve as an international, cross-cultural missionary.

## The Hidden Controversy

The controversy arising from Charlotte's appointment was not apparent in the public press. It was, however, far from over and arose from several issues.

One issue was logistical. The Baptist Board of Foreign Missions conducted its business under challenging circumstances. Its twenty-one members were dispersed across twelve states and the District of Columbia. They lived in communities from Massachusetts to Georgia, most of them a considerable distance from Philadelphia where the meetings were held. The Board therefore empowered a quorum of seven members to act on behalf of the whole. Given the difficulty and plodding speed of travel, most of the one-year-old Board's actions were taken by that seven-person quorum.

The votes to appoint Adoniram Judson, Luther Rice, and George Hough had been unanimous. But not the vote for Charlotte White. At least one prominent member disagreed. He was the Rev. Dr. Henry Holcombe, pastor of Philadelphia's First Baptist Church. Recounting the incident five years later, Holcombe frankly acknowledged, "I took an active part in opposing the appointment of Mrs. Charlotte H. White, as a foreign missionary."[2] In 1820 Holcombe published *The Whole Truth,* a book in which he compiled and arranged documents that affirmed his commitment to mission and defended his actions on the board. Each reference to Charlotte White in the book, however, seemed to advance a different reason for Holcombe's opposition to her appointment.

First, he claimed that Charlotte had purchased clothing for her voyage to India before she had formally asked for appointment. Holcombe characterized this as an "underhanded policy," even though the board had as yet formulated no policy, procedure, or sequence to be followed by missionary applicants.

Holcombe's second and rather astounding reason for opposing Charlotte's appointment concerned William Carey's oldest son, Felix. Although citing no evidence, Holcombe questioned Charlotte White's motives: "In the next place, I ventured to oppose the Rev. Dr. Staughton, in an attempt he made to influence the board in favour of engaging our funds to support Mrs. White, a young widow, in case she should marry the celebrated *Felix Carey*."[3]

Felix Carey, four years younger than Charlotte, had begun mission work in Rangoon, Burma in 1807 at age twenty-one. There he experienced multiple sorrows. Within a year of moving to Rangoon, his wife, Margaret, died. Felix's second wife, Miss N. Blackwell, was "Portuguese," a term in British India that meant one whose parentage was Indian and European, whether Portuguese, English, French, Dutch, or Danish.[4] Together they built a family of a son and daughter. At King Bodawpaya's invitation, which may have been perceived as an order, Felix agreed to move to the capitol city of Amarapura where he was to relocate the mission's two printing presses from Rangoon. On August 20, 1814, Felix and his family began making their way to Amarapura. Ten days into their journey, a severe squall struck their brig on the Irrawaddy River, causing it to capsize. Felix barely managed to avoid drowning but could not save his wife and children.[5] He also lost all his household goods and both printing presses.

Mr. William Burls, the British Baptist Missionary Society's treasurer, sent news of the tragic deaths to the Baptist Board in America in March 1815.[6] With that news freshly impressed on his mind, Holcombe suggested that the widow White wanted to go to India simply to marry the widower Carey.

Having objected to Charlotte White's procedure and motive, Holcombe then listed a third objection. He claimed that George Hough's wife had refused to proceed to Burma without a female companion for herself and the two small children. Holcombe contended that Charlotte had agreed to go to Burma as that companion but later changed her mind. According to Holcombe, Charlotte White insisted that "she would never live in the servile state of a companion for Mrs. Hough, nor go to India, except she were put on an equality with male missionaries."[7] In Holcombe's eyes, such equality amounted to Charlotte demanding an "elevation" of her role.

Holcombe's book also reprinted eight letters published in Philadelphia in 1818 that were written anonymously by "PLAIN TRUTH." The letters leveled scandalous charges against both Luther Rice and William Staughton. Henry Holcombe denied writing the letters under that pseudonym, although internal evidence suggested otherwise. The letters clearly represented Holcombe's views and defended his actions. The fifth letter in the series reviewed Charlotte White's appointment and summarized three reasons to oppose her appointment. They were "her sex, her delicate constitution, or want of qualifications for missionary service."[8]

Several others also opposed Charlotte's appointment because of her gender and assumed lack of qualifications. But "PLAIN TRUTH" was the only person who questioned Charlotte White's "delicate constitution." Ironically, despite the punishing south Asian climate and illnesses foreign to North America, Charlotte's health and strength enabled her to live to age eighty-two, twenty-one years longer than Holcombe, who died at sixty-one.

Henry Holcombe's fundamental opposition to Charlotte White's appointment concerned gender and was consistent with views that he had expressed about women during his earlier pastorate in South Carolina. Holcombe was moderator of the Savannah River Association and had written a circular letter to its churches titled "On the Duties and Privileges of Female Members of a Gospel Church." In it he cited Paul's letter to the Corinthians and concluded, "It is well known that a veil was worn in the Apostolic age as a mark of distinction betwixt the sexes, and as indicating the inferiority in some respects, of the woman to the man." According to Holcombe, that inferiority brought restrictions. He granted that women could exercise various ministries and that many women "have proved as useful as ornamental to the Christian church." But, he asserted, women were restricted from any role that might be "an usurpation of authority over the man." Most significantly, according to Holcombe, women were "excluded from sacerdotal honors." Giving the biblical examples of Miriam, Deborah, Priscilla, and Phebe, he noted that "none of these ladies ever departed from the characteristic modesty of their sex, by an assumption of those high and sacred privileges, comprised in the ministerial office, and peculiar, as we have seen, to the man, who is the image and glory of

God."[9] Women in ministry "were not less, but more profitable, from moving in a humbler sphere."

Henry Holcombe believed that most of the board shared his opinion and that they likewise would have refused to appoint Mrs. White had they been present to vote. Although the quorum's majority vote to appoint Charlotte was legal, at the next monthly meeting the men agreed to poll the absent members. Henry Holcombe and William White were appointed to prepare a letter for circulation to the board requesting their opinion about Charlotte's appointment.

When the Board of Foreign Missions met again five days later, Holcombe was not present and the jointly written circular was not available. Inexplicably, Holcombe had chosen to travel to New York rather than meet with White to draft the letter. In its place, Holcombe sent a circular to the meeting that he alone had written. William White likewise brought a draft circular. After both were read and considered, White's draft was unanimously adopted.

The circular letter to the rest of the board's members overcame the logistical issue and focused on the primary source of the controversy. That was a missiological issue that concerned a definition. The word "missionary" had been in use for three centuries after the Jesuits coined it in the 1500s. But what did the word mean? The circular letter said the majority of the quorum "were of opinion that the Term Missionary did not mean a Preacher only; but *one sent*" and "did not mean to restrict the Term [Missionary] to the male sex or Preachers only."[10] The quorum sought clarification from their Board colleagues by asking two pragmatic questions. First, could Luther Rice still be considered a missionary if he remained longer in the United States? Second, did Charlotte White, a nonordained woman, qualify to be appointed as a missionary?

Henry Holcombe had strong opinions about what constituted a "missionary" and believed it was an inappropriate designation for Luther Rice if he remained in the United States. Holcombe wrote, "I pressed the return of the Rev. Luther Rice to India…though contrary, as we have long known, to his intentions."[11] Furthermore, Holcombe believed that missionaries must be ordained preachers and ordained preachers must be male. Therefore, neither Charlotte nor any woman, single or married, could qualify for missionary appointment. But did the rest of the board agree that a missionary must be an ordained male?

The Board's question about Charlotte White was primarily rooted in a third issue: the era's assumptions about gender roles. What was a woman's proper role in society and in the church?

The Baptist commitment to soul freedom and congregational governance within the local church enabled considerable diversity of opinion on this and other questions. Local church governance was balanced, however, by the Baptists' equally historic commitment to interdependence with other believers of similar faith and practice. That interdependence was expressed as individuals covenanted with one another in local churches and as their churches entered voluntary associations with other congregations. Discussions leading to group action took place both within local churches and their associations. Such discussion often occurred in response to specific actions by their members, whether in church or in the wider society.

During the American Revolution, for example, a Middleborough, Massachusetts, Baptist named Deborah Sampson fought in battles disguised as a man and identified as "Robert Shurtleff." Her military service ended when she was hospitalized for fever in Philadelphia and discovered to be a woman. The First Baptist Church of Middleborough subsequently excommunicated Sampson from its membership on September 3, 1782, for "dressing in men's clothes, and enlisting as a Soldier in the Army."[12] It is not clear whether Sampson's church thought dressing in men's clothes or fighting in the army was the greater offense, but they clearly thought neither was acceptable for a woman.

As Baptists considered the appointment of missionaries, gender role assumptions and unresolved definitions combined to influence their expectations. All twenty-one members of the Baptist Board were ordained. Many of them anticipated that their appointed missionaries would likewise be ordained. Although George and Hannah Liele served without appointment or support by any mission agency, George was an ordained pastor. William Carey was a bivocational ordained pastor who supported his family as a cobbler. Dr. John Thomas had been employed by the East India Company as a surgeon but was ordained by British Baptists before being sent back to India as a missionary with Carey. All the British Baptist missionaries who joined Thomas and Carey in India were ordained. The Congregationalists in the United States ordained all five of their first missionaries before their departure. George Hough was considered one of the "first fruits" from the American Baptists as he was a Baptist at the time of his departure.[13] And George Hough was ordained.

Many early nineteenth-century American evangelicals assumed that missionaries would be ordained preachers and presumed that preachers would be male. Baptists with that presumption either ignored or were unaware of the gender egalitarianism that was a distinctive part of their own heritage. Seventeenth-century English Baptists were criticized for allowing "she-preachers" to exercise their gifts.[14] Roger Williams, the iconic founder of the first Baptist church in America, was "emboldened" to become a Baptist by Katherine Scott, sister of Anne Hutchinson. The colonial Massachusetts governor wrote that Hutchinson "exercised publicly," he but did not indicate whether Scott also preached publicly or convinced Rogers through private conversations.[15]

In the 1700s women preachers were known and affirmed among the Separate Baptists. Sarah Wright Townsend preached in her Separate Baptist congregation in Long Island in 1759 and for at least fifteen years following.[16] Along with their male counterparts, Baptist women preachers in Virginia were harassed by the established Anglican church. Margaret Muse Clay, an effective Virginia preacher, was arrested in the mid-1760s for preaching without a license. Clay was sentenced to the humiliation of a public whipping, but she escaped that punishment when an unknown man paid her fine.[17]

The formation and growth of Baptist churches in the South owed much to the gifted preacher Martha Stearns Marshall. Robert B. Semple described Marshall as a woman whose "surprising elocution, has, in countless instances melted a whole concourse into tears by her prayers and exhortations!" Semple's book, *A History of the Rise and Progress of the Baptists in Virginia*, was published in 1810. It reminded his generation of mission-minded Baptists that the famed success of Daniel Marshall was "ascribable in no small degree, to Mrs. Marshall's unwearied, and zealous co-operation." Perhaps aware that his positive statement might challenge his readers' gender role presumptions, Semple added diplomatically that Martha Stearns Marshall was a person of good piety and a "lady of good sense" whose ministry was exercised "without the shadow of a usurped authority over the other sex."[18]

Freewill Baptists were particularly open to women preachers. Mary Savage was preaching publicly as early as 1791. The Freewill Baptist 1797 Yearly Meeting at New Durham, New Hampshire, raised contributions to purchase a horse, saddle, and bridle for Sally Parsons to use as she traveled, exhorted, and prayed. The 1803 Freewill Baptist Quarterly Meeting in

New Durham listed Fanney Proctor, Hannah Lock, and Eliza More as "Publick Preachers and Exhorters."[19] Many Freewill Baptist women were invited to preach in churches beyond their own denomination. For example, Nancy Gove Cram preached in Christian Connexion churches from 1812 until her death in 1816.[20]

## Women in Ministry—Welcomed and Rejected

By the time that Charlotte White was appointed as a missionary in 1815, Baptists and others were of a divided mind about women in a preaching role. This division is evident by the contrasting public responses to two Baptist women preachers—Clarissa Danforth and Rachel Baker.

Clarissa H. Danforth was born in Weathersfield Bow, Vermont, in 1792, ten years after Charlotte Atlee's birth in Pennsylvania. Clarissa's father was a respectable community member who owned a tavern and an ashery. John Danforth took advantage of Weathersfield Bow's location on the Connecticut River to also own a wharf and several river flat boats.[21] The Danforths provided Clarissa a good education that equipped her well for her later ministry. Clarissa came to faith under the preaching of Rev. John Colby, a Freewill Baptist evangelist who passed through Weathersfield on horseback in 1809 en route to Ohio.[22] She preached first in Vermont, then in Massachusetts, New Hampshire, and Rhode Island where she had her most extensive ministry.[23]

Danforth served both as a local church pastor and an itinerating evangelist. Movements of spiritual revival emerged under her leadership. Several men and women who came to faith under her preaching also became prominent pastors and evangelists. Freewill Baptists were not alone in holding Clarissa Danforth in high regard. Churches of other denominations also opened their doors to her. From 1810 to 1820 Danforth was rightly called "the sensation preacher of the decade."[24]

At the mid-point of that decade, Charlotte bought a book containing prayers and seven sermons delivered by another Baptist woman preacher, Rachel Baker, who was two years younger than Clarissa Danforth.[25] While her sermons reflected a moderate Calvinist theology, Baker caused much debate because she was a woman who preached in her sleep!

Rachel Baker was born in 1794 into a pious Presbyterian family in Pelham, Massachusetts. The family moved to Marcellus, New York, in 1803. In 1811 while visiting a friend in Scipio, New York, Rachel witnessed an immersion baptism at the local Baptist church. Struck by what she had witnessed, Rachel became deeply distressed by "almost insupportable" thoughts of her own sinfulness and wretched state.[26]

Five months later, seventeen-year-old Rachel began talking in her sleep, begging for mercy. On January 27, 1812, she awakened in distress. That night she "gave herself up unreservedly into the hands of Almighty God and heard those heart comforting expressions: 'daughter, be of good cheer, thy sins are forgiven thee.'" From then onward when she talked in her sleep, her words were calm and celebrated God's grace.[27]

Rachel moved to Scipio in 1813 to live with an aunt and learn dressmaking. Soon after her arrival she joined Scipio's Baptist church. Her sleep preaching continued and followed a pattern. She began with prayer, followed with a sermon, and concluded with "a kind of ministerial prayer." She spoke calmly and expressively, at times quoting scripture, poetry, or Isaac Watts's hymns. When listeners interrupted her sermons to ask questions, Rachel gave appropriate answers and then resumed preaching.

Rachel's preaching became increasingly well known. Both individuals and groups were allowed to be present at night to witness the evening phenomenon. Stenographers were engaged to transcribe her prayers and sermons in shorthand.

People debated the nature of her preaching. Some felt her sermons were special works of the Holy Spirit, something Rachel explicitly disavowed. Others said Rachel was an impostor seeking to enrich herself, a contention that was undercut because Rachel received no compensation for her sermons. Others believed Rachel was ill and described her night preaching as a "fit," "disorder," "paroxysm," "disease," or "malady."[28]

Rachel claimed she was not asleep when she spoke in the night, but neither was she aware of what she was doing or saying until told by others. She said her night preaching was a heavy burden, and her parents increasingly felt she was ill. In October 1814 she was brought to New York to secure medical counsel. There was also hope that either the travel itself or New York's seaside atmosphere might moderate or stop her sleep talking. On her journey to New York City, the tavern inns in which she stopped for the night attracted the skeptics, the curious, and the believers. All wanted to witness her "involuntary prayers and exhortations." Her fame was spreading. In New York City, multitudes crowded into her chamber to see and hear for themselves.[29]

By now, Rachel Baker was drawing more than regional attention as newspapers in states as distant as Mississippi carried articles about her sleep preaching.[30] Her preaching was, to be sure, a "strange case." But while doctors visited to examine her mentally, clergymen visited to examine her theologically. Tellingly, the clergymen's questions seldom concerned *how* she felt she could preach since she was asleep, but rather *why* she felt she could preach since she was a woman. In early 1815, New York stenographers transcribed the questions that clergy asked Rachel over the course of four evenings:

By what authority do you undertake to preach the gospel?

Do you suppose you have received any supernatural revelation of divine truth?

The apostle says, "I suffer not a woman to teach." Why, then, do you speak in public?

By what authority do you presume to address men?

Do you not violate that command of the apostle, "Suffer not a woman to speak in the church," when you presume thus to address sinners in the name of the Lord?

Why should it be thought, in this enlightened age, the duty of an illiterate female to give instruction on religious subjects?[31]

Rachel's answers were both rational and disarming. She said that she neither preached nor presumed to preach, but the Lord had given her "a lesson to read to the children of men." She acknowledged, "I, in some sense, preach unto you; and in another sense, I do not. I do say that there is no other way to be saved except through the blood of Jesus Christ, the Lord; but what the Lord giveth me, I declare to the children of men."

Rachel dispelled the notion of having any other revelation than that of the Bible. She agreed that the apostle said, "I suffer not a woman to teach" and explained, "I only exhort each of you to be steadfast in the faith: shall I, therefore, presume to be a teacher? If I could do my own will, I would rather not speak to you!"

Rachel knew the clergy's objections were because of her gender. "Shall a woman be silenced because she is a woman, and not improve her gifts?" she asked. "I perfectly agree with the apostle, that it is not proper that she should stand up in the church; and I undertake not to speak."[32] The crucial distinction for Rachel was speaking *in the church*. She was, after all, speaking *in her bedchamber*. She had not gone forth to seek listeners. Listeners had come to her.

Rachel further assured the clergy that she did not speak on her own authority, but by the authority of scripture. Drawing their attention to Peter's words on the day of Pentecost, she quoted the prophecy of Joel that was now being fulfilled: "Behold, sayeth God, I will pour out my spirit upon all flesh, and your sons and your daughters shall prophesy, and your young men shall see visions, and your old men shall dream dreams, and on my servants and on my handmaids I will pour out in the last days of my spirit, and they shall prophesy."[33]

Rachel was a quiet introvert while awake. It was therefore remarkable that while asleep she could challenge her interrogators. She asked one clergyman if the Lord had not said he would "choose the weak thing to confound the things which are mighty." She bravely reminded him, "[E]very one shall stand before the bar of God. I expect to give an account for what I say unto you, and you must give an account how you have heard such a feeble worm as I am."[34]

Should she hold her peace? Rachel replied,

The apostle sayeth, let not a woman stand up in the church as a public teacher: but are you hard of believing; are you hard of understanding? I have told you that I cannot avoid doing these things: my God knoweth what they mean. I do not pretend to teach men; but I only tell them of their danger, and tell them that there is woe to them that are at ease in Zion. God forbid that I should be silent: I pretend to speak nothing but the truth, as it is in Christ Jesus my Lord. Shall a woman hold her peace, because she is a woman? Methinks the apostle meant not so; but meant that they should let their light shine before men. Is it a mystery to you my friends? Let it not be a mystery any longer, but rather leave it in the hands of the living God; he will do what is best and right.[35]

When asked why she preached in the night and not in the day, Rachel reiterated that she only spoke what the Lord gave her. She insisted, "You may say that I *preach*, but I do not say that I do. I only read the lesson which my God giveth me."[36]

Rachel did not hide her personal limitations. She had received only seven months of formal education and was not fond of reading.[37] "Truly I have not had the advantage of education," she said, "I am but a poor ignorant child." She simply spoke what God seemed to reveal to her, and while it seemed hard to understand, "yet it is easy with him to accomplish his will by the weakest instruments."[38]

How was she able to preach with such fluency and intelligence? New York stenographer Charles Mais reported that Rachel's father had frequently opened the Baker home to traveling preachers. As a child with a very retentive memory, it could be assumed that Rachel's theology and means of expression were derived from the language to which she was exposed both at church and in her childhood home.[39]

Ferdinando Fairfax, a Virginia landowner and justice of the peace, interviewed Rachel in New York while she was awake. He purposely questioned her religious beliefs and provoked her to defend them. He also interviewed those who knew her well about her personality, habits, and means of religious instruction. He observed her at night when she was not aware of anyone present and found that her behavior was consistent with the evenings in which people were present. Fairfax concluded, "All that Rachel expresses in her state of somniloquism, is the result of preconceived ideas and opinions, but delivered with a readiness and a fluency which is very far above her waking state."[40]

Rachel left New York City after numerous doctors had examined her. Rather than giving her a "cure," her time in the city had given her increased notoriety. Mais reported, "Curiosity was so strong, that, on the day of her departure, many persons followed her out of town to the place of resting until the morn, that they might witness the spectacle, not of a waking preacher and a drowsy audience, but of a preacher abstracted from outward things, holding forth to a wondering and staring company."[41]

Rachel's five years of night preaching ended in 1817 in Norway, New York, under the care of Dr. Rowland Sears, a relative. Sears treated her with two grains of opium before bed. Whenever she began preaching, "some cold water was dashed, with force, into her face." Sears also used camphor, castor, and "gum foetida" but primarily depended on the opium. He continued his treatments for ten days until Rachel stopped preaching.[42]

Unlike Clarissa Danforth, who received warm encouragement from Freewill Baptists and others, Rachel Baker was confronted by authority figures with negative attitudes about women preaching. Had Rachel felt God calling her to preach, it is reasonable that she may have repressed her thoughts and beliefs only to express them when she was quite unaccountable in an unconscious state.

Charlotte White, however, was not seeking to become a preacher or asking to be ordained.[43] She sought to be a missionary educator either managing schools or instructing Indigenous women. But even that plan was problematic. Most teachers in colonial America had been male. Following the revolution, much of society still believed that teaching was a man's profession.

By 1815, that attitude was just beginning to change. The U.S. population between 1810 and 1820 was 93 percent rural, and rural women worked to provide food and clothing for their families. One man reflected on this division of labor during his rural Indiana childhood in the 1820s by recalling, "There was no such thing as a woman teacher. It wasn't a woman's job any more than milking a cow was a man's job."[44] Urban women educators, such as Maria Staughton in South Carolina and Isabella Graham in New York, most often taught girls or tutored children in homes. The advent of common schools in the 1820s and 1830s, however, created a demand for teachers that could not sufficiently be filled by men. Schools began hiring women when male teachers were increasingly unavailable and when schools discovered they could pay women less than men.[45]

The majority of the seven-man quorum acting on behalf of the entire Baptist Board had appointed Charlotte White as a missionary. Their circular letter to the rest of the board outlined four reasons for their action:

> 1st. Not that she should preach, but teach a school of native children, and thus lay a foundation for future usefulness; 2nd. that females only could have access to the females of the East, and for such reasons are employed by the English Mission. 3rd. that Mrs. Hough should not be alone on her passage, and when arrived at India. 4th. that Mrs. White procures her own outfit, and only asks the Board to pay her passage, and then support her as a member of Mr. Hough's family. We have only to add, that Mrs. White is a lady of *education, refinement,* and *unblemished piety,* which is admitted by all the Board.[46]

Charlotte White had been appointed as a missionary on June 14, 1815. Would her appointment now be revoked?

## Chapter 6

# DRAMA IN PHILADELPHIA

No one traveled more miles on behalf of the Baptist Board of Foreign Missions than its first agent, Luther Rice. And his journal recorded the speed of his travel:

> March 13, 1817—I have long wished to obtain a horse, whose traveling gate would carry me 5 miles an hour—heretofore I have never been able to journey faster than about 4 miles an hour—If my present horse continues to travel as he has done today—it will save me 2 hours in every 40 miles—2½ hours in every 50—worth to at least $250 a year—& will render my services to the missionary cause worth at least an equal sum more than has hitherto been the case.— The matter appears to me providential—*"In all thy ways acknowledge Him, & he shall direct thy steps."*[1]

Rev. Richard Furman, the Triennial Convention's first president and a member of the Baptist Board of Foreign Missions, lived some 680 miles south of Philadelphia in Charleston, South Carolina. A messenger on horseback riding nonstop at Luther Rice's speed for ten hours a day would need a minimum of thirty-four days to shuttle the board's questions to and from Furman.

Although it took some time to receive the members' replies, the voice of the board slowly began to be heard. By September 4, 1815, the first four responses had arrived:

1. James A. Ranaldson (North Carolina) Yes, Luther Rice should stay in the U.S. as an agent of the board, and "He views the term Missionary, not confined to males only; that Mrs. White's appointment is proper providing her talents are suitable, and the funds sufficient."[2]

2. Thomas Baldwin (Massachusetts): Yes, Luther Rice should stay, and "Mrs. White's appointment is highly satisfactory to him; that the Convention did not intend to restrict the Board to appointment of Male Missionaries only."

3. John Williams (New York): Yes, Rice should stay, and "Mrs. White's appointment is constitutional, and pleasing to him."

4. Lucius Bolles (Massachusetts): Yes on Rice, and "he cordially approves of female Missionaries, and of the appointment of Mrs. White particularly."

By September 12 another reply had been received, this one from Judge Matthias B. Talmadge (South Carolina): "That the constitution does not confine the Board to one sex only: That the word Missionary does not mean a Preacher. That if he objects to Mrs. White's appointment, it is founded on the supposition that the Funds are insufficient. That if she be now dismissed, that the Board ought to make up the losses she has sustained by entering into our service."

Upon receiving Judge Talmadge's positive response, a majority of the Board of Foreign Missions had spoken. Charlotte White's appointment would stand.

Henry Holcombe had dissented in the vote to appoint Charlotte. Sensing the direction in which the majority was moving, he brought a written protest to the board and asked permission to read it. Permission was granted. After reading the protest, Holcombe refused to give the document to the board for inclusion in the minutes. Presumably Holcombe had protested women serving as missionaries. Representing the view of the majority, Rev. William White stated that no arguments should "prevent the association of our amiable widow, on grounds of reciprocity, with male missionaries."[3]

Facing a clear majority, Holcombe surprised his colleagues with a strategic maneuver. When the board met again the following day, September 13, seven men were initially present in the persons of Henry Holcombe, William Rogers, Burgiss Allison, William Staughton, H. G. Jones, William White, and William Moulder. However, before the minutes of the previous day's meeting could be read and approved,

Holcombe submitted the resignations of himself, William Rogers, Daniel Dodge, and Judge Moulder. Holcombe and two others then immediately departed, depriving the meeting of a quorum.[4] The Board had existed for only sixteen months, but contention over appointing a woman was already causing it to fracture.

Judge Moulder, an associate judge of the court of Common Pleas of Philadelphia, assured the four men remaining in the room that a lack of time was his only reason for resigning and that he would remain on the board until a successor could be found. He reassured his colleagues that he had "always gone with the majority of the board in the measures they have adopted."[5]

Holcombe later claimed that by submitting the resignations "we gained time to expose the unconstitutionality, and inexpediency, of the appointment in question.... We have, indeed, been blamed for resorting to the only means in our power to prevent the infraction of our constitution, as we conceived, and the misapplication of our funds by 'out-generaling,' as is said, in this instance, our opponents."[6]

Holcombe's resignation only temporarily delayed the board. Several weeks later it was evident that the board could form a quorum without him. Nine men were present for the September 30 meeting; they constituted a quorum of seven plus Holcombe and Rogers, who had returned and said that they (but not Dodge) wished to recall their resignations. They asserted that the board could not have accepted the resignations on September 13 because the board had lacked a quorum and thus could not have conducted business. That being the case, they argued that they now had the right to withdraw their unaccepted resignations. Their request to retain their seats was granted.

Two more responses had been received:

1. Richard Furman (South Carolina): Yes, Rice should stay, and "He is of opinion that the appointment of a female auxiliary Missionary is constitutional; that care ought to be had however, as to qualifications, & the State of the Funds."

2. Lewis Richards (Maryland): Yes on Rice, and "He is of opinion that Mrs. White ought to go out as attached to the family of Mr. Hough."

No other replies from board members, if received, were included in the minutes. All seven responses affirmed Charlotte White's appointment.

Several respondents, however, implied some reservations about appointing her.

Judge Talmadge confirmed that the convention's constitution allowed the appointment of both male and female missionaries. Furman agreed with that plain reading of the constitution, but added the word "auxiliary," suggesting that an appointed woman was something less than a full missionary.

Richards's approval of White's appointment was somewhat ambiguous. The phrase "as attached to the family of Mr. Hough" could suggest that she reside with the Houghs for reasons of safety. Or, it could suggest that her role in Burma should be that of a housekeeper and childcare worker.

Furman and Ranaldson raised the question of "qualifications" and "providing her talents are suitable." Notably, the question of talents and qualifications was not raised when the board appointed Adoniram Judson, Luther Rice, and George Hough. Perhaps this was because the three were ordained preachers, though only Hough had actual pastoral experience prior to appointment. Or perhaps their qualifications and suitable talents were presumed because they were men.

The men who voiced reservations about appointing a woman missionary all lived south of the Mason-Dixon line, as had Dr. Holcombe prior to his pastorate in Philadelphia. Their opposition to Charlotte's appointment may have reflected their region's more conservative view of womanhood and woman's role in church and society.

Then there was the matter of money. Three men conditioned their approval on the sufficiency of funds. Charlotte White had apparently been prepared for objections citing a lack of funds. In her June 13 letter to the board, Charlotte had rejoiced that "God has opened a way" for her to go to India. It was a very pragmatic opening, for God had provided Charlotte with a modest estate. As she gave her letter to the board, Charlotte also tendered property as a contribution that would be sufficient to fund her own missionary service.[7]

The cost of both her "outfit" and income was now covered. Funding to pay the passage for her and the Houghs had been approved at the board's June 14 meeting. But the means of the missionaries' transportation to India was not yet resolved. Attempts to book passage on ships departing from New England proved unsuccessful. The board then learned that two cargo ships owned by Philadelphia merchant Edward Thomson were about to sail for Calcutta. Mr. Thomson (also spelled Thompson) was approached about his willingness to take on passengers. Thomson's reply was a total surprise; he not only would accept the five passengers but would also accommodate them at his own expense. Nine years earlier, another Philadelphia merchant, Robert Ralston, had provided free transportation for the English Baptist missionaries William Robinson and James Chater from London to Bengal in one of his ships.[8] Now Edward Thomson, "an opulent merchant of Philadelphia, and a friend of Christian Missions," would participate in the missionary endeavor through similar generosity.[9]

Thomson's ship that was named in honor of a renowned Philadelphia physician was chosen. The *Benjamin Rush* was "a fine copper-bottomed vessel, nearly new, having gone only a single voyage." Thomson immediately ordered cabins built into the ship for the Hough family and Charlotte White.[10] The resulting accommodations would be "peculiarly comfortable."[11] In addition, Thomson offered to similarly accommodate any future missionaries when any of his ships were sailing to the East! In gratitude, the board elected Thomson as an honorary member of the Triennial Convention.

The financial objections that anyone could raise had now been removed. Through Charlotte White's willingness to fund her own missionary service and Edward Thomson's generosity in providing free transportation, God had indeed opened a way.

Thomson's wonderful provision had opened the door that some had tried to keep shut and locked against Charlotte White's service as an appointed missionary. It was the news that moved William Staughton on August 25 to send the twenty-five-word message to Charlotte White, "*God is with us!* The best ship in the harbor of Philadelphia is at the service of brother Hough and yourself. The passage *without money*." Charlotte could sail to India.

## Indignity and Inspiration

With both the money and her appointment in place, Charlotte White was indeed positioned to go to India. During its September 30 meeting, the board voted, "Resolved that our Missionaries go out in the *Benjamin Rush*, as it seems most congenial with the wishes of the owner." The resolution was stated in the plural. The Board's "missionaries," George Hough and Charlotte White, were now approved for departure.[12]

Approved for departure, but not without pain. Charlotte Hazen Atlee White had been orphaned, widowed, bereft of her only child, derided at her baptism, exposed to public controversy due to her gender, and accused of underhanded procedure, inconsistency, mixed motives, insufficient qualifications, and weak stamina. She would now be subjected to a final indignity.

The quorum's approval came only after Henry Holcombe extracted a price for use of the plural word "missionaries." Holcombe repeated his assertion that Charlotte White originally intended to go to India to assist the Houghs as a domestic helper, and anything more was tantamount to giving her a "promotion." Whether convinced by his argument or simply wearied by the controversy, five members of the quorum opposed the supposed promotion. Now William Staughton and William White were in the minority. Holcombe characterized his partial victory in the board's vote by writing, "Mrs. White, of course, was continued as Mrs. Hough's companion, and, contrary to her former determination, sailed with our missionary family, in the *Benjamin Rush*, for Calcutta."[13]

Charlotte made no public comment about Holcombe's political maneuvers. The Baptist Board of Foreign Missions had appointed her as a missionary, and she knew within herself the call that God had placed on her life. Meanwhile, there were final details that required attention that included discussion with a committee of the board concerning the disposition of her property and her yearly support.[14] And there were bittersweet departing conversations with family and friends.

Charlotte did not contest her own understanding of her call against the board's understanding of their appointment. On November 6, a committee that had been appointed to attend to "the case of sister White" met with Charlotte. They reported that "she informed them it was her intention to go out with Mrs. Hough." Furthermore, after providing her own outfit at her own expense, she expected to deposit about three hundred dollars in the treasury.[15]

Charlotte had more than once been described as "amiable."[16] Her willingness to accept the board's characterization that they were sending her to India "attached to" the Hough family, however, may have been based on more than her affable personality, for Charlotte White had understanding and encouraging advocates in William and Maria Staughton.

In the board's chief executive role as corresponding secretary, William Staughton had the task of encouraging the departing missionaries and delivering instructions to them on behalf of the board. In preparing his remarks for the missionaries about to embark on the *Benjamin Rush*, he exercised subtle diplomacy.

Staughton placed "in the hands of brother Hough and family" a document that would be made public in the board's *Second Annual Report*.[17] The instructions were the board's first official statement on the practice of mission. In seventeen brief paragraphs, Staughton began drawing both practical and theological contours of a holistic missiology. The practical matters addressed conduct on board ship, relations with the British Baptists at Serampore, prompt transition from India to Burma, relations with Adoniram Judson and Felix Carey, the priority of learning the local language, Scripture translation, establishing schools, and the importance, nature, and frequency of communicating back to America. Staughton also urged the missionaries to refrain from political involvement and to adopt a plan of common life similar to that at Serampore.

The theological base of this emerging American Baptist missiology was rooted in the missionaries' relationship with God, the centrality of the cross of Jesus Christ, witness to others through both words and deeds, and mutual accountability by walking together as members of a local church (which they would need to form).

The missiology was holistic, starting with the missionaries' personal lives. It envisioned them living in intentional community, holding all things in common after the example of the New Testament communism being practiced by the British Baptists at Serampore.

The missionaries were "called to preach the truth as it is in Jesus." As God's truth is not limited to the message of salvation, the missionaries were expected to "diversify your subjects as occasion may demand." Yet, in diversification they were to retain that which was primary: "...the cross of Christ will be your favourite theme. This is the power of God unto salvation."

The missionaries needed to be flexible. Their work should respond to the needs confronting them. For instance, if others had not already completed the task of Bible translation, the Hough party might need to set other work aside to become translators. In so doing, they were reminded that faithfulness to scripture was not the same as wooden literalism in translation. Instead, "Aim to come as near to the meaning and spirit of the Scriptures as possible." In the twentieth century, this approach to translation would become known as "dynamic equivalence."

Letters to America from the Houghs and White were to be frequent and to reflect a holistic interaction with their surroundings. They were urged to learn and communicate about "the soil, productions, customs, mythologies, animals, plants, literary works, &c. that prevail in Burmah."

The board was sending George Hough to Burma to set up and operate a printing press. This was holistic mission in that it was neither preaching nor forming churches. Perhaps Staughton thought Hough's task was self-evident since his instructions made no reference to establishing the press. Instead, Staughton gave prominence to another form of holistic mission: education. The subject of schools took up two paragraphs, twenty-six lines. This was more than Staughton wrote on any other topic.

It was important to start schools "extensively and as early as practicable." They could begin as elementary schools and widen with time. Education could prevent the children's minds from becoming "wedded to superstitious rites." Beyond personal enlightenment, education could fulfill an evangelistic role in the lives of students and parents alike. "Children from their communicative temper will impart to their parents what they learn, and may in this way become serviceable." Educational ministry would be a long-term investment, for "who can tell but that native missionaries, through the blessing of God, may by this means be created."

With the benefit of experience that he and Maria had gained from teaching and managing schools, William Staughton suggested pragmatic approaches to education. He addressed the power of literacy, the effective use of catechisms, the function of memorization, the benefit of Socratic questioning, and practical means to encourage attendance and diffuse information.

Most importantly for Charlotte White, it was in education rather than childcare that *her* important and strategic ministry was envisioned. Henry Holcombe had his own ideas about women in mission, but William Staughton was issuing the official instructions: "The Mahometans, by schools, have extended in Africa the doctrines of the Koran, and it cannot be doubted that such institutions may be greatly profitable in diffusing information and diminishing prejudice. *Females in this department may become useful; and in this sphere we think our sister White may be enabled materially to serve the common cause.*"[18]

Was it any wonder that Charlotte White could be amiable?

## Departure at Last

The days now seemed to move quickly as the missionaries anticipated their departure. On Thursday, November 2, Charlotte White requested a letter from Sansom Street Baptist Church dismissing her as a member and requesting her acceptance into the Baptist church that was yet to be formed in Rangoon, Burma. William Staughton wrote the letter on the church's behalf.[19]

A month later, on December 4, Maria Staughton gathered the Sansom Street Baptist Female Society for Promoting Evangelical Missions, the society of which Charlotte had been a founding member and vice-directress. The women voted to recognize the missionary service of Charlotte White and Ann Judson by designating them both as honorary members.[20]

Several days later, an ecumenical gathering filled Philadelphia's Second Baptist Church to pray for the missionaries. The crowd was huge, as churches from New York to Baltimore as well as ministers and members of other denominations had been invited.[21]

Dr. Staughton and six other preachers spoke, prayed, and commended the missionaries to God's care. The word "missionary" was in the plural. Dr. Edwin Augustus Atlee, Charlotte's brother, a well-known Philadelphia physician and "a publick preacher among the Friends," gave a short address and offered fervent prayer. As Charlotte White and Phebe Hough had not been commissioned the previous May when hands were laid on George Hough, this ecumenical gathering in effect became their commissioning service. It also took on the character of a funeral service. "On the impulse of the moment," Rev. Ezra Stiles Ely, pastor of Third Presbyterian Church, composed and sang a short hymn. The lyrics conveyed the clear expectation that Charlotte and the Houghs would serve, die, and rest buried in Burma:

> Thy servants pray with one accord,
>
> To Birmah waft thy servants, Lord;
> And may their souls in Birmah find
> A cov'nant God is ever kind.

Give them to see their hearts' desire
Millions of converts for their hire;
And then in Birma make their bed
'Till Jesus wake them from the dead.[22]

Events now broke with great speed. On Monday, December 11, with but several hours' notice, the missionaries were summoned to the wharf to board a steamboat operated by Capt. Whildin. Several friends, including Capt. Annsley, William, and possibly Maria Staughton, accompanied them on the forty-mile journey down the Delaware River to meet the *Benjamin Rush* awaiting their arrival at New Castle, Delaware.

Amidst the sound and vibrations of the steamboat moving against the water, the missionaries were "in excellent spirits, happy in each other, and happy in the blessed cause their hearts had been influenced to espouse." Their mood was elevated even more when Capt. Whildin said he would take no payment for their fare and accommodation.

Deep emotions comingled among those in the boat. Excitement for the adventure, grief at the parting, wonder, joy, and awe. And gratitude. Nine years earlier Charlotte White had broken forth into spontaneous song as she waded into the Merrimack River about to be baptized. Now in a steamboat on the Delaware River, she composed a poem on the spot in gratitude to God for Mr. Thomson whose ship she was about to board.

Seest thou yon scroll by Angel borne

Up to the azure gates of light?
What *characters* the field adorn,
Attracting nether mortal sight—
     'Tis THOMSON.

Now reach'd the sacred shrine of heav'n,
He lays the scroll at Jesus' feet—
A wreath to pious bounty given
He drops—the destin'd brow to meet
     Of THOMSON.[23]

The group that had accompanied Charlotte and the Houghs in the steamboat now grew to include people who had made their way to New Castle by land for the final farewell. To mark the occasion, Staughton composed and recited a seven-stanza poem.

ADIEU, lov'd friends! In Jesus' name

We bid the heart inspir'd adieu!
In yon fair bark descend the stream,
To Indian climes your course pursue.

Affection soft and Memory stand,
To hold you to your natal soil;
But Grace can stretch the parting hand
Possess'd of all in Jesus' smile.

A thousand pray'rs for you ascend;
A thousand blessings shall return;
Diffus'd by that imperial friend,
Whose Glory bids your bosoms burn.

Brethren belov'd on Eastern shores
Shall hail you welcome to the field;
Prudence unveil her sacred stores,
And Love her rich refreshments yield.

Go, firm in faith, maintain the fight,
Jehovah shall all nations know;
Veils shall be rent, and banish'd Night,
Where beams the sun or breezes blow.

Sustain'd of Heav'n, devoutly swear
Perpetual league of heart and hands;
Nor Hell, nor Earth, nor Time shall tear
The sweet inviolable hands.

A few more moons, and we shall meet;
Our labours and our suff'rings o'er;
And stand and sing at Jesus' feet,
Nor mourn dividing Oceans more.[24]

With Capt. Annsley now on board, the *Benjamin Rush* made its way
to Reedy Island. There it sat until December 20, 1815, when "a fine wind"
pushed it out to sea. Charlotte White, America's first appointed woman
missionary, was on her way.

## Voyage and Arrival

For almost a year, family, friends, and churches in the United States waited to learn the fate of the Houghs, Charlotte White, and the *Benjamin Rush*. What was happening to them on the ocean?

The *Benjamin Rush* had been at sea for almost four months. The passengers kept journals and wrote letters as they wondered about life ahead in Burma and pondered the life they had left behind in America. Although Charlotte White recorded her thoughts and experiences in a diary, its location is now unknown. She may have shared some of the feelings that Phebe Hough confided by letter to a friend in New York:

> The other evening I sat reflecting on the past, and my absent friends shared much in my meditations; sadness pervaded my mind, and I almost involuntarily poured forth my soul in song. Possibly the simple effusions of your friend may amuse you, and perhaps a sympathetic feeling will pervade your bosom as you read the following lines:
>
> ON MELANCHOLY.
> When absent friends invite
>     The silent tear, the tender sigh;
> When Memory throws her light
>     On scenes of joy passed swiftly by;
>
> Then Melancholy flings
>     A somber sadness o'er the mind;
> She strikes the tender strings
>     Of sensibility refined.
>
> She bids the tears to speak,
>     To tell the latent grief she feels;
> Their language is too weak,
>     'Tis what the deep-fetch'd sigh reveals.
>
> But, Melancholy, why
>     Hang all thy tender charms o'er me?
> I would not always sigh
>     For worldly joys, which transient be!
>
> Though time and distance join
>     To part me from the friends I love;
> If Jesus is but mine,

'Tis joy which changes cannot move.

Then, Melancholy, go—
    Thy power can never bind my soul;
Thou tender nurse of wo,
    I yield thee not supreme control.[25]

Finally, on Tuesday morning October 8, 1816, almost ten months after her departure, a parcel of letters from Charlotte White arrived at the Philadelphia home of William and Maria Staughton. Reading the letters with relief and joy, William Staughton then immediately wrote to share the good news with Dr. Baldwin in Boston, president of the board.

The *Benjamin Rush* had been blessed with good winds during the voyage and encountered no accidents, ship damage, or pirates. The missionaries had been made comfortable in the new cabins that Mr. Thomson had fitted out for them and also by the attention they had received from Capt. Annesly, who was "a polite and attentive friend."

They had arrived safely in Calcutta on April 23, 1816, after 129 days at sea, and the British Baptists had received them "with open arms."[26]

Charlotte included an update from Burma. Felix Carey was now remarried, was no longer part of the Baptist mission, and was living at the royal court in Amapura. The Judsons were both speaking and writing Burmese in Rangoon where they expected to stay. Charlotte reported that Ann Judson was highly respected among the Serampore missionaries and "is spoken of with astonishment for her fortitude, her silent acquiescence under trials, and her strength of intellect."

Charlotte's packet of letters also brought comments addressed privately to Dr. Staughton, her pastor and friend. Indeed, she felt close enough to Staughton to call him her father. For two days he pondered the thoughts she had confided to him. Then he answered, trusting that she would accept and act on his advice.

Charlotte was well aware that her appointment had stirred controversy. She had borne the brunt of argument over whether a woman, a non-ordained woman, a *single* woman could be appointed. However bluntly or diplomatically the conversations had proceeded, they had not remained focused on the philosophical question of policy. Instead, some had personalized the issue by asking whether *Mrs. Charlotte White* should be appointed, questioning her ability and integrity. Staughton knew that he could not provide helpful advice without first acknowledging the very personal nature of the controversy. He also knew, as Charlotte could not, that contentious discussion had not faded away after she had sailed away. There could be no denial that a growing number of people were talking about her and expressing their opinions, pro or con. He counseled her to use caution, "Your character, my sister, from the opposition of enemies and the interested feelings of friends, has acquired a publicity, that will require much prudence, circumspection and prayer."[27]

Staughton then offered Charlotte advice that would be fitting for every missionary. She should respond as a peacemaker. "Cherish to the utmost possible extent a conciliating temper," he wrote. "Study only and ever, the things that make for peace." This would require at least three kinds of action. First, a readiness to forgive "not only seven times, but seventy times seven." Second, a maintenance of self-respect without letting it "degenerate into self-importance." And third, flexibility. Staughton's advice was reminiscent of the apostle Paul's words, "I have become all things to all people, so that I might by any means save some."[28] As Staughton expressed it to Charlotte, "Be willing to be any thing, provided the cause for which you have given up the endearments of your natal soil and home, may be promoted."[29]

Staughton sent off his letter to Charlotte in Burma, urging her to be explicit about her living expenses in Rangoon. She would not receive a stated salary from the board since she was funding herself. But Staughton assured her that the board would send her remittances appropriate for her needs. His letter closed with caring words of encouragement: "Never despair with Jesus for your leader."

If blessed with good weather, the ship bearing Staughton's letter would take four months to reach India plus additional days to be carried from Calcutta to Rangoon. But even before the letter had been written, Charlotte's life had taken a dramatic turn.

The British Baptists had indeed welcomed Charlotte White and the Hough family with open arms. They had hosted the American missionaries with joy and presented a printing press they were sending to Burma to replace one of the two lost in the tragic 1815 boat accident in which Felix Carey's wife and children were drowned. Then came the unexpected. No ship could be found to take the Americans, the press equipment, and type to Rangoon. The delay would last for two months.

By then, Charlotte White had met the Rev. Joshua Rowe.

# Chapter 7

## THE WOOLCOMBER'S SON

Joshua Rowe was born into poverty on September 24, 1782, at Foxton, Leicestershire, in England, two months after Charlotte Atlee was born in Lancaster, Pennsylvania.[1] His parents, Adam and Ann Rowe, moved their family to Bristol and then to Southmoulton in Devonshire due to economic need. By that point, Joshua had two younger sisters, and the woolcombing trade was "very dead." Desperate to feed his family, Adam Rowe applied to the parish for relief. To receive the assistance, the Rowes were forced to enter the workhouse.

Joshua's father chafed under the experience while he sought ways to again support his family. Several months later, he left for Poole in Dorsetshire where he found woolcombing work. The pay for the hot, dirty work was minimal. Through the long workday, Adam stood before an upright metal comb bearing five- to six-inch teeth. The comb was mounted over coals to keep the apparatus at high temperature. It also kept the dusty room hot and fetid. Adam's hands became slippery from "wool fat," the lanolin from the raw tangled wool that he repeatedly pulled through the metal teeth. Once separated into parallel strands, the fiber would be spun and woven. Merchant houses selling cloth or clothing made most of the profit, while woolcombers like Adam struggled to feed their families.

While Adam Rowe sought to regain financial independence, Ann and the children lived in a house separate from the other buildings on the Southmoulton Workhouse grounds. Ann was attentive to Joshua's spiritual nurture and frequently welcomed "two or three serious persons in the Workhouse" into her house for prayer and fellowship. The small group sought to meet secretly, as the workhouse master was "a great persecutor of Religion." Joshua listened in on the meetings and "felt a pleasure in hearing them converse about Divine things." But there was a cost to be paid. Whenever the workhouse master learned that Ann had attended a spiritual meeting, he vented his anger by beating Joshua.

During his early childhood at Southmoulton, Joshua learned to read. His mother's "pious instructions" made a lasting impression on him. He frequently "engaged in secret prayer," enjoyed learning hymns, memorizing catechism, and reading the Bible. He was strongly affected when one of his first cousins died and was further impressed by life's fragility when a young man was crushed to death under a falling wagon soon thereafter. He long remembered the funeral sermon from Psalm 119:9, "Wherewith shall a young man cleanse his way? By taking heed thereto according to thy word."

In 1789 Adam Rowe called Joshua to join him at Poole. There he enrolled Joshua in school to learn writing and arithmetic, skills to fit him for more than woolcombing. Meanwhile, Joshua's mother and two sisters were able to leave the workhouse to live with a cousin in Southmoulton.

When Joshua was twelve, his father took him from school to become a servant of Mr. Neave, a Quaker who was a draper, hosier, and Newfoundland merchant. There Joshua soon "became connected with low companions." Despite a troubled conscience, he stopped attending church and began frequenting alehouses. He gave full scope to "carnal inclinations," including the habit of cursing and swearing, imagining that it made him "appear more manly." Despite his employer's numerous warnings, Joshua's conduct lost him the opportunity for promotion and led to his firing.

Without a job, Joshua returned to Southmoulton. Though he wanted to learn the woolcombing business, he was unwilling to apprentice himself and gave it up. He now resumed regular church attendance, attempting to reform himself. His misconduct, however, had become ingrained and "corrupted others." During a worship service, Joshua and his companions were so disruptive that the pastor "burst out in tears, shut up the book, went home and left us in the Meeting house." Joshua became so ungovernable that his mother persuaded him to return to live with his father at Poole, which he did in 1796.

At Poole, Joshua worked as a weaver, rejoined his former companions, and followed his "old course." Weaving provided a meager income and no promising future, so Joshua sought to advance himself vocationally, if not spiritually. He attended an evening school and worked to improve his writing, mathematical, and accounting skills.

Later, he became employed by "a seafaring man of Poole" and went to sea. Joshua later recounted that his shipboard experiences led to remitting and relapsing attempts to reform himself: "About this time, the terrors of God seemed to get hold of me. When I had engaged to go to sea, I thought within myself that I must leave off cursing and swearing; which arose from this idea, that God could easily drown me, if he pleased."

Three harrowing incidents nearly sent him to the bottom of the sea. During each of the terrors he made solemn promises to God and, after surviving, attempted to reform his life. But his changes repeatedly wore off, and he "returned like a dog to his vomit." After his first stint as a seafarer, he wavered between sinning and repenting, between meetinghouse and alehouse. He then gained employment as a ship merchant's clerk and expected to sail to Newfoundland. His plans were frustrated, however, because England was at war and the ship owner refused to risk the French capturing his ship.

Joshua now began to worry about his future since he had no training beyond weaving, which was a low-wage trade with much drudgery and little future. He considered the military and was accepted into the sea fencibles, the militia consisting of small commercial vessels converted to defend the British coast. Here too he met frustration. He was soon discharged when officials learned that he was too young to qualify for militia service.

In 1798 Joshua's father moved to Dorchester. Disappointed and disillusioned, Joshua joined his father to learn his father's trade. There he encountered something unexpected—something far beyond the life of a woolcomber, something that began with a side comment in a sermon.

About this time the Lord was pleased to open my eyes, to see the awfulness of my state. A remark that was droped [*sic*] from the pulpit seemed to make an abiding impression upon me; which was concerning the folly of spending youthful vigour in the service of Satan, and then expecting God to accept of us; and the unreasonableness of such expectations as wishing God to accept of us when we have devoted our all to Satan.—Such a view of the holiness and purity of the divine character appeared to me as I never experienced before: and such a sense of the necessity of the mediation of Jesus Christ.

Joshua made a radical turn toward Jesus, whom he saw as his only refuge, his last and only defense. His first outward change was to leave his former companions. As a result, he "became a laughing stock, was often pelted with stones, and became the subject of their derisions." At times, the outer and inner struggles were almost too hard for him to bear.

> Satan often tempted me to disbelieve the being of a God: and at others, that my sins were too great to be pardoned. Not having much acquaintance with the people of God at Dorchester, I had no bosom friend to relate the exercises of my soul: and I was so uncomfortably situated in other respects, that could have no retired moments for prayer at home: therefore when the weather permitted, I retired into the fields and poured out my soul to God.

In 1799 Joshua moved to Salisbury to take a job as a woolcomber. Although the person with whom he worked "proved great snares" to him, Joshua continued attending church, this time in his parent's Baptist tradition. The Rev. John Saffery, pastor of Salisbury's Baptist church, provided spiritual guidance for a year, when Joshua took another step in his spiritual journey.

> After attending about 12 months; and being persuaded that baptism was a positive command, that immersion was the way in which it ought to be administered, and that those and only those who believed in Jesus Christ ought as a means of manifesting their attachment to the Dear Redeemer, to obey him in this command; as also in that of the Lord's supper: I proposed myself as a candidate to the Baptist church over which Mr. Saffery was pastor. I felt a willingness to cast in my lot with the people of God, and to give myself up to the Lord: persuaded that I could not be bound with too strong cords to the object of my regard.

Joshua Rowe gave testimony of his faith to the church, was accepted, and was baptized by Saffery on December 28, 1800. He would later come to know three other men who were baptized on that same day: John Biss, Krishna Pal, and Felix Carey. John Biss was baptized at Plymouth Dock (renamed Devonport in 1824) and would sail with Rowe as a fellow missionary to India. Krishna Pal and Felix Carey were baptized in the Hooghly River at Serampore, India. The former was the first Hindu to become a Christian under the ministry of the Baptist mission, and the latter was William and Dorothy Carey's oldest son.

Though unaware of how it would foreshadow his future, Rowe felt a strong concern "for the rising generation," and joined a friend voluntarily teaching children reading, writing, and arithmetic. Their school grew to almost forty children when the "deadness of trade" forced Joshua to move from Salisbury to find woolcombing work at Milton. Joshua continued assisting the Salisbury school though the three-mile evening walk from Milton proved very fatiguing after his day's work. After several weeks at Milton, Joshua moved to Bristol for a much better job. There he found work as a clerk, employing his mathematical skills and keeping accounts in his characteristically clear, precise penmanship. On Sundays he worshiped at the Broadmead Baptist Church. He now began sensing a desire to enter ministry but shared his thoughts with no one. He was, after all, only a woolcomber's son. Still, wanting "to do something for the rising generation," he volunteered to help teach in a school being led by John Chamberlain, not knowing how Chamberlain's life would yet intertwine with his. Now he sought ways to help his students with their spiritual as well as mental formation.

When Joshua heard Dr. John Ryland, Broadmead's pastor, read accounts from the English Baptist missionaries in India, his sense of call began taking more definite shape. He had heard about the work of the Baptist mission before. In Salisbury, Pastor Saffery was "a plain but powerful advocate of the mission from the pulpit."[2] But Saffery's words had been like seeds. Only now did Joshua truly begin to reflect on the lives of the people of India. Only now did he begin to feel "a tender and affectionate concern for them." Yet, the woolcomber's son had doubts. Were his thoughts "airy flights of an hasty or indiscreet Zeal" that would soon fade away? Once again, Joshua told no one about his growing sense of God's call.

As Joshua prayed, he weighed the implications of mission service, being wary of "rushing like the unthinking horse into battle." He also took another step in his process of discernment by writing to his parents, expressing his thoughts, and asking for their consent. His father's reply provided reassuring encouragement.

But what shall I say unto you, on the chief subject of your past Letter? Shall I attempt to dissuade or discourage you from entering upon the work in the places and manner indented [*sic*]? No, by no means! Go and the Lord be with you and bless you. You must be sensible that Natural and Parental affections must work upon the minds: but when we consider the nature and design of the work you purpose to enter upon, we would endeavor to act as Hannah and Elkanah did by their son Samuel; they gave him up to the Lord, not with reluctance, but willingly and cheerfully: so would we do by you our dear and only Son!! When we look and take a view of what the providence of God has done for you, from your Infancy to the present moment, in a variety of instances, we cannot help concluding that the Lord has, (if we may use the expression,) a more than common claim to you: But if to Providential Kindness and care; we unite sovereign Love, and Mercy, how is the obligation increased: How forciably [*sic*] does Gratitude demand all your strength and abilities in the service of so great, so glorious, and so loving and kind a benefactor and friend.

Finally, Joshua sought either affirmation or redirection from the body of Christ as represented by the local church. He wrote, "I considered it my duty to make it known to the people of God, and to leave myself entirely at their disposal." Joshua spoke to Henry Page, assistant pastor at the Broadmead church, who arranged for him to meet with the pastor, Dr. John Ryland. Joshua noted that "after having some conversation with me, [Ryland] gave me some books to read, *History of Missions in America*, Horn's *Letters on Missions* and Brainerd's *Life*. By this means I attained greater knowledge of the nature of Missionary service." Joshua also began to preach as opportunities arose.

Mission seemed to be in the very air Joshua and those around him breathed. First, the Baptist Mission Society appointed his fellow teacher John Chamberlain to serve in India. Then on April 27, 1802, Chamberlain married Hannah Smith, a member of Rev. John Sutcliff's church in Olney. For three years Hannah had corresponded with Chamberlain and had "always believed that sometime or other he would be engaged in the Mission." Initially, Hannah could not say that she was willing to go if he were to be called into missionary service, yet neither did she discourage him from going. During those three years, Hannah educated herself about mission. She read David Brainerd's *Life* and a church history written by

Thomas Haweis, a founder of the London Missionary Society. She also read the current *Periodical Accounts* of the Baptist Missionary Society as well as the account of the first voyage of the ship *Duff* that the London Missionary Society purchased and used in 1796 to send a group of its missionaries to islands in the south Pacific.

In an April 3, 1802, letter of appreciation to John Sutcliff her pastor, Hannah confided, "now as the society are desirous of sending Mr. C. and as he is willing to go, I also am willing to be his companion." Hannah was not naive about what missionary life might entail, but she had breathed the air of mission.

> I can truly say, I do not feel my mind elated, or carried away in the vain expectation, as to think that I am now going to enjoy perfect happiness, nor that I shall now have done with the cares and anxieties of life. A thought of this kind has not entered my mind. [I am] willing to go and be and do wherever & whatever the Lord appoints [and to] meet new trials, difficulties & anxious cares, but the Lord reigneth…and whether I live in England or India, his eye will behold me, will guide, defend, protect, support & comfort me.[3]

Following a sermon that Chamberlain preached at Olney shortly before he and Hannah departed, a young man named William Robinson was baptized. No one, including Joshua Rowe and John Chamberlain, had any hint of the young man's future. Robinson's own father had doubted William's ability to learn his own trade as a lace pattern maker, so he had apprenticed him to a shoemaker. But Robinson, too, had breathed the air of mission. Four years later in the Baptist Chapel at Oxford, John Sutcliff, Andrew Fuller, and John Ryland laid hands on William Robinson and James Chater, commissioning them as missionaries to India.

After the Chamberlains sailed for India, Joshua was left with the sole care of one of Chamberlain's schools. Ryland then consulted the Baptist Mission Society concerning Rowe, and it was agreed that John Sutcliff would mentor Joshua as he had mentored William Carey seventeen years earlier.[4] On September 30, 1802, Joshua arrived in Olney to live and work with Sutcliff at the Baptist church. This began Joshua's close, lifelong friendship with the Sutcliffs and other Olney friends. Meanwhile, Elizabeth Walker, yet another member of the Olney church, sailed for missionary service as Robinson's wife. From India, Robinson would four times attempt to establish a mission in Bhutan before successfully doing so in

Java. Later, he would return to India and serve alongside John Chamberlain.[5]

As a reflective exercise while awaiting missionary appointment at Olney, twenty-one-year-old Joshua wrote a ten-page account of his life. He particularly reflected on God's grace in his experiences of spiritual regression and growth. Joshua understood the gospel to be holistic, relating to both temporal and spiritual life. He expressed a sense of his own unworthiness and God's corresponding holiness and grace. "When I reflect on my past conduct, the wonderful dealings of the Lord towards me and the little gratitude I manifest; I am an astonishment to myself." While he still struggled with doubt, he sought to be closer to God and to serve faithfully.

> I long to imbibe more of the spirit, and temper of the blessed Redeemer. I long to experience more of the influences of the Holy Spirit in my soul. To be inspired with an apostolic ardour: to be emptied of self, and as it were swallowed up in love to God and love to man.... If I can contribute the smallest assistance as an instrument in the extention [*sic*] of the Redeemer's cause in a distant land, I am ready, I am willing...I long to embrace a Hindoo in my arms, and esteem him as a brother in the Lord!

Two months later, the pace of events increased. The mission society decided to send Joshua Rowe to India along with pastors John Bliss, Richard Mardon, William Moore, and their wives. Joshua went to London to get outfitted for Indian service. On November 7, 1803, he married Elizabeth ("Betsy") Noyes,[6] who was a member of Rev. John Saffery's Baptist church in Salisbury.[7]

The Broadmead Baptist Church was "well filled" on December 8, 1803, when Rowe, Biss, Mardon, and Moore were commissioned for missionary service. Drs. Andrew Fuller and John Ryland as well as Revs. Saffery and Sutcliff led the service. Fuller preached,[8] expounded on Genesis 28:3-4, and showed how God's work to bless all families of the earth started with Abraham and continued to the present generation and its missionaries. His exposition gave way to specific, pragmatic advice.[9] The "day much to be remembered" culminated as hands were laid on the new missionaries, blessing them for their future ministry. As would be the case in America, only the men were appointed and received the laying on of hands. Not their wives.

## Voyage to America

Andrew Fuller had cautioned the missionaries to expect many difficulties and discouragements. "You do not expect a smooth sea throughout your voyage," he said, speaking figuratively of the years of ministry yet to come. Unfortunately, his words were also an apt description of their voyage to America. Captain Ryan had planned to sail on December 5,[10] but a fierce storm kept them from boarding the *Hannah* and departing on that day. They were wise to have waited. Joshua wrote from aboard the ship while still in the Bristol Channel, "Thro: mercy we did not sail at the time appointed, a vessel that sailed at the time we intended was lost!"[11]

Though all were safe as they finally departed on January 3, 1804, their first day did not bode well. Joshua wrote,

> On my left hand is Mrs. Moore very sick, calling out lustily for a pot: bro: Moore holding her head and calling for a bucket. Complains of being sick himself. Mary Biss vomiting upon her Mother. Bro: Mardon ascending the ladder for fresh air, but obliged to discharge the contents of his stomach before he could get on the deck. Mrs. Biss very sick: bro: Biss holding her head, and very quamish himself. Mrs. Mardon sitting down on the floor of the state room casting up her accounts.—Betsy looking pale, and putting on a kind of sham cheerfulness, saying she is not sick—The vessel begins to heave much now. I do not know what kind of a night we shall have.[12]

The winter crossing threw many strong headwinds, gales, and squalls at the *Hannah*. While seasickness recurred throughout the voyage, the ship's violent rocking caused even greater discouragement. On their second night the missionaries "lost near 2 gallons of liquor by Mrs. Biss's falling off a box on which it was placed." Joshua noted that they would soon have plenty of room for their dishes, plates, bowls, and teacups as so many of them were thrown from the table and broken. Eating often had its challenges since "at dinner the potatoes frequently rolled out of one plate into another." Chests were smashed, articles were broken, books and papers became waterlogged. Bumps and bruises were regular occurrences.[13]

Captain Ryan granted the missionaries permission to conduct worship on deck or in the cabin, although the weather on a third of the Sundays made that impossible. Driving storms, heavy winds, and mountainous waves often required the ship's glass windows to be replaced with solid wood "dead lights." Even that did not prevent seawater from spraying upon them through the crevasses. For days on end, they were confined below deck in their rooms, sitting or lying in darkness. Captain Ryan confided that he had never "experienced such a season as we have had."

After thirty-five days at sea, the *Hannah* encountered an American ship sailing from Bordeaux back to America. The *Hummingbird* had also struggled against the storms, been seventy-one days at sea, and was very short of provisions.

> We hove to; and they put out their boat & came on board. Capt. Ryan collected all the provisions he could spare, wh. was enough to serve them, with care, 40 days; & had Brandy in return: could give them no water, being too much sea to get it into the boat, but promised that if they wd. accompany us, they shd. have ½ a cask the first fine day. We also, collected what we could spare of our private stores & gave them.

As the *Hannah* neared the Azores, it was nearly captured by a French privateer and escaped only because the vessel withdrew when another sail came into view. Joshua's journal noted that after seven weeks of rough sea, the group needed an outlet.

> Thursday [February] 23rd. Gale continued all day. The vessel in wh. we are, with a *head-wind*, wh. is now the case, is like a log of wood, will go but about 2 miles pr. Hour, & rolls like a great tub: A curious scene presented itself at dinner-time. A sudden roll thro' many things off the table upon those at leeward; & Bro. Mardon broke his plate. No sooner were we fixed, than she gave a second roll, wh. topped Bro. Mardon's chair & threw him backward: Capt. Ryan endeavoured to save Bro. Mardon's place and pease soup, in wh. attempt he failed, fell on Bro. Mardon & upset his soup: Mr. Weston seated next to them, laughing & throwing his soup down the Capt's back & Mrs. Biss seated next to Mr. Weston laughing, looking at him and throwing her soup on the table!

The hilarious diversion relieved pent-up tension because at dinnertime four days later, Mr. Weston "got at his old work, throwing his pease soup down Bro. Mardon's back."

Hilarity aside, the storms continued to slow the *Hannah*'s progress. Dwindling food supplies led Captain Ryan to assign allowances of potatoes, salt fish, beer, and water. By March 2, the drinking water smelled "exceeding bad."

By March 10 some of the ship's sails were completely blown away; others were shredded by the winds, and its bowsprit had been broken and repaired. The *Hannah* looked like a wreck. After seventy days at sea, the relationship between Captain Ryan and the missionaries deteriorated. Ryan said he was sure there was a "Jonah" on deck. The ship should have reached New York before that time. He used to be able to damn the ship along, but now he could not. That evening during a headwind and gale they saw what the captain called "a Complisant."

> Its appearance was of a shining nature, much resembling that of a slow worm, and about the size of a man's fist, wh. being dark, we could see plainly: it came up out of the sea at the beginning of the gale, and continued ascending the [rigging], gradually, till the height of the gale; then fixed on the *highest* part of the *main*-mast for a few minutes, and as the gale decreased that descended into the sea again!

Joshua chronicled the ship's worsening condition in his journal. March 14: "Are much troubled with rats." March 21: "Head wind continues. Capt. *sold* Bro: Moore some Porter, & charged him 1 shilling per bottle: by so doing he not only broke his agreement, but took an advantage by over-charging." April 3: "Mr. Weston seems to be almost broken hearted, on account of our not yet being arrived." April 8: "Wind in our teeth. Capt. found that the rats have eaten & destroyed a [barrel] of brown biscut; therefore have but one barrel of white biscut left, for the whole ship." April 16: "Are very short of bread & meat: what little bread we have is much moulded & what meat we have is rotten." April 17: "The rats are in great want of provisions, consequently they are greater thieves than ever: stole Bro: Mardon's Breakfast."

By March 23 the *Hannah*'s proximity to its destination was such that Joshua could write, "Have a fine fair wind. Conceit that we partake of N. York air." But there was to be no easy final arrival. Heavy winds blew the ill-fated brig off course and periods of calm prevented her final approach. On April 18 they met three ships and communicated with all three by speaking trumpet. One of them, the *Alleghany*, was returning to America from Calcutta and Madras with a full cargo of sugar, pepper, ginger, twine, and piece goods.[14] Its encounter with the *Hannah* was reported to New

Yorkers in the *Evening Post*: "April 18, spoke the brig *Hannah*, Ryan, of Newburyport, 110 days from Bristol for N. York—during which time she had experienced several very heavy [gales] and much bad weather: carried away her bowsprit, and lost some of her sails. She had been blown off the coast by the late heavy gales from the westward, and kept out for several weeks by head winds and calms."[15]

Though not mentioned in the *Post*, the *Alleghany* gave desperately needed provisions to the *Hannah* as the *Hannah* had similarly shared with the *Hummingbird*. The *Alleghany* provided more than basic foodstuffs.

> After hearing our situation they hove to & put out their boat: some Ladies being on board one of wh. proved to be the supercargo's wife, who observed that there were some females on board us, collected some wine, spirits, tea, sugar, plumes [*sic*] &c. for them, sea being smooth the supercargo came on board, and presented the things to our wives, as also provision to the Capt., but wd. accept nothing for them.

Andrew Smith, the *Alleghany*'s supercargo, also gave the missionaries something that was real but intangible: encouraging hope. Smith knew William Carey and the brethren at Serampore! He had been a guest at the Serampore mission house for several days and "spoke highly of them & their situation." Smith gave the missionaries his address and invited them to visit him in the United States if they were able. As it happened, Smith was Mrs. Isabella Graham's son-in-law, who would return to India via London later in 1804. On board would be Mrs. Graham's beloved former student, Sarah Farquhar, who would marry Englishman William C. Loveless and become America's second woman foreign missionary following Hannah Liele.

Meanwhile, the *Hannah* continued onward with its missionary passengers refreshed in body and renewed in spirit. Two days later they landed in New York where Joshua wrote, "Thus thro' the inexpressible kindness of the Lord, we are safe arrived after a passage of 109 days!" The passage should have taken less than half that time.

The missionaries remained in New York City for a month where the local Baptists provided them food and lodging. There they attended the New York Baptist Association, preached in local churches, and met a number of the area's leading pastors such as Dr. Thomas Baldwin of Boston. Their presence was sufficiently known throughout the region for

William Staughton to greet them by mail from his Burlington, New Jersey, home thirty miles from Philadelphia.[16] They felt "a shock of an earthquake" in New York and saw the city bear the shock of the recurring yellow fever epidemic. And they took the pulse of America's interest in mission. Joshua's assessment was disappointed but hopeful: "Think that the people of God in America do not seem to feel so much of a missionary spirit, in general, as those in England; but the spirit appears to be fast increasing."[17]

## Onward to India

The missionaries secured passage on the American ship *Sansom* and departed New York on Monday morning, May 28, 1804, in better accommodations than those in the *Hannah*. The cargo vessel was armed with twelve guns along with a "great number of small arms, swords, &c." and looked on the water "much like a sloop of war."

Among its well-stocked provisions, the *Sansom* carried forty dozen chickens, ducks, and turkeys as well as two goats and two sows that would produce litters en route. On June 4 Capt. Stephen Minot ordered a grand dinner so his British passengers could commemorate King George's birthday.

Capt. Minot owned the *Sansom*, and though he was "a man of no religion," he was exceedingly considerate.[18] He permitted the missionaries to conduct Sunday worship on deck and ordered the crew to don clean shirts and attend. When later in the voyage some refused to do so, Minot stopped their allowance of grog.[19]

Nine hundred miles from land, the *Sansom* sprung a serious leak. To avoid returning to New York, the crew rolled the ship's guns to the opposite side. The action tipped the vessel enough for them to stop the leak that had been underwater.

The ship moved at a good pace as the days of good weather exceeded those of squalls. As the journey progressed, Joshua read an account of John Eliot's mission to the Native Americans.

On Saturday, July 28, as the *Sansom* crossed the Equator, King Neptune, his wife, and constables appeared on deck to conduct the customary initiation. Many of the sailors were shaved and dunked in a large tub of salt water while the officers doused the missionaries with water. The custom was not repeated when the *Sansom* re-crossed the Equator three months later.

On November 12, 1804, the *Sansom* arrived in Madras after five and a half tedious months at sea. The Rowes settled into a rented house within the Madras fort as they searched for a ship to carry them on to Calcutta. Betsy was pregnant, and in Madras at the end of her second trimester she delivered a stillborn son. Though two doctors despaired of her life, Betsy survived.

Although the Rowes and their missionary colleagues received encouragement from others at Madras, they faced frustrating difficulty in getting to Calcutta. French privateers seized several ships on which they had attempted to sail. Finally, on February 4, 1805, after three months in Madras, the Rowes and Moores departed on the *Juno*. The Mardon and Biss families planned to follow later. Wary of privateers, their ship hugged the coast as long as it could. Seemingly chased for several hours by a menacing ship, the *Juno* found a pilot schooner to follow until they were safe from privateers. Moving up the Hooghly River, the *Juno* ran into and sank a local boat; two people drowned. On February 20 they anchored about eight miles from Calcutta. Since the winds were calm and the ship could not move, Joshua Rowe and William Moore went ashore and walked to Calcutta where they met William Carey ahead of the others. By February 22, the ship reached Calcutta where the missionaries moved their luggage through the Custom-house, procured a pass, and proceeded to Serampore.[20]

The joys and sorrows of missionary life in India were about to begin.

## Mission in India

Joshua and Elizabeth worked with the mission press and school at Serampore as Joshua learned and began preaching in Bengali. Meanwhile, Carey progressively implemented a plan to disperse "European brethren" throughout India. Carey's plan envisioned each missionary occupying a circle of one hundred miles in diameter in order to "journey from home fifty miles in every direction with tolerable ease."

> I recommend that native brethren, preachers, readers, &c. be stationed around him at convenient distances, to labour continually in preaching, reading the word, conversation, &c. and that the European brother superintend them, and strengthen their hands in the work. By this, or similar methods...a considerable degree of light may be spread through a wide extent of country by a few persons;

and if a divine blessing accompany their labours many souls may be converted.[21]

In pursuit of the plan, a property with several bungalows was purchased in 1809 at Digah where the Moores established the new mission station. The Rowes moved to Digah in 1811 where the evangelists Brindabund and Hedut Ulla joined them and the Moores.[22] Digah was a village on the southern bank of the Ganges some 360 miles northwest of Calcutta. Nearby along the river stood two cities of importance to Digah's residents: the ancient city of Patna less than ten miles to the east and Dinapore less than a mile to the west. Dinapore's cantonment for British troops had been constructed for the defense of Patna, which was an important commercial center for the East India Company.[23] Patna had long received boatloads of salt for sale throughout India and shipped out saltpeter for production of gunpowder.[24] In 1799 Britain established a monopoly on opium production in British India. Within two decades, the Honorable Company was generating its greatest profit through its opium trade. All poppy growers were required to sell their raw product to the company, which oversaw its processing into opium and then sold the drug to agency houses in India that in turn resold it in China.[25] "Patna Opium" was of high quality and extremely profitable. English novelist Emily Eden wrote that the Patna opium storehouses "wash every workman who comes out; because the little boys even, who are employed in making it up, will contrive to roll about it in, and that the *washing* of a little boy well rolled in opium is worth four annas (or sixpence) in the bazaar, if he can escape to it."[26]

Even though "Patna Opium" was clearly produced under East India Company control, the use of intermediaries protected its trading rights and kept its ability to buy tea at Canton, China, from being jeopardized.[27]

Digah stood between these centers of commerce and the military. As a result, the mission was in position to serve not only Indigenous people but also soldiers, administrators, merchants, and others related to the Crown and the Honourable Company.

The Rowes organized a church, reached out to local families, and established schools while also becoming parents to a daughter and three sons. Elizabeth Rowe mastered the local language and wrote a Hindustani grammar. Then on October 19, 1814, Elizabeth died after giving birth to the couple's second daughter, Elizabeth Maria. Joshua buried his wife and child next to their daughter Eliza.[28]

Joshua Rowe was overwhelmed as the pastor of the mission church, manager of six Hindustani language schools, and single parent to three young sons ages eight, six, and five. Rowe wanted to remarry. His search for a partner was exceedingly difficult, in part because he could find few eligible English women in India who shared his commitment to Jesus. He therefore turned to the leadership of the Baptist Missionary Society in London and asked them to help him find a wife. Rowe wrote to John Saffery that he was desperate and might be tempted to marry "an indifferent Christian, a doubtful character, or an unconverted woman" to provide for his motherless children.[29]

Rowe recalled that Miss Sarah Wollingshead was a member of Saffery's congregation. He asked Saffery to show Sarah a copy of the account of his wife's death if Saffery and the society thought Sarah might be a suitable spouse. Months later Rowe learned that Sarah was already married. Rowe hoped that the society would continue to help him find a wife and had already provided criteria. Rowe wanted someone not over thirty-five, who had a good constitution and would be able to keep a good boarding school to support the station. And who would be pious.[30]

Meanwhile, Rowe's loneliness continued.

# PART 2

≪֍

# INDIA—THE TESTING OF A MISSIONARY

Charlotte formed her first impressions of India as the *Benjamin Rush* made its way up the Hooghly River, the branch of the Ganges on which Calcutta was located. The river scene some miles below Calcutta elicited images out of her classical education. Tree-lined riverbanks called to mind Greek mythology's Arcadia, the paradise in the silver age, and Elysium, the place of eternal bliss in the afterlife: "Suffice it to say, the clumps of round mudwalled, straw and leaf-thatched cottages of the poor natives, shaded by various kinds of trees, differing in colour, and verdure, and formation, novel to my eye, afforded pleasure, while it seemed to carry the mind back to ages of primeval life and rural contentment."[1]

As the *Benjamin Rush* drew closer to the city, however, reality began to displace mythology. The city, she wrote, "consists of straw huts like haystacks, divided by narrow offensive streets or lanes. Besides these there are elegant edifices, with generous areas divided in pail by broader streets, which are constantly crowded with servile natives, palankeens, and various equipages."[2]

Two opposing images—shaded cottages with contented, primeval rural life or haystack huts with crowded, offensive streets and lanes. Which kind of country was she entering? Charlotte would soon discover a real India that was far more delightful and disappointing, bewildering and beloved than any fleeting first impressions.

## Chapter 8

## A NEW LIFE IN INDIA

Charlotte and the Houghs arrived in Serampore on April 26, 1816.[1] The Judsons had entered Burma three years earlier. Ironically, just eight days after the Judsons' July 13, 1813, arrival in Rangoon, the British crown approved Parliament's act to renew the East India Company's charter. Due to the work of political leaders such as William Wilberforce and a massive number of petitions sent to members of Parliament, the renewed charter included "pious clauses" that allowed evangelical missionaries to live and work in India.[2] Charlotte did not fear the threat of expulsion by the Honourable Company that the Judsons had faced. Instead, she could encourage other missionaries to follow her into India.

After her first week in Serampore, Charlotte sent a letter to Philadelphia urging American women who wanted to serve in mission to "not waste time on employments of housewifery or labour, which must be laid aside here." Instead, they should acquire knowledge of "the political concerns, geographical situation and religious interests of their country and the world." In addition, they needed to gain the skills necessary to effectively operate schools, because "*they will be of little use without them.*"

Her specific advice indicated that Charlotte expected other women to follow her as educational missionaries:

The support of schools is the bread of the mission, and the *power of truth*. In this respect, the labour of females is highly important. In the *fitting out* of missionaries, bear it in mind, that all English and European goods are more expensive in India than in America, as I find needles, thimbles, scissors, pins, and linen threads, are scarcely to be had here. A few bombazets,[3] dark ginghams, and old silks for the voyage. Let everything be of the best quality; for if put up dry, seen to, and aired, they will sustain no damage in a good vessel.[4]

Charlotte noted how mission stations had expanded from Serampore, including the mission in Rangoon where the Judsons were serving. She and the Houghs had been delayed in traveling on to Burma because they had not yet found a ship that could take them in that "boisterous season." She also offered another quite interesting reason for their delay in joining the Judsons. "We should proceed to join them without delay," she wrote, "but for the desire of our brethren of this little Eden (the mission house and families) to form a tie to us by acquaintance."[5]

On the very day that the Serampore missionaries heard of the Americans' arrival in Calcutta, they sent a boat to convey Charlotte and the Houghs upriver to join them. Two single men brought the boat. One was the Marshmans' twenty-two-year-old son John. The other was Joshua Rowe.[6]

Twelve years earlier when Joshua and his first wife, Elizabeth, had visited the United States, he and Charlotte had moved in separate worlds. While the Rowes spent five and a half weeks in New York City, Charlotte and her husband Nathaniel were in Rutland, Massachusetts, preparing for the birth of their son.

After meeting in India, a tie formed quickly between Charlotte and Joshua. Within two months, the tie became permanent. On June 11, 1816, in Calcutta's Cathedral Church of St. John, the Rev. Joseph Parsons pronounced them husband and wife.[7]

Despite the availability of the Baptist churches and pastors at Serampore and Calcutta, it was not unusual for the two Baptist missionaries to be wed at St. John's. Whether or not Charlotte's Episcopal background may have inclined her to an Anglican wedding ceremony, British law in India virtually compelled it. Parliament had ended common law marriage in England by passing the 1753 Marriage Act (often referred to as Lord Hardwicke's Marriage Act), which set the age of consent at twenty-one and required marriages to be solemnized by Church of England clergy. While Quakers and Jews were exempt from the requirement, the same was not true for others. Baptist, Independent, and Church of

Scotland clergy in England petitioned Parliament for the right to solemnize marriages, and by the 1820s several bills to that effect had passed in the House of Commons. All the bills, however, failed in the House of Lords.

When Charlotte and Joshua prepared to marry in 1816, the question existed whether or to what extent the Marriage Act applied in British India where some marriages were being solemnized by military officers and non-Anglican clergy. Even several decades later, Baptists would lay a case before a member of the Calcutta bar and receive the opinion that when a dissenting minister, judge, or magistrate celebrated marriages in India, those marriages were "not valid for many important civil purposes."[8] Given the uncertainty, it was prudent for Charlotte and Joshua to marry at St. John's, a church built by the East India Company in 1784 and designated as a cathedral on Christmas Day 1815.

Charlotte and Joshua were neither the first nor the only Baptist missionaries to be married there. Six months earlier, William Yates married Catherine Grant, daughter of the deceased Baptist missionary William Grant, at St. John's. In 1822, William Carey himself went to St. John's to marry his third wife, Mrs. Grace Hughes. At least three of the Carey children were also married there.[9]

In some respects, Charlotte and Joshua were an unlikely couple. Charlotte was two months older than Joshua. No physical description of him survives beyond his reference to himself as "being little."[10] Charlotte was the last child of a Supreme Court judge, whereas Joshua was the first child of a woolcomber. Hers was an upper middle-class family. His was lower working-class. The Atlees were Episcopalians. The Rowes were Baptists.

The two, however, shared powerful life experiences. Both had lived through childhood traumas. Charlotte had lost her mother at age seven and her father at age eleven. By age seven, Joshua had endured beatings from the master of the parish workhouse. Both had mourned the deaths of their spouses and children. Charlotte had lost her husband and son. Joshua had lost his wife, two sons,[11] and two daughters. Both were committed followers of Jesus who had gradually discerned God's call to cross-cultural, international mission. And both saw education as a means to enlighten the mind while opening the spirit to a living relationship with God.

News about Charlotte quickly made its way through the British Baptist community in India and on to England. John Chamberlain wrote from

India to a prominent London Baptist pastor, "Bro. Rowe has met with a wife very opportunely who I hope will be a blessing to the school. I have not seen her but I hear things of her which shew that she is a complete Missionary. She is in every respect well qualified for the school, which was in great necessity. The Lord be with them for good."[12]

Chamberlain's recognition that a woman could be "a complete Missionary" differed from the gender expectations of Baptist Missionary Society in Britain which, like the Baptist Board of Foreign Missions in America, was not appointing women missionaries. Andrew Fuller was the society's first secretary and one of the founders when the society was organized in Kettering, England, in the home of one of his deacons. As a pastor, theologian, and mission leader, Fuller's views on mission were highly influential. By 1808 he had written *An Apology for the Late Christian Missions in India* defending mission endeavors in the realm dominated by the East India Company. Noting that the London Missionary Society was said to have three women missionaries, Fuller mused, "Are women then to be reckoned as missionaries? If so, we have considerably more than eleven in Bengal." Fuller's remark about women as missionaries proved to be rhetorical, for when he went on to list the eight Baptist missionaries in India, all of them were men. Fuller then quoted an extract of a letter from the London Missionary Society listing that society's missionaries including several married couples. Fuller concluded, "but, as their wives do not preach, they ought not to be called missionaries."[13]

Some of Chamberlain's missionary colleagues shared Fuller's gender bias. John and Hannah Biss, who had traveled to India with the Rowes, Moores, and Mardons, came to have two daughters. It was at the birth of a son, however, that John Biss wrote Andrew Fuller with elation, "We hope and trust that the LORD has now given us a young Missionary."[14]

From Burma, Adoniram Judson expressed his thoughts about Charlotte White privately in a letter to Lucius Bolles. His words seemed strikingly critical: "Mrs. White very fortunately disposed of herself in Bengal. Fortunately, I say; for I know not how we would have disposed of her in this place." As Judson elaborated, it became clear that his objection was not specifically against Charlotte, but more generally against the sending of any single woman missionary to Burma.

> We do not apprehend that the mission of single females to such a country as Burmah, is at all advisable. Nor do we think that our

patrons would have adopted the measure, had they been acquainted with the habits & ideas of this people, & the circumstances in which we are placed. Had she resided in the same house with us, it would have been impossible to have prevented the impression on the minds of the Burmans that our preaching & practice on the subject of polygamy were directly the reverse. A man, also is here considered to own his wives, his sisters (if the father be dead), & his daughter, as a part of his live stock; & as we could have laid no other claim to Mrs. White, it is not improbably [*sic*], that some Burman viceroy would have conceived it improper, that such a female should long remain without a proprietor & protector. In regard to the instruction of native women & children, we apprehend, that if every missionary is married, as he ought to be, these departments will be adequately supplied.[15]

Despite Judson's concerns about the propriety of single women missionaries serving in Burma, the work of his second wife, Sarah Hall Boardman, provided evidence to the contrary. After her missionary husband George Dana Boardman died in 1831, Sarah remained in Burma, effectively preaching in Karen jungle villages and supervising mission schools until she married the widowed Judson in 1834.

Judson's comments had been made about Burmese culture, and Sarah Boardman had served among the Karen. However, single women also served with distinction among the Burmese. Lovell and Marilla Baker Ingalls began mission service in Burma in 1851, the year following Judson's death. When Lovell died in 1856, Marilla settled in Thongze, an isolated jungle village a week's distance from Rangoon. The work she established in Thongze was staffed entirely by single women and became a major Baptist mission station in Burma. Ingalls built friendships with Buddhist monks that were unique in a religious setting that held women to be inferior beings. Marilla Ingalls died on December 17, 1902, and was buried in Thongze. During her funeral, a former monk said that Marilla's witness had led more than one hundred monks to "throw off the yellow robe" and become followers of Jesus.

Sarah Boardman's and Marilla Ingalls's life circumstances as widowed, single missionaries were comparable to those of Charlotte White. But the ministries of Boardman, Ingalls, and other single women occurred years later and thus could provide no guidance for the convention or its board in relating to Mrs. White, now Mrs. Rowe.

The General Missionary Convention held its first triennial meeting in Philadelphia, May 7–14, 1817, at the Sansom Street Baptist Church. There the board formally reported the news of Charlotte and Joshua's marriage.

> Mrs. Charlotte H. White, who accompanied Mr. and Mrs. Hough, had her views, in common with theirs, directed to Burmah. Her expectations, by a controlling Providence, have been disappointed. An important missionary station is established at Digah, near Patna, between 3 and 400 miles above Serampore. Mr. Joshua Rowe, of the English Baptist Mission, is there engaged. He solicited, and obtained a union in marriage with Mrs. White. The step appears to have been approved by the brethren of the Serampore Mission House.[16]

Beyond mere approval, the British saw the marriage as a symbol of the intimate relationship between the two mission societies. Dr. James Hinton, assistant secretary of the Baptist Missionary Society, wrote, "England and America have plighted hands, at a missionary altar, by their respective representatives, Mr. Rowe and Mrs. White. Everyone augurs good from their union." William Carey believed the marriage would bless not only the two individuals but also the work of the mission station. "I consider her marriage as a very providential circumstance," he wrote. "At Digah she cannot fail of being useful."[17]

As its corresponding secretary, Charlotte's friend and former pastor William Staughton delivered the board's address to the General Missionary Convention. His report did not simply depict Charlotte White in her new role as a missionary's wife. Instead, Staughton took pains to place her in her own role as an educational missionary. He also swatted down the earlier insinuation that she lacked the needed qualifications by stating, "She has now the care of a large school, a station for *which she is excellently qualified*, where a directress was greatly needed, and is introduced into a sphere of respectability, usefulness, and comfort [emphasis added]."

Staughton's report offered a gracious benediction upon Charlotte White Rowe: "May she prove, in her new situation, like Priscilla, a helper in the Lord Jesus." *Like Priscilla!* The comparison bore a subtle but powerful message. Readers of scripture would know of Priscilla's ministry as a theological educator. Attentive readers could also note that Priscilla's name superseded that of Aquila, evidence that in writing the Acts of the

Apostles, Luke believed Priscilla's effectiveness in ministry exceeded that of her husband.[18]

Staughton knew that many convention delegates opposed the appointment of women missionaries. Indeed, such opposition had already swayed most of the board. On June 22, 1816, by a vote of eight to two, the board had passed a resolution that "it will not be expedient in the future, as far as they can now Judge, to make appointment of an unmarried female missionary."[19] The board had not known that several days earlier, their first appointed woman missionary had married a British Baptist missionary.

Now a year later and knowing about her marriage, would the 1817 Convention delegates object that its board had spent the society's financial resources on her? Perhaps to forestall any such complaint, Staughton reported, "The Board consider it their duty to state to the Convention, that not a cent of expense has arisen to the institution from sending Mrs. White (now Mrs. Rowe) to the East. She supported herself entirely while she continued in America, and from her own funds procured her outfit."

Rather than having spent any money on Charlotte, the board found itself in the awkward position of holding funds that she had contributed to support her own work. In order to honor the intent of its donors, the board concluded that Charlotte had donated funds which, "as she is now connected with the English mission, the Board is of opinion ought to be returned to her."[20]

Meanwhile, Charlotte's future relationship with the Baptist Board of Foreign Missions remained to be clarified. After the board marked its fiftieth anniversary in 1865, it published *The Missionary Jubilee* as a record of its first half-century of mission. The book included a list of all the missionaries it had appointed. Charlotte's name appeared twice in the list. The entry under ROWE stated: "closed connection, Dec. 1816." The entry under WHITE stated: "resigned, 1816." Taken together, the entries suggested that Charlotte White Rowe had closed her connection with the board by resigning in December 1816. This would have been news to Charlotte, who wrote to William Staughton on April 21, 1817, to ask about her status.

"I know not in what relation to themselves, the Board now consider me;" she wrote, "or whether my union with the English mission by marriage, will, in their estimation, dissolve the bond between them and me." Charlotte hoped that a means could be found that would enable the relationship to continue. "I can only say, I wish still to be regarded as a daughter of the American mission, and to hold some filial affinity and intercourse with it, though I need not its pecuniary supplies."[21]

In the 1990s almost two centuries later, the board would approve joint appointments for some of its missionaries. In such relationships, a formal partnership would be established with the other appointing mission agency, institution, or church. In each instance, both bodies would fully claim the person as one of its own missionaries. The missionary would be employed by and primarily accountable to the major appointing partner while fulfilling specified accountabilities to the minor partner. In 2017, 18 percent of the American Baptist International Ministries missionaries were serving under such joint appointments.[22] In Charlotte's time, however, the board had not yet considered such a concept.

The evidence from *The Missionary Jubilee* suggests that the board unilaterally closed its connection with Charlotte White at the end of 1816. More than two years later, on April 16, 1819, the society finally returned Charlotte's donation.[23] The funds would prove critical for her.

*Chapter 9*

# THE NEW MISSIONARY AT DIGAH

The new Mrs. Rowe arrived at Digah on September 12, 1816, three months after she and Joshua were married in Calcutta. There she would meet her mission colleagues, the Moores. She never forgot the peace she felt upon approaching the mission station at eleven o'clock that night: "I remember it well, for the mission family having retired to rest, Mr. R. and his children with myself, walked about the garden, until the other family rose and joined us there. I was a stranger, but made welcome. The planets shown brightly on the station that night, and all seemed lovely."[1]

Charlotte quickly entered into mission work while simultaneously acquiring the tools needed for that work. Charlotte had said that she intended "to pursue such studies as are requisite to the discharge of missionary duties." Now settled in Hindustan, she reaffirmed that her sole desire was "to devote my every talent to the gracious Giver, and to serve his cause all my days and hours."[2] Immediately she began to study Hindi. When John Chamberlain had visited the Moore family and the widowed Joshua Rowe in Digah in early 1816, he had observed that a language barrier hindered their work. In Serampore, Joshua had been reading and preaching in Bengali, but after four years in Digah, he was still struggling to learn Hindi.[3] "They are not perfectly acquainted with the language," Chamberlain noted, "and hence cannot be expected to do much among the natives."[4] Upon returning in March 1817, Chamberlain saw a changed picture. "Sister Rowe," he reported, "is very assiduously studying the country language;

and if she is able to prosecute her design, she will doubtless become a proficient in it beyond many."[5]

Charlotte's determination to learn Hindi required both linguistic skill and hard work. Seven months into her studies she confided to readers in Philadelphia, "It requires the most persevering diligence to make any progress in the Hindoo language; as there is no dictionary or spelling-book printed with the characters." It also required a pioneering spirit. Charlotte noted, "For a female to read Hindoo is a very extraordinary thing. They all talk Hindoostanee to their servants, yet I have never either seen or heard of any who could read it."[6]

John Chamberlain's astute observation proved to be prophetic, for Charlotte soon began to speak and write Hindi. By December 1816 she had read the Gospel of John several times to her moonshee (her language instructor) and had translated nine chapters of John into Hindi.[7] Two years later George Hough in Rangoon was still struggling to learn Burmese and wrote, "I sometimes think it folly for one past thirty years of age to attempt it."[8] By contrast, Charlotte began acquiring Hindi when she was thirty-four, and a month after Chamberlain's visit she was teaching others. Charlotte informed Maria Staughton, "I have one native scholar, a little girl, whose parents brought her to me, requesting that I would teach her to work and read Hindee."[9]

Charlotte had begun conducting the station's English-language school for local boys upon her arrival in Digah. She and Joshua also boarded and taught English-speaking Eurasian children in their home.[10] Charlotte soon began fulfilling her desire to provide similar educational opportunities for girls. By the time she completed her letter to Maria Staughton, Charlotte was teaching a second local girl along with Simatria, her first female student. In two years she would be teaching eleven girls, five of whom were "Portuguese" children of mixed parentage.[11] Now Charlotte was conducting three schools: the boarding school for Eurasian children and the Hindi-language girls' school, both of which were in the Rowes' bungalow, as well as the English school for Indigenous boys in a separate bungalow.

Other British Baptist missionaries also observed the change that was taking place in Digah. John Lawson wrote to the board in the United States that Mrs. White (Rowe) seemed to be very happy and useful at Digah. "That station was much in want of such a person."[12]

Indeed, "such a person" was now building relationships with a growing circle of Indian neighbors and expatriates. Every morning about a dozen people gathered in the Rowes' bungalow for Hindi-language worship that Charlotte helped to lead. The schools, however, remained her primary work. In October 1817 her small "native female school" consisted of three girls and two women. By now Charlotte had partnered with several British ladies from nearby Dinapore who agreed to provide yearly subscriptions for native female education. The contributions greatly helped the Rowes, who otherwise funded the enterprise from their own limited resources. Since more help was needed, Charlotte appealed to friends in America. "The known friends of the cause who possess means, are too few to form a society for its support to any great extent," she wrote. "Should any society in America be disposed to contribute towards the support and enlargement of this infant native female school, a little pecuniary aid from time to time, will be acceptable in its behalf."[13]

Soon Charlotte had written *Mūl Sūtra,* or *A Hindee Spelling Book,* as an aid in teaching the local children to read their mother tongue. The Calcutta School Book Society (CSBS), newly founded in 1817, published the book. By 1820 Charlotte had also compiled a small Hindustani grammar that the CSBS likewise printed.[14]

Charlotte and Joshua believed that schools were an important form of mission and saw them as "an excellent method of spreading divine truth." They recognized the distinction between intellectual knowledge *about* Jesus and a personal relationship *with* Jesus. Education about the Christian faith could prepare students to enter that living relationship. It could also be a means of introducing the good news of Jesus in students' villages and families.[15]

Similar to Sarah Farquhar Loveless several years earlier in Madras, Charlotte faced resistance to schools from local people as well as expatriates. In Digah and nearby communities, female education and women schoolteachers were novelties that aroused suspicion in the minds of conservative traditional villagers. In one community, girls fled their school when a rumor circulated that "as soon as the girls had received a competent education, they were to be kidnapped, tied up in bags, and shipped for England!"[16]

Sometimes resistance came not from novelty or rumor but from a basic prejudice against girls' education. Except for the women in Dinapore who pledged annual subscriptions for native female education, Charlotte found that most of that town's European inhabitants discouraged instruction of both native boys and girls.[17] This attitude seemed to reflect the Honourable Company's long-standing views.

A decade earlier, Carey, Ward, and Marshman in Serampore knew that European missionaries could not introduce Christianity throughout India by their own efforts alone. They needed to train and partner with Indigenous evangelists, pastors, and church leaders. In a similar manner, the Rowes and their colleagues worked with Indigenous teachers to bring education to children throughout their area. Men were more likely than women to be literate and were therefore in greater supply as schoolmasters. Charlotte therefore taught adult women along with girls, strategically looking for potential teachers to place in schools that she started and superintended.

Schools needed students, teachers, and places to meet. Sometimes local zamindars (Persian for "landholders") supplied the school locations rent-free to benefit the families living on their land. In North India where Moghul administration had been most powerful, zamindars typically were hereditary tax collectors who were part of the ruling class. British officials treated them as landowners and used princely titles such as Raja (King), Maharaja (Great King) or Nawab with some who were wealthy and influential. Nawab became Anglicized as "Nabob" to refer both to the Indigenous landowners and to English men who made fortunes working for the East India Company and returned to England to buy seats in Parliament. "Nabob" thus became synonymous with a person of great wealth or prominence.[18]

Charlotte negotiated sites for schools, trained teachers, recruited students, solicited funding, and supervised the schools. She also taught the Rowes' boarding students in English and local girls in Hindi when their numbers were not large enough to have their own school mistress.

Student retention was no less a task than student recruitment. This was a particular challenge among girls whose parents were not fully convinced about the value of educating their daughters. Charlotte labored to assure parents that education would equip their daughters to better care for their families. Parents nevertheless tended to remove their children from school to place them in jobs or in marriage as soon as they had rudimentary skills in reading and arithmetic.[19]

An imbalance of power existed between the Western expatriates (including missionaries) and the Indigenous population. Permission to live in India and safety in doing so were both due to British colonial rule. Upon witnessing a frenzied, religious street parade within her first year in India, Charlotte acknowledged, "I should have trembled for our safety, had it not been for the military force at Dignapore."[20] Expatriates tended to be associated with powerful entities such as the East India Company or the British military while their Western education and access to money further contributed to the power imbalance.

Expatriates could use their political, educational, and economic power either to advantage themselves or the people among whom they lived. The missionaries sought to do the latter by providing opportunities for economic development, opening schools for children, and seeking to abolish the practice of widow burning. However, actions particularly related to money sometimes had unintended consequences.

Charlotte did not want poverty to keep children from the opportunity of an education. In a report to John Saffery about schools that Charlotte was overseeing, Joshua Rowe wrote, "Some of the girls in this school [at Moinpoora] are very poor, and Mrs. Rowe has had to furnish them with a piece of cloth to enable them to appear decent."[21] And to counteract their being removed prematurely from school, Charlotte experimented by offering a small reward of money or cloth to girls who remained in school. The Rowes asked the society for advice about this practice but appear to have received none.

Money also inadvertently became an issue associated with conversion to Christianity. Similar to many Indian families and other expatriates, the Rowes employed people to work in and around their home and mission station. They paid modest stipends to Indigenous itinerant evangelists from funds provided by the society. They employed male and female teachers for the native boys' and girls' schools from gifts given to the society designated for native education and from donations contributed directly from other expatriates in India. In addition and largely from personal funds, they employed Miss Sarah Bacon (a British teacher for their children), a moonshee (Hindi language teacher for Joshua and the Rowe children), a chokidar (watchman) for the station grounds, a sincar (steward), and bearers to carry them when traveling by palanquin. The Rowes and their missionary colleagues were naturally inclined to employ Indigenous Christians for those jobs. This practice, however, contributed to an increasingly common expectation that if a person were to become a Christian, the missionaries would find them employment.

The expectation of employment became a significant missiological problem.

Did missionaries have an obligation to provide for Hindus who gave up their caste to become Christians or for Muslims who professed Jesus as Lord? What kind of support should the mission provide to new believers whose faith caused them to be shunned by family, fired by employers, excluded from their community, or otherwise isolated socially or economically?

There were situations in which missionaries did perceive an obligation to care for specific people whom they sought to serve. In Burma, Felix Carey came upon a man being crucified who was yet alive after hanging for six hours. Felix intervened and saved the man, who then became his responsibility.[22] Dr. Jonathan Price, American Baptist medical missionary working with the Judsons, was especially known for his skill in removing cataracts from the eyes. While his failures were infrequent, his surgery on a young Burmese woman named Mah Noo left her permanently blind. Price, whose wife had died almost a year earlier, married and cared for Mah Noo.[23]

The Rowes took on an obligation of care through a different situation. An inquirer named Ramkisoon from the city of Lucknow lodged for a considerable time at Digah, then left after he was refused support. Several years later he returned with his wife and family. She along with her twelve-year-old daughter began learning to read at Digah and showed great interest in knowing more about Jesus. Meanwhile, the soldiers' church at Dinapore hired Ramkisoon as chokidar to watch over the brick chapel that they had erected behind the barracks. Ramkisoon was eager to be baptized, but he clearly believed that Joshua Rowe would then be obliged to find him employment if he should find himself without work in the future. The Rowes wrote to the society seeking advice, and their question appeared in the British publication *The Baptist Magazine*: "How ought a Missionary to act, when he sees something really hopeful in an inquirer, but by baptizing him he is necessitated either to find him employment for his support, or to turn him out into the world in great distress?"[24]

When the Dinapore chapel was later given to Joshua Rowe to hold in trust, Ramkisoon became Joshua's employee. Charlotte began teaching Ramkisoon's wife and children daily at the Digah Native Female School while Joshua put him under a course of spiritual instruction.[25] In autumn 1822, Ramkisoon was struck with cholera. Within one day he died with a prayer on his lips to Jesus as his Lord and Savior. His widow and four children were left dependent upon the Rowes.[26]

The relationship between the Rowes and Ramkisoon's widow differed from the question of whether mission stations should generally become sources of employment for new believers. On that question Joshua and Charlotte seemed to receive no counsel.

On October 20, 1818, Charlotte gave birth to twin daughters, Charlotte Elizabeth, named for her mother, and Esther Anna, named for her grandmother. The infants were so small at birth that Charlotte had exclaimed, "O! They cannot live a fortnight!" The two were virtually identical, and Charlotte noted that at age four they looked "so much alike that strangers can discern no difference."[27] The girls grew the family to five children, joining their half-brothers Joshua, William, and Josiah who were twelve, ten, and nine years older.

## Partners in Mission

Charlotte referred to Joshua not only as her husband but also as "my dear partner."[28] As partners in ministry, they supported one another in giving primary effort to separate language spheres.

Joshua taught their Eurasian boarding students in English. In addition, he ministered to the soldiers stationed in the nearby Dinapore cantonment. Regiments of His Majesty's army were often stationed in the cantonment for up to two years before being transferred elsewhere and replaced by another regiment of foot soldiers or artillery. At other times, the regiments at Dinapore were from the East India Company.

Joshua also reached out to civilian expatriates who included invalid former soldiers living in the cantonment, civil servants of the Honorable Company, European estate owners, merchants, and tradespeople. While he sometimes accompanied the Indigenous evangelists as they itinerated among the villages, he considered his work among the soldiers to be his most fruitful ministry.

Some of the soldiers were Protestant dissenters, but only Anglican chaplains were provided to serve the military and company regiments. Dinapore had no place of worship for dissenters, so the soldiers walked to the Rowes' bungalow in Digah for that purpose. Meanwhile, several soldiers in His Majesty's 24th Regiment stationed in Calcutta became Christians, were baptized, and formed a church within their regiment. The church had grown to about eighty members when it was transferred to Dinapore in summer 1814. After initially going to worship at the Digah mission station, the soldiers decided to erect a chapel in Dinapore that would be more convenient and might encourage additional soldiers to come to the services. Behind their barracks the soldiers built a chapel of bamboo and grass with room for 250 people. The structure was immediately dubbed the "Grass Tabernacle." Joshua Rowe preached there twice on Sunday and twice on weekdays. Some months later the regiment was sent about ninety miles north to fight on the Nepal border. Joshua visited them there for three weeks, preached in a structure they had built near the front of their lines, and conducted the Lord's Supper. While there, the soldiers dug a hole and lined it with mats to hold water so that Rowe could baptize those who professed faith.[29]

Other regiments and the families of the 24th Regiment worshiped at the Grass Tabernacle while the 24th was at Nepal. When the regiment returned to Digah, the chapel was in poor repair and was now too small. Rowe's congregation in the regiment therefore dismantled the Grass Tabernacle and constructed a building on the same site with walls of bamboo that they plastered with mud and then whitewashed. Rowe's services filled the chapel with up to 400 worshipers. Before the regiment was sent south to battle, the regimental church formed a Branch Society as an auxiliary to the Baptist Missionary Society in Serampore.[30]

In 1821 His Majesty's 59th was stationed at Dinapore where it found the chapel needing much repair. With the permission of Major General William Toone, believers in the 59th tore down the structure and replaced it with a more durable brick building. The congregation in the 59th contributed to the mission in Serampore and financially supported the native female school in Digah. When the 59th left Dinapore for Cawnpore in 1822, the congregation gave the building to Rowe to hold in trust and ensure that it would continue to be used as a place of worship.[31]

Joshua Rowe was saddened that relatively few Indigenous people had professed Christianity as a result of the Digah station: "If in the institution of a gospel ministry, God had nothing in view but the conversion of sinners and the building up his people on their most holy faith, I should certainly conclude that nearly all my labours were in vain; but when I consider that he has a design even in an unsuccessful ministry, I take encouragement, and hope that my labours are not in vain."[32]

Rowe's ministry among expatriate Englishmen, however, was far from barren. It was one of many instances in which missionaries discover fruitful ministry among a different group of people than those among whom they had expected to work. Rowe suggested to Rev. John Sutcliff that his evangelistic and pastoral work among the British soldiers "ought not to be overlooked in reviewing the fruits of missionary labours in this heathen land. Many a hardened sinner from the shores of Britain has been converted in India."[33]

Joshua Rowe discovered opportunity and fruitful results among British soldiers rather than among the Hindus and Muslims to whom he had been sent. It was a de facto change of assignment. Such changes had theological and organizational implications that shaped and illuminated the missiology of the missionaries and their sending agencies. The missionaries could either embrace the work in which their ministry was proving to be fruitful or remain solely focused on their original assignment. Similarly, the sending agency could either affirm the missionaries' ability to alter the focus of their work or mandate adherence to the agency's operational plan. Such decisions were rooted, consciously or not, in understandings of the work of the Holy Spirit and discernment of God's leading.

## Charlotte's Ministry

Although Charlotte helped Joshua teach the English-speaking Eurasian students boarding in their home, both regarded this as a hindrance to Charlotte's broader work that was in Hindi. When financial restraints forced severe cuts in their household expenses, Joshua gave up employing his moonshee. He lamented that it was "a great loss to me and my children, who were studying some native language under him."[34] By contrast, Charlotte had been speaking, reading, and writing Hindustani for four years. She could read both the Nagree and Persian scripts. She called the former "Hindoo" or "Hindee," the latter "Oordoo," and used both in her ministry.[35] Then as now, the term "Hundustani" held differing meanings depending on the user. Broadly understood, Hindustani had arisen as a fusion of Hindi and Urdu after Muslim rulers arrived in India in the thirteenth century. Thus, spoken Hindi and Urdu tended to be mutually understandable and led the British to promote Hindustani over either pure Hindi or Urdu. In written form, however, the Nagree (Nagari or Devanagari) script, written horizontally left to right, and the Persian (Perso-Arabic) script, written horizontally right to left, were mutually unintelligible.

Joshua recognized that Charlotte was truly "in her element" when engaged in what he distinguished as her "missionary work."[36] He felt that her involvement in the school (presumably their boarding school) curtailed that wider work and told John Saffery,

> I wish she were freed from her school altogether, and had the whole of her time to devote to Missionary work among the native females. She is becoming more qualified for such an employment every day, and I hope something will turn up to free her from her present engagements in the school, and to enable her to devote herself *entirely* to *Missionary* work. This is the specific object for which she came to India, and this is the work in which she wishes both to live and to die.[37]

Again he wrote to the society telling of Hindustani-speaking women around them "who at present are much neglected. I wish Mrs. Rowe had sufficient leisure to be enabled to go about among them doing good."[38]

The following year Charlotte was instructing twenty-seven girls and one woman with the prospect of getting more. Joshua told Carey, Marshman, and Ward in Serampore, "Missionary work increases upon her hands as well as upon mine. Her soul is in the work, and she is daily becoming more qualified for it. It is her desire to give herself wholly to missionary work."[39]

Charlotte's work with Indigenous students and especially with the girls was a world set apart from Joshua. He mused that "It must be an interesting object to see a number of native females busily employed in reading and writing; this, however, is an object that I am as yet denied the privilege of seeing. If I were to venture to peep in upon them, it would probably spoil the whole."[40]

On Sundays the Rowes worked in separate locations. Joshua preached in English at Dinapore, while Charlotte "presided" in Hindi at worship services in their bungalow. When Joshua reported this to the society, he was conscious of controversies about women preachers and immediately added, "Do not put a wrong construction on the last sentence, by supposing that she is the *preacher*." He then continued in a suitably ambiguous manner, "She is indeed a preacher, but she does not preach on those occasions. One of our native brethren preaches to our Servants, and to as many others as we can induce to come to hear him, and she presides to keep order as well as to hear."[41]

The Rowes' concern to be accurately understood by the society was only one of their communication challenges. Letters could take from five to seven months traveling between Digah and London, and their posting and delivery were both uncertain. The Serampore missionaries knew when ships were about to depart and could make sure to get their correspondence on board; however, the Rowes in Digah never knew ship schedules. Their letters left Digah via the land-bound postal service with no control over the speed with which their letters would be conveyed to Calcutta. They never knew when ships were departing with their mail to London, nor did they know the reliability of the ships or their captains. Furthermore, the Rowes never knew when and by which ships the Baptist Missionary Society was replying to them. When they heard that Calcutta-bound ships were lost at sea, the Rowes always wondered if the ships had sunk carrying letters or goods intended for them.

Charlotte and Joshua had difficulty receiving general information from the society as well as answers to their specific questions. They repeatedly asked how the society intended to care for missionaries' widows and orphans. In 1820 Joshua wrote, "We have never seen the Regulations relative to Widows, Orphans, &c. you mention as having been sent to all the stations, though we have heard of them and written respecting them. You forgot to enclose the copy you intended to forward."[42] In 1822 he reminded the society that it had never told Charlotte how much funding it would send to support the female schools. He also told them, "I have never seen the Missionary rules, some of which you said were applicable to stations circumstanced like Digah, so that I have nothing whatever to guide me in their concerns."[43]

The Baptist Missionary Society was eager to receive stories about the results of the work being undertaken. In 1805 William Carey had already complained that too much was being published in London about his work, and therefore he sent very few profiles of new converts "for fear they shd. be published."[44] While the missionaries were eager to write about lives being transformed because of the gospel, the society needed to remember that newspapers and magazines printed in England made their way back to India, sometimes with negative consequences. Joshua explained, "Our communication generally return in print and by this time it may be that many of the things mentioned have no existence. Without considering the nature of the communications, an Infidel will then triumphantly ask where are your hopeful converts? Where am I to look for the expected fruits of your labours?"[45]

The missionaries cautioned the society to be prudent in its public relations. Letters written in a given context could become misleading as events unfolded over time and could be disastrous if used in ways for which they were never intended.

Charlotte learned this through great pain.

## Chapter 10

# THE AFFAIR OF THE REPURPOSED LETTER

Charlotte had been in the practice of writing to Dr. Edwin Augustus Atlee, her brother in Philadelphia with whom she had a close relationship. Edwin had preached at the public prayer meeting before Charlotte had set sail for India, and she undoubtedly felt it a comfort to have a brother an ocean away in whom she could confide.

Charlotte knew from experience that missionaries serving on location often have perspectives that differ from those of their sending agency. As she observed to Edwin, "A society in England or America is in the dark. Things in India are, and must necessarily be, different from their views."[1] A prime example occurred when William Carey, Joshua Marshman, and William Ward became estranged from the Baptist Missionary Society. Differing perspectives had emerged over several issues including property. The "Serampore trio" felt it was their right to make decisions regarding the Serampore mission property inasmuch as they had purchased and developed it from income generated by their own secular labor in India. The committee in London felt the property belonged to the society because the missionaries were the society's agents.

News of the disagreement circulated with more or less detail and accuracy among the "junior missionaries" in India. The potential conclusions were alarming. Were the "senior brethren" stealing society property? Was the society defrauding the missionaries of that which was rightfully theirs? How might this strongly held difference of opinion be resolved?

Some details of the contentious relationship found their way to Digah through various communications. Based on those reports, the Rowes felt indignant at the way in which they perceived the senior missionaries were treating the society and by extension, the rest of its missionaries. The issue lay heavily on Charlotte's mind, and she shared some confidential thoughts with her brother "bearing hard on the brethren at Serampore." To their later astonishment and distress, Charlotte and Joshua received an "affectionate though afflicting letter" from John Saffery, Joshua's former pastor and the society's chairman. Saffery informed them that extracts of Charlotte's letter had appeared in an American publication, copies of which had made their way to England. Saffery questioned the wisdom "to even communicate this even to a *brother unconnected with the Society?*" Charlotte was absolutely dumbfounded. Joshua replied to Saffery,

> We are at a loss to know how to account for it. Nothing could have been farther from her intention in writing the remarks. She has great confidence in her brother who is a respectable Physician and a leader among the Quakers. She expressly prohibited his publishing *anything* she wrote to him, and cannot yet believe it was done with his knowledge. The only way in which we can account for it is by supposing some one did it in a clandestine way.[2]

Saffery had not quoted the extract nor identified the publication in which it appeared. Charlotte therefore wrote two letters to her brother asking for an explanation. She could not conceive that he would have had any part in releasing her letter to the press and wondered what enemy could have done such a thing behind his back. Edwin's reply reached her about a year later and provided the details.

Writing in the distinctive Quaker speech pattern, Edwin wrote, "I acknowledge that I received strict injunctions from thee more than once, not to publish any thing communicated by thee relative to affairs in India, on pain of never, afterward, receiving a letter from thee." He then claimed that Charlotte had given publication permission "in particular cases, left to my own discretion, provided thy name was suppressed."[3]

Edwin asserted that he had "religiously observed" his sister's injunction. When he had shown Charlotte's letters and journal to his or her friends, he had frequently reminded them of her aversion to any part of them being committed to the press. Nevertheless, Edwin had shared Charlotte's letter with Theophilus Ransom Gates, editor of *The Reformer:*

*A Religious Work*, a radical monthly Philadelphia newspaper.[4]

Gates was a visionary and itinerant preacher whose wanderings had brought him from Connecticut to Philadelphia. Gates advocated a primitivist approach to faith that rejected all organized forms of religion including denominations, theological seminaries, ordained clergy, Sunday schools, Bible societies, mite or aid societies, houses of worship, and mission societies. The inauguration of *The Reformer* in 1820 coincided with the publication of works by two Baptists who opposed the nationally organized mission movement: *Thoughts on Missions* by John Taylor and *A Public Address to the Baptist Society, and Friends of Religion in General, on the Principle and Practice of the Baptist Board of Foreign Missions for the United States of America* by Daniel Parker. Both criticized the Triennial Convention and its Baptist Board of Foreign Missions as being unbiblical since mission societies were not mentioned in scripture either "by precept or example." Gates reprinted Taylor's writings and was a ready market for other criticism of mission boards and their missionaries.

Gates eventually published four newspapers in Philadelphia: *The Reformer* (1820–1830), *The Christian* (1830), *The Reformer and Christian* (1830–1834), and *Battle-Axe and Weapons of War* (1837). In 1834 he concluded that Jesus' second coming had taken place in 70 AD and that perfection was now attainable for members of God's kingdom on earth, a sinless state that he now claimed to have achieved. Gates believed that as he spread this message, he was fulfilling the prophecy of Jeremiah 51:20, "Thou art my battle-axe and weapons of war."

Gates's utopian vision of preparing sinless people to enter the millennium attracted about thirty followers.[5] The Battle-Axe members practiced free love, scandalized their neighbors, and caused their farming valley between Pottstown and Coventry, Pennsylvania, to be dubbed the "Free Love Valley." The Battle-Axe movement rejected any form of organization and did not outlast its first adherents.

The Battle-Axe venture began in the mid-1830s. A decade earlier, however, Gates was wholly engaged in producing monthly issues of *The Reformer* as his public forum against organized religion. His October 1821 issue began with a ten-page diatribe against Princeton Theological Seminary and paid clergy. Gates then printed portions of a letter from the late Harriet Newell that he used as evidence that the Serampore missionaries were living in "princely style." Then, "to cap the climax of the three famous Missionaries at Serampore," *The Reformer* reported the news that Carey,

Marshman, and Ward had "pronounced themselves *disconnected from, and independent of the Society in England;* and *declared the premises at Serampore, to be their own exclusive property.*"[6]

Two months later, Edwin had placed portions of Charlotte's letter in Gates's hands.

Gates reprinted them as anonymous extracts in December 1821 to prove *The Reformer's* October report. In a concluding editorial note, Gates assured readers that, if required, he could provide evidence from his "most respectable source" certifying that the extracts were truly "contained in a letter from a Baptist missionary, now in India, who could have had no inducement to state things incorrectly."[7]

Edwin Atlee felt justified in releasing portions of his sister's letter that were critical of the Serampore trio. In his judgment, these were things that "the *honest* public have a *right* to know." He pointed out that he had not exposed her name to *The Reformer*. Further exonerating himself, he asserted that he had never promised to refrain from publishing her words, then adding legalistically, "and thou knowest that no agreement can *exist*, much less be *coercive*, unless by mutual consent of the parties."

By early 1822, however, Charlotte's authorship of the letter had become known to some in America and England and had occasioned Saffery's letter to the Rowes. Therefore, Edwin felt vindicated in permitting *The Reformer* to identify her in print. Edwin also showed Gates portions of the two letters Charlotte had written to him seeking an explanation of the affair. Furthermore, Edwin provided Gates with a copy of his reply to Charlotte including the full text of her critical remarks about Serampore that had been published earlier.

Gates reprinted this exchange of letters between Charlotte and Edwin in the April 1823 issue of *The Reformer*. Gates introduced the article by stating, "[T]hrough some channel unknown to us, the author of the Letter from India, giving an account of the transaction of the Missionaries at Serampore, has been ascertained." He then identified Charlotte, painting her as a victim of Carey, Marshman, and Ward.

> Mrs. Rowe superintends a native female school at *Digah*—is zealously, and we believe sincerely devoted to the cause of missions—and is the wife of one of the English Baptist Missionaries. The letter was written to her brother, Dr. Edwin A. Atlee, of this city. Letters lately received from her by her brother, show that she has every thing to fear from having it known that she communicated

any thing of a disparaging nature respecting Missionary proceedings in India. It would seem, indeed, that it is a concerted plan among the [Serampore] Missionaries, to present only the *bright side of the picture*, and keep from the public every thing wearing a different aspect; and that whoever departs from this rule, becomes a victim to their displeasure.[8]

By republishing the critical extracts and naming Charlotte H. Rowe as the author, *The Reformer* intimated that it was honoring her as a person of integrity telling truth in the face of opposition. It did so, however, with the subtle but persistent gender bias of the era. Rather than identify Charlotte as a missionary, it introduced her as a school superintendent who was the wife of a missionary.

Charlotte had said of the publication of her letters, "Suffice it to say, I am injured by it throughout the world." If anyone ever informed her that *The Reformer* had republished the extracts as well as portions of her two follow-up letters to Edwin, she must have felt doubly injured.

Gates concluded with editorial remarks of regret that Mrs. Rowe should become a sufferer on account of *The Reformer's* articles but asserted the public's right to know. He hinted that even if the Serampore missionaries might persecute Mrs. Rowe for telling the truth, *The Reformer* would not be silenced. "If they are able to control the press in India, they are not able to do it in this country."

For his part, Edwin's letter to Charlotte professed sincere regret that the publication had wounded her feelings and reputation. She was "so valuable and devoted a labourer in the vineyard of reformation" and his "much-loved sister." He was ready to take on himself "all just censure which the public may see fit to impose."

Edwin Atlee knew that putting her words yet again before the public would most certainly wound his sister, "whose devotedness to the cause of the Redeemer I have never doubted." Yet he closed his last letter to her with assured rightness in his actions and singular deafness to her wishes.

As to thy recommendation and *command*, "that all thy letters and diary from the first of thy correspondence from India be consigned to the flames," I may affectionately tell thee, that we are not prepared to *obey*. They are too valuable, not only as future *vouchers*, but as mementoes of a dear relative whom we never expect again to see in this state of mutability. And I freely resign to the sad alternative, on which thou art resolved, never hereafter to favour us with a single line: concluding this, probably *my last* to thee, (which, if not in print, might share the fate of *many* heretofore sent and not received,) with the fervent breathing of my spirit, that being preserved stedfast, [*sic*] "in *evil report* and *good report*," thou mayest keep thine eye *single* to the glory of God, loving "His praise more than the praise of *men*; and when thy work of *Faith* and labour of *Love* shall have been accomplished, thou mayst be privileged to "enter into the joy of thy Lord."

With the salutation of brotherly and Christian love, I bid thee farewell.

EDWIN A. ATLEE[9]

Charlotte warmly admired her brother. In mid-April 1823 she gave birth to her last child and named him Edwin Atlee Rowe.[10] With strong winds and smooth seas from Philadelphia to Calcutta and ready land or river transport from Calcutta to Digah, Edwin's letter could have reached Charlotte by July.

It changed her world.

Stunned by Edwin's arrogant attitude and actions, Charlotte renamed her baby. From that time on her son would be called Judson Ward Rowe. Rather than look to his Uncle Edwin, Charlotte encouraged him to emulate her fellow missionaries, the courageous Adoniram Judson, who was laboring in Burma, and the warm-hearted William Ward, who had died of cholera in Serampore a month before little Judson's birth.

View of one side of the Main Street in the Indian city of Patna.
*Watercolor by Sita Ram, 1814–1815, The British Library*

Charlotte Hazen Atlee was recorded
to be a resident of Rutland when she married
Nathaniel Hazen White on November 17, 1803.

*Rutland, Massachusetts, Town Clerk Records, 1626–2001*

Charlotte White married Joshua Rowe
at St. John's Cathedral in Calcutta.

*Painting by James Baillie Fraser, The British Library*

The ancient city of Patna ten miles east of Digah was an
important center from which the East India Company
shipped goods for export down the River Ganges.

*Painting by Thomas Daniell, The British Library*

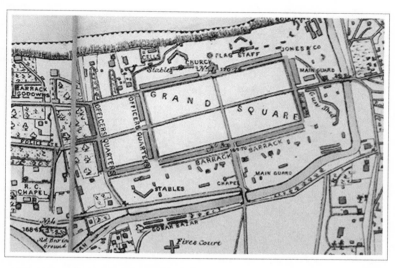

The Dinapore (Danapur) Cantonment located one mile west of Baptist mission in Digah housed soldiers from His Majesty's Army and from the East India Company. Joshua Rowe preached in the "Grass Tabernacle" behind (south of) the barracks. The brick chapel then replaced it.

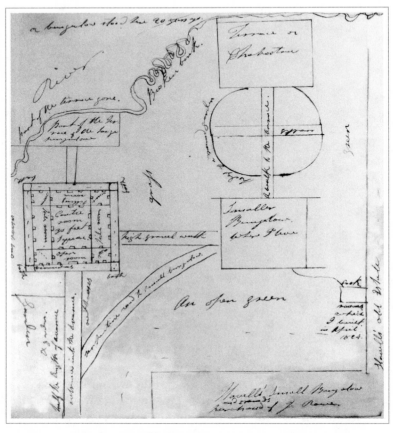

Charlotte sent her hand-drawn map of the Digah mission
property to the Baptist Missionary Society in London in 1824.

*Courtesy Angus Library and Archive, Regent's Park College, Oxford, UK*

The "Grass Tabernacle" on the Dinapore Cantonment
was constructed with bamboo walls and
grass roof similar to this school from the era.

Charlotte Rowe initially used a palanquin to reach villages where
she started and supervised schools. Charlotte replaced
her palanquin with a small horse-drawn cart due to the
disrespect often shown to the bearers.

The Calcutta School-Book Society that published Charlotte's
Hindi language spelling book and grammar usually met in the
Town Hall of Calcutta shown here.

*Painting by James Baillie Fraser, 1826, The British Library*

tained. A concealment of the name being no longer enjoined upon us, we inform the public that the writer is Charlotte H. Rowe. Mrs. Rowe superintends a native female school at *Digah*—is zealously, and we believe sincerely devoted to the cause of missions—and is the wife of one of the English Baptist Missionaries. The letter was written to her brother, Dr. Edwin A. Atlee, of this city. Letters lately received from her by her brother,

The *Reformer*'s article identifying Charlotte Rowe as author of the repurposed letter was reprinted in newspapers from New York, Vermont, and Connecticut to the District of Columbia.
Reformer, *1 April 1823*

A CARD.

MRS. C. H. ROWE, late Missionary in India, having located at No. 101 Wood street, above Seventh, gives notice to her friends and the public, that she is about opening an English School for Young Ladies and small Children; intending to admit a few select pupils as boarders.

Being a native of Pennsylvania, she trusts that her fellow citizens will forward her humble efforts to support a rising family.

N. B. For farther information, apply to Rev. Mr. Brantly, Gen. Duncan, and Dr. E. P. Atlee.

Jan. 29th, 1830.

Charlotte Rowe's advertisement for her school in Philadelphia.
Columbian Star and Christian Index, *Philadelphia, 31 January 1830*

The "Grass Tabernacle" on the Dinapore Cantonment
was replaced by this brick chapel in 1821. The building
now houses an Indian Army printing press.

*Courtesy Reid Trulson*

Charlotte was buried in the St. James Episcopal Church
cemetery next to her twin daughters.

*Courtesy Reid Trulson*

## Chapter 11

# DEATH, DISARRAY, AND DETERMINATION

In the summer following Judson Wade's birth, Charlotte felt "very poorly." In reality, she was approaching death.[1] By early fall, her health was still "extremely bad." Joshua contemplated sending the two oldest boys to school or work in Serampore or Calcutta as he labored to care for the family and continue the ministry. In mid-September Joshua developed a cold and began feeling unwell as he was carried home at night in a palanquin after preaching at Bankipore, a community immediately west of Patna. He became seriously ill and was confined to bed. On September 21 he preached to his congregation at Dinapore and bade them farewell. It was his last sermon. After three weeks of struggle, he called his children around him, kissed them for the last time and assured them that he would meet them in heaven and that God would be their father here. On October 11, 1823, he died. He was forty-one.

Soldiers bore Joshua Rowe to a grave in the Dinapore cantonment's burial ground where he was interred beside Betsy and their two daughters.

Charlotte was now back on the sorrowful path she had walked nineteen years earlier when her first husband died just months after their first son was born. She must have worried that little Judson might soon follow Joshua in death as her first son Nathaniel had followed his father. Still very weak, Charlotte was scarcely able to care for herself, much less six children aged seventeen years to seven months. To build back her strength and have help with her children, she took the family to Calcutta. There in Bengal she was careful to secure mentors and jobs for the three older boys. Joshua began proofing manuscripts and helping with the school at Serampore. William entered a mentorship to become a doctor. Charlotte proposed that if he could find no prospects in India after his studies, he could go to America as a surgeon on a ship. Then he could "go on to a little farm belonging to me in Luzerne County, which is the property of my youngest child—and thus settle himself as a County physician, if nothing else, for a few years." Josiah started training to become a surveyor for which there were ample jobs in India.[2]

Charlotte recuperated in Calcutta until March 1824 when she returned to Digah.[3] Her months in Calcutta had "resuscitated" her with physical, emotional, and spiritual renewal.[4] She would need it.

The Digah mission station to which Charlotte and the three youngest children returned was in great disarray. The large bungalow that the Rowes had previously rented out to others stood vacant and seriously damaged by thieves even though she had left a watchman to guard it.[5] The roof of the smaller bungalow into which she and the children moved had serious damage from the seasonal rains. Other buildings and the public gateway to the campus stood in serious disrepair.

The Rowes' boarding school was nonexistent. None of the girls' schools survived although the boys' schools that they had started with local schoolmasters continued to function. The house church that met in her home had only five members including Charlotte. Digah's itinerant evangelists, the brothers Hurree Das and Roop Das, had stayed at the station. No other missionaries remained, and all the station's male workers had left. Charlotte assessed the situation with simple realism: "Having been left to act alone, I have had to direct things according to the best of my own understanding."[6]

And act she did.

The six-year-old twins needed an education, one-year-old Judson needed watching, and forty-two-year-old Charlotte needed an income. Since the British Baptists were not appointing women missionaries, she could expect no financial support from the Missionary Society. Although she qualified for a grant from the widows and orphans fund, the society's grants were very modest because it expected widows to either re-marry or return to England. Charlotte knew that the widows' grant was inadequate and rooted in mistaken reasoning, so she wrote to John Dyer, the head of the society whom she had never met but addressed as "my dear friend."

You I trust, will pardon my being so particular. I do it for the just information of the Society, who, intending to make due provision for missionaries widows & orphans, have been misled, or induced to adopt rules which necessarily must be overreached. We are fully persuaded of their paternal feeling toward us—and we are grieved, that we cannot, with all our economy, come within their allowance, unless we descend to a mode of life, at once distressing to ourselves and them. I have no doubt, they will affectionately consider these things.[7]

Charlotte's call to mission remained as vibrant as it had been when she sailed from America as its first appointed woman missionary. Characteristically pragmatic, she knew that following that call meant continuing to self-fund her mission. She explained to Dyer that she intended to take in two pupils as boarders. Miss Sarah Bacon would teach the boarders and the twins at Charlotte's expense. Ramkisoon's widow, who lived in the bungalow as a family dependent, could give some attention to little Judson. Meanwhile, the tuition from the two boarders would supplement the widow's grant from the Missionary Society.

Many buildings at Digah needed repair for which the society had provided no specific guidance and no funding. Like the wise business-woman of Proverbs 31, Charlotte used industry and investment to tackle the problems. She renovated and repaired the vacant bungalow and rented it to a Colonel Boyd. She then used the rental income along with materials salvaged from failing or collapsed structures to repair and maintain other buildings at the mission.

The Missionary Society owned the Digah property, and Charlotte sought their advice before proceeding much farther. She knew, however, that annual repairs were not sufficient. Entire roofs needed to be replaced if the buildings were to remain usable. The smaller bungalow into which Charlotte had moved her family was almost uninhabitable. During the rains, she and the children "could scarcely find a dry corner to sleep in" even though the roof tiles were being placed and replaced daily.[8] She wrote, "The insects have eaten the beams and rafters so that it sinks in places, and lets in floods of rain upon the tops of the walls which it washes away, and rots the cloth which serves as a ceiling. The old straw is rotten under the tiles and breeds innumerable insects which fall continually over tables, dishes, &c."[9]

In addition, the larger rented bungalow was in imminent danger. The house stood on the bank of the Ganges, which flowed west to east along the north side of the property. The monsoon rains each June through September increased the current and steadily cut into the bank. When Charlotte returned from Calcutta, only two yards of earth remained before the encroaching river might undermine and collapse the entire structure.

In the past, Joshua Rowe had annually sunk pillars and fastened bamboo lattice to attempt to protect the bank, but virtually every year the floods washed it all away. There were several options at hand: continue erecting ineffective lattice-work fences, follow the example of the Honorable Company and face the bank with a brick wall, sell the property and leave the problem to the buyer, or keep the property but build or buy a replacement bungalow. As Joshua had done before to no avail, Charlotte pleaded for the society to decide.

Charlotte knew that the question was not simply about property. It was about mission. Digah was a prime location for meaningful ministry among Hindus, Muslims, and, indeed, Europeans of Hindustan. She envisioned the society sending three missionary families to join her at Digah. The mission ought to expand.

> There ought to be an English School for Hindoos, and a printing press here; and a School for European children. But several missionaries are requisite to do all this. A number of missionaries combined, may render a station less expensive to the Society than only one missionary, because they may unite in keeping a boarding school which will nearly support themselves, while the Society bears only the outward expenses.[10]

Charlotte forged ahead to restart her educational and evangelistic work while simultaneously dealing with Digah's most urgent property needs. Always proactive regarding schooling for girls, she immediately reopened a girls' school at Moinpoora. She named it the "Liverpool School" because Baptists in Liverpool, England, had donated the funds for girls' education. She was equally ready to reopen the similar "Lyme School" for girls if Baptist supporters in Lyme, England, would contribute funds as they had in the past. Meanwhile, she started a girls' school at Digah that she funded herself.

To guide the teachers and assure accountability, Charlotte went to the schools in regular rotation. She generally visited two schools every morning, the weather and her health allowing.[11] During her recuperation in Bengal she had observed that school facilities there were far better than those she supervised in Hindustan. Topography contributed to some of the poor conditions. The highest ground along that portion of the Ganges was at Dinapore on which the military cantonment was located. For miles around, the land stretched out as a flat and poorly drained plain. This led to significant flooding during the rainy season.[12]

The Liverpool School at Moinpoora was a prime example. The local zamindars had requested a school for the community and provided a building rent-free for that purpose. Charlotte described it as a mud hut with two inlet-like doorways that was "small and so dark and close that it is quite disgustful." In dry weather, the yard was crowded with feeding cattle that filled the hut with suffocating animal fumes. When Charlotte visited the school in mid-September 1824 following the rains, the condition was even worse. The yard overflowed with muddy water. Men waded waist deep to carry Charlotte to the hut's door where she "ascended with difficulty, having no dry place for my foot."[13] Thirty-five boys and ten girls awaited her inside the hut.

Determined that children in and around Digah deserved better learning conditions, Charlotte resolved to replace the inadequate schoolhouses with healthier structures on sites less prone to flooding. Again, she solicited funds from the expatriate community, and again she encountered resistance. Some were willing to loan money if it were to be used for Charlotte's personal needs, but most believed that "the improvement of the natives will be pernicious to the national tranquility." Local children didn't need schools. "They are better left as they are."[14] Undeterred, Charlotte continued reaching out to the expatriate community until she found several individuals who endorsed her vision. One was Lady Maria Toone, whose husband, Major General Sir William Toone, commanded the East India Company's troops in Dinapore.[15] Lady Toone provided funds for a girls' school on the local Nabob's compound where a boys' school already existed.

By 1826 Charlotte was supervising nine schools: four for boys, three for girls, and two coeducational. She had put a new roof on Daoodpore's boys' school and had succeeded in the greater challenge of reviving Daoodpore's Lyme School for girls. That school now had a woman teacher and a young male assistant and operated in a new brick house that Charlotte had financed by raising subscriptions.

The coeducational Liverpool School at Moinpoora was perhaps her greatest construction challenge and victory. This was the mud hut school where on two visits her palanquin bearers had waded to their waists in floodwater. On a third visit she had been unable to get to the school at all because of the slime remaining after the floods. By early 1826, however, construction was underway, and the foundation had been laid for a new building.[16] The foundation and floor were raised above the neighborhood's usual level of flooding. The structure would have a tile roof supported by brick pillars. Lattice walls of bamboo admitting light and air would provide the decent learning conditions that Charlotte so wanted for the children.[17]

Charlotte financed the school projects at Moinpoora, Daoodpore, and elsewhere by raising subscriptions for those purposes. To gain support she first needed to convince people that girls as well as boys could learn and benefit from education. So she offered proof. On Saturday, October 16, 1824, a select group of expatriates came by invitation to the Digah mission station. Each was a person of influence: Lady Toone and her family, Colonel Boyd, Captain and Mrs. Wilson. They had been invited to witness something new—the first public examination of mission school students. Charlotte planned to hold a public examination annually, if not every six months. She knew that without seeing for themselves, many European expatriates would not even believe that such schools existed, much less be convinced of their utility. All her invited guests were impressed that 55 girls and 159 boys were under instruction.[18]

Charlotte had to arrange everything by herself. Some children would demonstrate that they could read in one syllable, some in two syllables, while others were literate in three and four syllables, grammar, and full reading. Students recited Watts's Catechism and the Ten Commandments. Some showed their ability to write on paper or on boards with chalk water while all the rest could write the alphabet and write on the earth with chalk. Nearly all showed competence in "Hindoo arithmetic."[19]

> The similar classes in each school were formed into one, and brought into the room, examined and dismissed alternately, and all done quietly. The girls presented their needlework, and gained much praise, as well for that as their other performances, for they wrote, and read in print before the Ladies & Gentlemen. After the work of examination, the children were all called into the rooms, and brother Roop Das read to them a few verses from Scripture, and explained them very clearly respecting what really defiled a man, and *that knowledge* which was necessary to their enjoyment,

both in this world and that which is to come. And having sung a native hymn in which many joined, brother Hurree Das closed with prayer. The children were then dismissed with the trifling reward of 2 pice or a penny each, to get themselves a morsel to eat on their way home, as many had come six miles.[20]

Charlotte's educational philosophy was never limited to the "three Rs." Hers was more holistic and included spiritual formation and domestic skills. While she could have grown discouraged that few students were quickly becoming Christians, she believed that spiritual fruit would emerge over a longer term. "The word of God bids us cast our bread upon the waters, and after many days we shall receive it again. I would apply this to native female instruction," she wrote in 1824. Of the nine or ten girls whom she had begun to teach in 1817, seven had learned to read and sew, and over the course of time, five had become Christians. One of those students was now the teacher in "Lady Toone's School" at the Nabob's compound. While none of the sixty girls who had been taught to read from 1821 to 1823 had come to faith, she likened their instruction to "sown wheat in frigid climes" that would eventually "spring forth vigorously when the Sun of Righteousness shall shine over these sown fields...."[21] "If half of every school should thus become converts, through Christian instruction, how great would be the rewards of those who extend it to them!"[22]

## Making Changes

Charlotte was managing the Digah mission work by herself. "My own head and hand have every thing to decide and to perform," she wrote as she began making changes.[23] Landowners and village leaders had requested all the schools she supervised, and they provided places and sometimes buildings for the schools without charging rent. They also permitted teaching of the Bible and Watts's Catechism as well as weekly gatherings for Christian worship in which large numbers took part. This had never happened prior to Joshua's death.[24]

Meanwhile, Charlotte's missiology continued to mature. After his first three years in India, Joshua Rowe had recognized that experience was teaching him things about mission that he "could never have learnt in theory."[25] The same was true for Charlotte. She had long been concerned about offering financial inducements in education. The experiment of paying small rewards to girls to encourage their parents to allow them to attend initially seemed to be effective. Before Joshua's death, the Rowes had increased the rewards based on students' performance. In 1822 Joshua reported that five girls

> obtained a new suit of clothes, made of cotton cloth dyed blue, for having learned the first half of the Hindee Spelling book. Three of these have since gone through the whole of the Spelling book and have commenced the Gospels. The other girls in this school are advancing in their respective classes. These rewards have a very perceptible influence on their exertions. In the present state of things, such an influence appears indispensable.[26]

Although the Rowes had asked the Missionary Society for advice about this practice, they appear to have received none. Now, however, Charlotte saw that the practice was both unsustainable and counterproductive. In 1825, parents at the aforementioned school colluded to demand that all the girls should receive higher payment and a suit of clothes at the end of the term. Only under those terms would they allow their daughters to return to school. Charlotte held firm against their demands even though all but two of the girls then stopped or were prevented from attending.[27]

Charlotte was equally uneasy about the role of money in evangelism. She and Joshua had long been concerned that many enquirers expected to be employed by the mission if they became Christians. On one occasion a Muslim had come to Digah to offer his services as a preacher. When asked in the presence of another Muslim if he had made a profession of Christ, he replied that he knew nothing of Islam or Christianity but, if employed, he would do anything that was asked of him.[28]

Muslims were not alone in expecting employment for conversion. Hindus expected and sometimes demanded compensation for throwing off their caste. In either case, Muslim and Hindu inquirers often faced expulsion from their communities and were thus deprived of work that provided for themselves and their families.

The pervasive employment expectation was neither limited to Digah nor to the Baptist mission. In 1821 when William Ward asked why

Hindustan seemed to yield fewer converts than Bengal, Joshua Rowe's diplomatic answer included the money issue,

> I know not how it may be in Bengal, but in Hindoosthan I have never known a native convert but what had been supported. Our two brethren are supported as native itinerants. The native brethren at Monghyr are supported in the same way. I am also informed that most if not all the native converts belonging to the Church Missionary Society are likewise supported, and that those labourers who have not the means of doing this, meet with little or no success. I know that refusing to do this has operated powerfully in sending off inquirers from Digah.[29]

The Rowes consistently refused to promise employment to converts. They did, however, provide free lodging to adult enquirers who wanted to stay at the mission station to read scripture, ask questions, and otherwise consider the Christian faith. They also gave their guests "daily pice," coins worth one sixty-fourth of a rupee, with which to purchase their own food. The concept had seemed to be an appropriate form of Christian hospitality. As Joshua had described it, "The place we appropriate to the accommodation of inquirers, much resembles a missionary inn. Travellers are frequently turning in to rest themselves, which affords a favourable opportunity of directing the attention of many strangers, from all parts of the country, to the word of life."[30]

Direct experience, however, gave Charlotte insight to address this issue that seemed to elude mission leaders who were immersed in their home culture in England. Charlotte observed that giving pice to enquirers did not encourage true conversion but led to the charge that missionaries were purchasing converts. When she returned to Digah after recuperating in Calcutta, she stopped the practice. With no daily pice and no promise of employment, most of the enquirers left.

Charlotte also dared to exchange the hospitable offer of free lodging for an approach that more adequately fit the culture. She reasoned that people seeking to learn about Christianity could follow the practice of Hindu or Muslim pilgrims. If coming from a distance, they could bring supplies with them. If living nearby, they could continue their trades and come to Digah at intervals to learn.[31]

Experimentation and cultural contextualization shaped Charlotte's missiology, and the results of changing the payment practice were positive.

She could report, "Since [making the change] there have been a number of persons to sit and hear the word explained, but no complaints on the part of such persons, for not getting pice daily."[32] Citing the example of a man who remained close to them at Digah and intended to support himself by his own labor after being baptized, she wrote, "So much for refusing to deal out 4 pice per day to enquirers, who yielded no fruit."[33]

Charlotte also experimented as she sought to demonstrate the powerlessness of idols. At Serampore during her first months in India, Charlotte had witnessed the festival of Juggernaut. She described the idol, the car with multiple platforms on which it sat and the massive wheels under which worshipers were sometimes crushed as the heavy car was pulled to the Ganges. Juggernaut was only able to descend platform to platform from the car's summit by being "let down by a rope around his neck."[34] Nevertheless, the festival was neither the time nor place to help people consider an idol's impotence,

A building in which one of the mission schools met was a more conducive setting for Charlotte's experiment. The schoolroom had niches in the wall that held little idols. One day, despite the risk, Charlotte took one of them down. To the students' surprise, she held it high over a wooden chair and said she was going to "make their God fly to pieces." Experiments are not always successful, and on her first try the hard-baked earthen statuette refused to break. The students' looks of alarm now changed to triumph. On the second try, however, it shattered. Charlotte then asked the students how an object made by human hands could help them when they were in need, if it could not save itself from her hand. The demonstration changed the way her students thought about the objects. Charlotte was gratified that "in a few days, they all came to me and repeated the whole ten commandments, in their own language."[35]

As Charlotte worked to open more schools, she also expanded her Hindi language worship and evangelism work. Worship in Hindi was held twice in the "native brethren's place" and twice in her bungalow every Sunday. Her Sunday mornings began before breakfast when she went to the native chapel to read a chapter of scripture or commentary after which one of the Christian Indian women prayed. At ten o'clock Charlotte held Hindi worship in the center room of her bungalow. In the afternoon she held a service for those who worshiped in English. The household consisted of herself, her children, the boarders, and the Indian widow for whom she provided care as a family dependent. Then on Sunday evening and every evening of the week in her bungalow, she held family worship in Hindi. She did this to include the household servants who either could not or did not like to attend during the day. In the evening, however, they all attended.

Charlotte saw the evening worship as particularly effective. The cook was especially attentive and often interrupted as she read to ask the meaning of the passages. "He seems to enjoy hearing of the scriptures," she wrote, "and acknowledges without hesitation, the folly of all Hindoo rites &c. The old native woman who lives with me and teaches the small Digah family native female school, takes her turn alternately at prayer, being I think, a sincere lover of Jesus."[36]

Students and teachers also often attended the Hindi services. Two schoolmistresses, twenty girls, and several boys attended worship regularly while those from farther distances came on occasion.[37] Ten Rookhampore boys might come with their schoolmaster one Sunday, seven Moinpoora girls and their schoolmaster the next Sunday, and so forth.[38]

Hurree Das and Roop Das preached at numerous places in schools and homes as well as the native chapel on the mission station grounds. They brought questions and difficulties to Charlotte to be settled and called her "their pastoress."[39] While she felt inadequate and prayed that a trained pastor would be sent to serve their church and community, she was happy that she could serve until such a time. Interestingly, *The Baptist Magazine* reprinted a letter in which Charlotte acknowledged that Indigenous Christians considered her to be "their pastoress." The editor said the letter would show "how serviceable Christian females may be, when under the influence of a right spirit, in keeping things together at a Missionary station, during a state of bereavement."[40] Though undoubtedly intended as a compliment, his words suggested that it was unusual for a bereaved woman to be able to continue mission work while the unspoken assumption was that it would not be unusual for a bereaved man to do so.

In her bereavement, Charlotte did more than "keep things together." From the start, Indigenous itinerant preachers had partnered with the missionaries to staff the Digah mission station. Given her language ability and role in the Hindi worship services, Charlotte, rather than Joshua, had had the greater interaction with them. After Joshua's death, Charlotte's role with the "native brethren" Hurree Das and Roop Das deepened, for Indigenous partners were central to her missiology.

Charlotte closely followed Hurree and Roop's ministries, adding what she could to their training, encouraging them and paying careful attention to their needs. The brothers were aging. The strain of itinerant ministry was taking its toll. Hurree had become "nearly grey bearded." Roop struggled with a withered leg and was "almost disabled from walking the shortest distance," his other leg and hip being very painful and helpless. The men had walked from place to place but were becoming increasingly "unable to endure the toil upon their own feet." To provide a measure of relief, Charlotte bought them a pony at her own expense so they could take turns riding to their most distant preaching places.

The brothers received very modest wages from the Baptist Missionary Society, the lowest paid to anyone at Digah. Charlotte pointed out that the income was inadequate and advocated that their wages be increased. She cited five reasons supporting higher wages and concluded, "Something is due to the dignity of their office." They should not be made to feel that they were viewed "upon a level with hawkers and Cooks, by receiving the same wages."[41]

In addition to a wage increase, Charlotte urged the society to also encourage the preachers in non-monetary ways. She told London, "Brother Hurree Das and Roop Das hold a great share in my respect and affection. I should be pleased if the Society would notice them by addressing a short letter to them, which I will give them a translation of, if I am here when it arrives. It will be attended with great good, both to themselves and the cause here."[42]

Charlotte's concern to show respect for Indigenous workers was not limited to religious workers such as Hurree and Roop Das. It also formed much of her unease about bearers carrying her in a tonjon[43] or palanquin, though "all gentlemen and ladies, both European and Asiatic, resort to these modes of conveyance."[44] To be sure, Charlotte found the palanquin distinctly uncomfortable. She wrote, "The posture of reclining on the back or sitting like a sailor in a palankeen shaken on the shoulders of four men, has heretofore brought on great weakness and indisposition."[45] She likened a palanquin to "a *hearse* carried by men."[46] Quite apart from her own physical discomfort, she anguished over the toll that carrying others exacted on the bearers' bodies and abhorred the disrespect they were shown.

It was never without pain of mind that I beheld streams of sweat glisten on the backs of those poor fellow men—but most, when it was by my own weight, that their pores wept; and though many years residence there had accustomed my sight to many things for a while repugnant to it, yet I could never remain unmoved when I sometimes heard the allusion in jest, to "six black horses for the palankeen" being kept.[47]

She faced the dilemma that refusal to use a palanquin would leave the bearers without employment. Nevertheless, for the sake of conscience even more than comfort, she made the change. When funds allowed it, she replaced her palanquin with a small horse-drawn carriage.

Charlotte's maturing missiology was enriched by her reflective observation. She observed that Hindus and Muslims were interested in passages from Hebrew scripture, and she deduced that this was due to similarities between their cultures and that of the ancient Hebrews. "The history of those times describes customs similar to the present in this country," she wrote. "Some of the servants of the house and Station *like to hear* the Old Testament, others *nod*." As a result, she increasingly used such texts and found various settings in which to employ them such as reading them publicly from her house in the early evening. People who seldom came to the ten o'clock Sunday worship services often assembled in the evening to hear her read and comment on the Hebrew texts before being dismissed from work.[48]

By mid-1826 Charlotte had established more places for regular Hindi preaching such as the Liverpool School, the Lyme School, and the work yard of Stephen Rolt, a trusted merchant and shopkeeper in Patna. Charlotte now met for worship with the Digah schoolgirls on weekday mornings as well as on Sundays.[49] In addition to weekday preaching in various locations, Hurree and Roop Das now preached six times every Sunday: twice at Patna, once at a village mid-way between Patna and Digah, once on the Digah mission compound, and twice in Dinapore.[50]

Finally, Charlotte challenged the society's linguistic preparation for its new missionaries by insisting that language was best learned experientially on location from native speakers. She warned that new missionaries who attempted to learn "Gilchrist's *Englishized* Hindustanee," in England would be forced to unlearn it after their arrival in Hindustan. Charlotte could have urged this change in a generalized way. Instead, she named John Borthwick Gilchrist, Britain's recognized Hindustani authority, and addressed the inadequacy of his language learning system.

Scottish-born Gilchrist had arrived in Bombay and subsequently become an assistant surgeon in the Medical Service of the East India Company in 1784. While marching with the company's Bengal Army, he observed that Hindustani could be understood in various parts of India. This led to his systematic study of the language and to his 1786 publication of *The Hindoostanee Grammar and Dictionary*.[51] Gilchrist urged that military officers and company employees be taught Hindustani in order to communicate with Indian troops, officials, and other foreign nationals in a common medium without translators. Fort William College in Calcutta was started for that purpose. Gilchrist became the school's Hindustani lecturer, and William Carey became its instructor in Bengali and local languages. It was Gilchrist to whom the society would turn to attest to the accuracy of the Hindustani New Testament that they were using.[52]

Gilchrist authored numerous books on Hindustani. His work to reform and systematize the language strengthened its role as the *lingua franca* of Hindustan. In 1820 he issued his third edition of *The Stranger's Infallible East-Indian Guide*. In it he discussed the origins of Hindustani, noting that its more appropriate name was "Hindee." Gilchrist prefaced his book by acknowledging the "irksome situation" of having to unlearn language pronunciation and lessons that have been previously learned. He prescribed that acquisition of Hindustani "should always be done at home when practicable, or on the outward voyage to any one of the british indian presidencies." Then, during the first three months in India, learners should perfect the language's difficult sounds "from some of their well-informed European friends." Learners should "make their selves complete masters of every word, technical term, and rule in this minute volume at least, before they sit regularly down to study the language with any moonshee."[53]

Charlotte emphatically challenged Gilchrist's approach. "*It is fully ascertained, and to the deep regret of some, that it is learning this language twice over, to commence it in England; since the false pronunciation they require through a foreign educator, or an English teacher, is more painful to leave off than to acquire the right. Such scholars may talk Hindu in England, but they will not be understood in Hindusthan, by any except learners like themselves.* I wish all who come to this country with a view to be useful to the natives would let the Hindu alone until they arrive, unless they have a *native* teacher."[54]

Charlotte was diametrically opposed Gilchrist's language learning system because the two were pursuing different goals. Gilchrist was serving colonial government and commercial interests and was addressing "the military, medical, and all other gentlemen of the king's or company's service" stationed throughout British India.[55] Gilchrist divided Hindi into three distinct forms: the pristine, familiar, and court dialects. Pristine Hindi was most nearly related to each area's original dialect and had the least foreign influence. Familiar Hindi had a greater mixture of foreign and original words while court Hindi contained the most numerous instances of Arabic and Persian words. Gilchrist reasoned that the language of the courts and provincial capitals would be known in the largest number of places throughout India and thus was the dialect "most worthy of attention and cultivation by foreigners, wishing to live, move, and have a comfortable being" among inhabitants in any part of British India.[56] Use of Persian script was part of Gilchrist's "reformed mode" of Hindustani that was taught at Fort William College.[57] Local people wishing or needing to interact with expatriates who had learned Gilchrist's Hindi would have to use standardized, reformed Hindi.

Charlotte's missiology, on the other hand, focused on the interests of Indian people in their specific locations. Her advice that missionaries should learn from Indigenous language guides speaking their mother tongue put the onus of cultural and linguistic adaptation on the missionaries rather than on those they had come to serve. Charlotte was addressing a missiological issue that would far out-live her time. Should mission agencies prepare missionaries for deep immersion in a specific culture and language group or for broad influence across a variety of cultures and languages? William Carey was on record affirming the former. To be fit instruments of God, missionaries needed "a competent knowledge of the languages current where a missionary lives."[58]

# Chapter 12

## ALONE

Even as Charlotte became ever more deeply involved in education and evangelism, she found herself spiritually isolated. She missed Joshua, her partner in life and ministry. She also missed the communication she previously had with three women who uniquely understood mission.

Charlotte had corresponded with Phebe Hough with whom she had sailed from Philadelphia to Calcutta and who had then proceeded on to Burma while Charlotte remained in India. Their correspondence faded when the Houghs became less engaged in the Burma mission.

Charlotte's exchange of letters with Maria Staughton ended abruptly with Maria's death on January 10, 1823, nine months before Joshua's death. Charlotte was not alone in mourning Maria's passing. The students at Columbian College in Washington, D.C., honored Maria by wearing black armbands for a month.

When Charlotte arrived in India in 1816, she began exchanging letters with Ann Judson in Burma. Ann told Maria Staughton that she found Charlotte to be "an interesting correspondent."[1] The sentiment was mutual. Charlotte enjoyed receiving news from Burma, such as Ann's July 3, 1819, letter reporting the baptism of the first Burmese convert.[2] Charlotte and Ann's conversation by mail was disrupted in 1821 when Ann sailed to England and then on to the United States to recuperate from ill health. When Ann returned to Rangoon in December 1823, she and Adoniram immediately relocated to Ava, which had displaced Amarapura as the royal city. Her contact with Charlotte continued to be disrupted by the onset of the Anglo-Burmese war, Adoniram's arrest, Ann's desperate struggle to keep him alive during his brutal twenty-one-month imprisonment, and finally by the severe illness that led to Ann's death.

Charlotte felt these losses. She confided to John Dyer, head of the Baptist Missionary Society, "I have no spiritually minded friends or friend to strengthen me." Charlotte was a spiritual mentor and leader among the Indigenous believers at Digah but had no one with whom she felt she could unburden her soul and from whom she could receive intimate counsel. That included her European expatriate neighbors. "I have kind, the kindest of neighbours, but none of them can enter in to the feelings or conceive the thoughts of a renewed mind. These are thoughts which almost make me drop my pen."[3]

Though Charlotte knew John Dyer only through their correspondence, she felt he had become a "valued friend." She knew it was critical for her to speak Hindi to help those around her relate to God in their own "heart language," but she experienced that same need for herself and begged Dyer to uphold her in prayer.

> I need strengthening by the secret influences of the Spirit—for I never hear a prayer or sermon in English, but what I pray or read myself at home. Nor have I a single *spiritual* friend to converse with at Dinapore. I have good *friends* but none who know how to reciprocate a *sinner's* feelings. If I did not enjoy the common ordinances of religion in the native language, I should be destitute indeed. In that I have continued work in doing or serving.[4]

Charlotte also felt intellectually starved. She urged Dyer to send books whenever he could, saying, "I live apart from the sources of Intelligence." Her sense of isolation at Digah had become more intense by the absence of adequate food for the mind.[5]

Her family's isolation, combined with her children's illnesses, prompted Charlotte to make plans for their care in the event of her death. The three older boys, Joshua, William, and Josiah, were adequately situated with trusted British friends in and around Serampore, but she had no one in India to whom she could entrust the care of her three younger children. "Who have I in India to take my tender plants to rear, if I drop into the dust—Indian Habits alas! must then ruin them. Indian diseases consume their rising strength, and instead of the sweet blooming, cheerful mind of England, they must become *mushrooms* of a day." Charlotte had originally thought that her brother Edwin Atlee would take her twin daughters and little Judson into his home in Philadelphia should they become orphaned. However, after Edwin revealed his role in the affair of the repurposed letter, their correspondence had abruptly stopped. Charlotte confided, "He and his family *used to be* the place I should choose for them to board. I feel no ties that way any longer."[6]

In December 1824, little Judson almost died.[7] Several months later the twins Charlotte and Esther both became sick, with Esther suffering three severe bouts of illness. Her children's health had become an increasingly serious matter. Charlotte had harbored few illusions about mission service when she sought appointment in 1815. She wrote in her application letter to the board, "Having found no period of life exempt from trials, I do not expect to leave them on leaving my native land, but rather add to their weight and number."[8] However, it was one thing to accept "difficulties, dangers, and new privations" for oneself and quite another to see them visited on one's children.

After her children recovered from their illnesses, Charlotte was prepared to bring them to England if she could settle them with a proper family with secure, suitable arrangements for their education. "I should feel much happiness concerning them, if I could see them across the ocean and placed at School in England myself." She thought it might be best for them to live with a Baptist family in England. If they could not live with their grandmother, perhaps Rev. John Dyer could keep them under his care. Scotland might also be a good location for the children, but Charlotte had no connections there. Whether in England or Scotland, Charlotte wanted "a plain, virtuous, good Lady to keep and to instruct them." If they could not be tutored at home, then she hoped they could live in a private home and go to school as day students, rather than live in a boarding school. "I abhor *Schools* so called, everywhere, if a child must be thrown into it," she wrote, "but the hourly attendance at a *good* school, is what I desire."[9]

## The Fog of Ambiguity

When Charlotte White married Joshua Rowe in 1816, she entered into an unclear relationship with the British Baptist Missionary Society. Charlotte was a missionary's wife, but did British Baptists also recognize her as a missionary? Joshua never doubted that she was. He regularly reported her "missionary work" to London. Signaling their partnership in ministry, his letters referred to Charlotte by her first name as often as by her married name, "Mrs. Rowe." He valued Charlotte's desire to "give herself wholly" to missionary service and asked the society to appoint her and to support her work at an appropriate level. He told Carey, Marshman, and Ward, "Nearly twelve months ago, I begged the Society to allow her to effect what was in her heart, but have not yet received their answer."[10]

The society's answer never arrived.

London's silence did not deter Charlotte. She steadily continued her educational and evangelistic ministry in Hindi both before and after Joshua's death. While *The Baptist Magazine* printed extracts of Charlotte's letters, its references to her missionary status were ambiguous. The magazine's 1824 obituary of Joshua Rowe used Charlotte's nickname by recounting that "Mrs. Susanna White" had come to India "in the Missionary service from our Sister Society in the United States." Noting that she had been "eminently useful in the school department at Digah," the magazine expressed the hope that she would "be disposed to remain at the station with a view of continuing her exertions in that much needed work." The magazine spoke with language from the "separate spheres" gender ideology, even as it subtly encouraged its readers to support Charlotte's ministry: "The friends of the Society will not, we are persuaded, withhold their sympathy from this family, thus unexpectedly deprived of their earthly head and protector!"[11] Later that year, however, *The Baptist Magazine* overlooked Charlotte's very presence at Digah by stating that the Digah mission station "became vacant" at Joshua Rowe's death.[12] That phrase reflected the view of the society's executive committee. At its September 26, 1824, meeting, the committee had agreed to let Carey, Marshman, and Ward determine whether William Moore should be asked to return to Digah from Monghyr "as the station of Digah, where Mr. Moore formerly resided, has been vacant."[13]

In 1825, the Baptist Missionary Society acknowledged that the Digah mission station, "has been maintained by the persevering exertions of Mrs. Rowe, who superintends the schools, and directs the proceedings of the native itinerants residing there."[14] In 1826 under the caption "Missionaries, &c.," *The Baptist Magazine* listed Mrs. Rowe as "Superintendent of Female Schools."[15] Male missionaries who superintended schools were not so designated. At least in the pages of the magazine, Charlotte seemed to be regarded as less than a missionary. She appeared to have become an *et cetera.*

After Joshua's death, Charlotte took over the task of writing to the society's leaders in London whom she had never met. Seven years earlier she had written to William Staughton in Philadelphia seeking clarity about her relationship with the American Baptist mission. Now she wrote to John Dyer in London asking a similar question of the British leaders. She wrote, "I am personally unacquainted with them or their feelings towards me."[16] Despite the society's ambiguous attitude toward her, Charlotte never lacked clarity about her identity: she was their missionary at Digah.

And it mattered.

It mattered because of the mission. Despite *The Baptist Magazine*'s notion that the station had become vacant upon Joshua Rowe's death, Charlotte both continued and expanded the mission. She increased the number of schools and negotiated with local zamindars for rent-free locations for those schools. She identified, trained, and placed women teachers. She oversaw the opening of new preaching sites and proactively attended to the needs of the itinerant preacher evangelists.

It mattered because of finances. Charlotte administered funds for education and evangelism. She received grants sent from England for "native female education." She deposited and withdrew funds from Alexander & Sons, the society's financial agent in Calcutta. She developed effective relationships with Indigenous and expatriate donors who pledged subscriptions for building and education projects.

It mattered because of property. Charlotte managed the society's assets. She preserved and repaired buildings. She secured renters for the empty bungalow. She fenced the premises to ward off those wanting to acquire it, much as she sought to defend the riverbank against the encroaching Ganges River. Only an official agent of the society was legally entitled to undertake such tasks. Charlotte recognized that fact and wrote, "I have acted conscienciously [*sic*] with the Society's proper[ty] and trust in divine aid to do so still.... I will not abandon the station, nor resign it into any hand but that of an *appointed* missionary."[17]

And it mattered if she was to continue ministry in India.

# A Conditional Future

Mission societies in England and the United States always struggled to receive adequate funding from supporters in the churches. The British Baptists had set a fixed compensation of 120 rupees per month for William Carey, Joshua Marshman, and William Ward. In 1800 the Serampore missionaries resolved "that no one of us do engage in private trade; but that all be done for the benefit of the mission."[18] Five years later, the resolution was expanded into a Form of Agreement for communal life in which all income was pooled in a common fund from which individual needs were to be met.

> Let us for ever shut out the idea of laying up a cowrie (mite) for ourselves or our children. If we give up the resolution which was formed on the subject of private trade, when we first united at Serampore, the mission is from that hour a lost cause. Let us continually watch against a worldly spirit, and cultivate a Christian indifference towards every indulgence. Rather let us bear hardness as good soldiers of Jesus Christ. No private family ever enjoyed a greater portion of happiness, even in the most prosperous gale of worldly prosperity, than we have done since we resolved to have all things in common. If we are enabled to persevere in the same principles, we may hope that multitudes of converted souls will have reason to bless God to all eternity for sending His Gospel into this country.[19]

It is noteworthy that the first sermon the Rowes and Moores heard William Carey preach after their 1805 arrival in Calcutta was on the text, "Ye cannot serve God and mammon."[20] Joshua Rowe joined those who willingly participated in adopting the Form of Agreement.

The 1805 Form of Agreement lasted for seventeen years. During those years, however, it became apparent that the missionary communism practiced at Serampore was largely unworkable for those serving at mission sites located considerable distances from one another. Furthermore, the opening of the new sites in India exceeded London's ability to make stated salary commitments for new missionaries. Joshua Rowe believed that if a third missionary family could be appointed for Digah, they could adopt a communal life like that of Serampore, but it was simply impractical to attempt it with only the Moores. The Rowes and Moores therefore served under an entrepreneurial self-support arrangement. They would raise the income needed to pay their families' living expenses while the Baptist Missionary Society would cover their work expenses. To that end, the Rowes and Moores supported themselves by conducting the boarding school at Digah. Because the society's remittances often failed to cover the work expenses at Digah and were frequently slow to arrive, Charlotte and Joshua covered the deficits out of their own personal resources.

The system of generating adequate income from the boarding school at Digah fell apart when William Moore moved to Monghyr to support his family through private work and investment. Moore proposed that the boarding students should choose whether to remain at Rowe's school in Digah or to transfer to his school at Monghyr. Joshua Rowe felt this would make their relationship competitive and instead suggested that the boys should transfer to Monghyr and the girls should remain at Digah.

At this point, expatriates nearby began opening competing boarding schools. Since the new schools advertised adherence to the Anglican liturgy, they tended to undercut the school options offered by Baptists.

Further emphasizing the fragility of the Rowes' financial situation, the society established a provisional resolution concerning widows. Upon the death of a missionary, his salary would continue for a time to his widow. The resolution, however, did not apply to the Rowes, for, as Joshua reminded London, "we have *no salaries allowed us*, and what are we therefore to do if placed in such circumstances?"[21]

Charlotte now found herself in those very circumstances. Joshua had received no salary that could be continued to her. And because the society had not recognized her as an appointed missionary, she had no salary of her own. For ten years, first under American Baptists and then under British Baptists, she had self-funded her missionary service. Her dependents included her three stepsons, her twin daughters, her son, and Ramkisoon's widow. The society had given some modest grants to support the nine mission schools under her oversight, but as the grants were not sufficient, she supported the Digah girls' school herself. Charlotte also paid the wages of Sarah Bacon, who taught Charlotte's children and two young girls Charlotte had taken in to educate.

Charlotte was ready to live and die a missionary in India. She told John Dyer, "I am content to be here for life. Nay I expect to bury my bones here."[22] She was torn, knowing that her resolve to follow God's call to be a missionary also affected her children. She confided this inner struggle to her mother-in-law: "I remain in the mission because I am a missionary, and would prefer dying such—but out of the mission I could lay up a little future support for my babes. My duty to them, might urge the latter, to a worldly mind—but I have a trust in God, that though we remain poor, he will keep my children alive and from the examples of the wicked, this is my chief concern."[23]

Charlotte's meager income came from several sources. She had purchased a house, "the little bungalow *I bought to make peace* and keep out proud and anxious intruders on the mission premises." While she rented it out hoping to gain on her investment, the proceeds were consumed by the building's repair and upkeep.[24] Therefore, she depended on three other revenue sources. Although she could not receive the equivalent of a husband's salary from the society, London did send her a reduced widow's allowance. She supplemented that with modest revenue from the tiny English boarding school in her bungalow. It was now that Charlotte's 1815 donation to the Baptist Board of Foreign Missions in the United States came into play. She had given the gift to cover her own costs in mission, and to its credit, the board had returned the donation to her after she married Joshua Rowe and came under the auspices of the British Baptist Missionary Society. Charlotte subsequently invested the money in Calcutta to draw interest. Those earnings were the critical third income source that kept her family solvent.

Charlotte's ability to self-fund her family and ministry from such limited resources required great care. She told John Dyer, "I have studied to bring both the mission and my private expenses into the smallest compass possible." To ensure that she was not missing some place to economize, she asked another missionary if they could compare their accounts. Upon examining their expenses, the other missionary "over and over again observed, that she did not know how I with so much larger a family, could keep [my expenses] so low."[25] Indeed, she could only manage so economically by foregoing some basics related to food and heat. She wrote, "I have not purchased any liquors, tea or coffee since I came from Calcutta. My friends send me a little wine and beer sometimes—as well as a good joint of meat. The war with Rangoon has made everything very dear."[26] While others used fires to warm themselves during the winter, Charlotte went without. "I have never had a fire to sit by," she confided to John Dyer, "though without a sheepskin under my feet, I should often suffer with cold."[27]

Charlotte's capacity to maintain financial viability could be disrupted by the slightest emergency, yet she willingly committed to maintain that delicate balance:

> If the Society will continue to me the allowance which the Serampore [brethren] have allotted me with a view of increasing it a little when my children get older—and a house to live in, and make me superintendent of native female schools....and expect me to attend to no other missionary concern, I would in that case engage to remain their missionary. At the same time, I should connect a few female boarders, *on my own private account and independent of the Mission*, with my family.[28]

The disruptive emergency arrived when the society informed Charlotte that she would need to keep the mission bungalows in repair at her own expense. That extra expense threw Charlotte's finances off balance. Her careful efforts at self-support were now unsustainable. Some expatriate friends advised Charlotte to "take a fine house and open a Public School for young Ladies, as I have been applied to, to take pupils to a larger extent that I now can." A large school could resolve her financial dilemma. It would, however, divert her from missionary work, the very purpose she had come to fulfill and was unwilling to abandon.[29]

Instead, Charlotte proposed a means by which she could remain in service and the mission could be strengthened. In 1826 the society had finally sent a missionary couple, Richard and Mary Burton, to join the work at Digah. Charlotte proposed that the society send another missionary couple to work with them. The new couple along with the Burtons and Charlotte would constitute a five-person missionary team. That team could resume the European school for boys and girls that the Rowes and Moores had once profitably operated. Charlotte identified the bungalows in which the students could reside. The school's success would be aided by other assistance from England, and Charlotte suggested, "Perhaps my mother-in-law and her daughters would come out as assistants to earn their living in that way."

Charlotte proposed that the society provide "a suitable salary" for herself and the additional male missionary. With that investment, the society could "cast the support of the native schools upon us—for if we have a large School of European children—we ought to aid the Society in turn." Softening her proposal with a slightly amusing aside, Charlotte nevertheless did not mince words:

As an old missionary and the head of a large family, I feel my rights, & I suggest them for the sake of mutual good understanding. If my situation and my mind are rendered comfortable, I can have no motive (except a suitable Marriage) to leave the mission, so long as I enjoy health in India. I would not be understood to wish to *dictate* to the Society, but merely to inform them, on what terms they may retain my services if they think them of any value.[30]

Before Charlotte's letter reached London, sorrow again visited Digah. In the preceding months, Richard and Mary Burton had suffered the deaths of two of their four children, their daughter Phoebe and their son Richard. Then Mary Burton contracted stomach cancer in her sixth month of pregnancy. Dr. Dickson, the superintending surgeon of the Dinapore military station and Dr. King, the senior civil surgeon at Patna, both determined that her illness was "beyond the reach of human aid." Charlotte was often at Mary's side offering physical care and spiritual consolation. She and Rev. Burton were repeating texts of scripture and hymns to Mary when she spoke what would be her last words, "Come, Jesus Christ, come, Jesus Christ." On Saturday, April 1, 1826, Mary Burton died with the child she was carrying.

Two days later, Rev. Burton suffered a severe fever attack while Charlotte continued to be the family's caregiver. When Burton's fever raged into a third day, Charlotte wrote to Monghyr urging Rev. Leslie to come to Digah as quickly as possible. On the day of Leslie's expected arrival, a letter appeared with the news that Mrs. Leslie had just died. Burton eventually recovered. He expressed his deep appreciation for Charlotte's presence and care, saying, "of [Mrs. Rowe's] kindness and attentions to the dear departed, myself, and children, I cannot speak in terms sufficiently strong."[31]

Still grieving the three deaths in his family plus that of his unborn child, Burton was deeply concerned for the survival of his two remaining children.[32] He resolved to send his four-year-old daughter and three-year-old son into the care of relatives in England and asked Charlotte to take them there.

Several factors led Charlotte to agree. Her own children had barely survived illnesses the previous year. Her twins were seven and little Judson was three. Burton's request gave her an opportunity to place her girls with a family in England where they could access decent schooling. Charlotte acknowledged, "I do not expect to get them out of the reach of sickness or death in England—but the chance of their living and growing up useful women is much greater there than here." She did not expect to remain long in England, but to return to her work again "in as short a time as possible."[33] Presumably she would bring little Judson back to India for several more years before he, too, might be placed into schooling in England.

More than this, ten years of nonstop work in India had affected Charlotte's health. "My health and spirits are depressed by too much exertion alone in the mission," she confessed to her diary. "Labor has become painful to me, on account of a weakness on my chest." Indeed, her appearance shocked a soldier and a Baptist woman from the 59th Regiment who came to be with her on her final Sunday in Digah. They had last seen her when she had accompanied Joshua as he preached at the church in Dinapore. In the three intervening years, her appearance had so altered that they no longer recognized her.[34] For good reason Charlotte may have welcomed a physical respite in the land of her grandparents' birth and the place where she could meet Joshua's mother and sisters.

Diminished health was the publicly cited reason for Charlotte's trip to England. But despite her need for recuperation, her primary reason was to meet the society's leaders to secure their official support and a salary that would enable her to continue ministry at Digah. She simply could not negotiate with them through letters that took five or six months to travel from Digah to London while she accumulated debt in India awaiting a clear response.

Moreover, Burton had calmed her lingering concern about the length of time she would be away from her work. Although most of Burton's time since arriving at Digah had been consumed with language acquisition, he now spoke Hindi well enough to no longer need Charlotte as his interpreter and well enough to assume her work of superintending the schools during her temporary absence. She wrote, "The only drawback that I should feel to taking a trip to England is leaving my native charge so long—but Mr. Burton has promised to supply my place there, and I have no doubt, would do *much* to improve the method of instruction, but he will not *interfere* while I am on the spot, or able to go on duty. It might be benefitting them to leave them to him for a while."[35]

Charlotte began planning the voyage to England for herself, her twins, her son, and the two Burton children. She had always taken great pains to pay all personal expenses from her own resources thus assuring the society that its money was used exclusively for society purposes.

Although the trip to England manifestly served the needs of the mission and its personnel, Charlotte did not leave until she could travel without exposing the society to any expense. Even in this, she paid her own way.[36]

October 29, 1826, was a day of grieving for Charlotte. It was her last Sunday at Digah. The thought of leaving gave her "a whole day in agony of mind." That morning, as usual, she had gone to the row of cottages or huts just inside the mission gate that they called "the native brethren's place." She had always found great pleasure in reading and explaining the scriptures, singing hymns, and leading prayer. Although she fully intended to return, she was aware that this could be her last time. She confided to her diary, "This morning when I attempted to pray in Hindoo, my mouth was shut—my heart was full and large with desires, but I could not utter them: but I trust in hope and faith, that the Holy Spirit, which needeth not words to acquaint him with our wants, will return upon them and me, such things as my soul craved."[37]

On Tuesday, October 31, Charlotte paid all the bills associated with her work at Digah. Later that day, the local men and women with whom she worked at the mission walked up the avenue with their children and pupils in a long solemn procession to bid her farewell. While Charlotte was in a back room busily packing, Richard Burton met the crowd on the steps. Without informing Charlotte of their arrival, Burton told the people they should not try to see Charlotte at that time because she was too busy to be interrupted. The crowd dispersed sorrowfully with Charlotte unaware that they had come.

When Burton told Charlotte what he had done, he said that it was to spare her "the pain of so formal a farewell." Although Charlotte wrote in her diary, "I felt thankful for it," her actions as she departed suggested something different. When Charlotte quietly boarded the boat that would take her down the river to Calcutta, none of her Indian co-workers were present. By the time they and friends returned to say farewell, the boat had already moved out into the stream. As the boat bore her away, those lining the shore brought their right palm to their foreheads and bowed repeatedly, almost touching their foreheads to the ground. Charlotte returned their loving farewells by bowing to them, her hand pressed tightly against her heart. Her feelings were too deep for words. "My heart was *still*," she wrote, "it was benumbed."[38]

Presuming to know what was for her own good, Burton had deprived Charlotte of the opportunity to speak departing words to those with whom she had shared the past decade of her life and to whom she hoped to return. Although Charlotte wrote that she was thankful for Burton's intervention, the style of her diary suggested that Charlotte was not writing exclusively for herself. She anticipated that other eyes would see her words. Her trust had been betrayed three years earlier when her brother allowed her confidential words to be repurposed for public use. Never again would she write about a fellow missionary in any way that could be seen to be negative.

Charlotte left Digah on November 1, 1826, in a budgerow, one of the cumbersome, rudderless river barges that plied the Ganges operated by a crew of eight boatmen and two servants. With her were her seven-year-old twin daughters, her three-year-old son, and Sarah Bacon, who had been her children's teacher. Their shelter on the barge consisted of a room constructed of mats with a thatched roof. The recently bereaved Burton followed with his daughter and son in a smaller boat. The weather was good and the river was smooth as they made their way to Calcutta. There Sarah Bacon would return to teach at the Orphan Asylum from which Charlotte had recruited her, and the Burton children would join Charlotte for the trip to their relatives in England.

One of the barge's first stops was several miles below Patna at the riverside town of Monghyr. There John Chamberlain's widow gave Charlotte two items to deliver to missionaries' families in England: a copy of the *Memoirs of Mr. John Chamberlain, Late Missionary in India* and some of the deceased Mrs. Leslie's hair.[39] The barge continued down river during the day and moored alongshore each night. On the journey, Charlotte became involved in two dramatic encounters that seared themselves into her memory.

The first occurred at the close of a day when the barge stopped at a place known locally as Phoolwarree (flower border). The boatmen laid a plank between the boat and bank and held a pole as a makeshift banister so the passengers could steady themselves as they stepped off the boat. After climbing the steep bank, they encountered a neat white-washed cottage, a shaded grove, and a number of footpaths. The children, now freed from the confines of the barge, immediately scampered off among the paths. A "grizly looking" man stepped from the cottage and bowed courteously as the adults passed by and strolled with the children until dusk.

As they returned to the boat where they would spend the night, they heard the loud sounds of conch shells. There, standing in a sort of piazza in the midst of numerous hanging lanterns, was "a hideous Idol" about three feet tall. The image had staring white eyes and a black mouth. It was painted in a flame color and appeared in the glaring light "like a red hot iron." Charlotte stopped and attempted to speak to the men, but they continued blowing the conch shells and conversation was impossible. The children were horror-struck and clung to their mother. Charlotte confessed that in all her years in India, "It was the most frightful spectacle I had ever seen."[40]

The second dramatic encounter would draw attention from people in London and New York City four years later.

Meanwhile, Charlotte traveled to Serampore where William Carey and Richard Burton gave her a letter to bring to the society's leaders. Although Charlotte was traveling unbidden to England, the Carey-Burton letter confirmed their approval of her journey and expressed their hope "that she will meet with that reception among you to which her labours entitle her."[41]

In Calcutta she took her leave of the British Baptist missionaries, including Burton, who would continue her work at Digah. "Mr. B assures me," she wrote in her diary, "that he can and will keep both [the native girls' school near the mission-house] and the other female schools in operation."[42] Secure in that assurance, Charlotte shepherded the five children aboard the "fine teak ship" *Palmyra* and departed.[43] After a stop in Ceylon, the *Palmyra* sailed on to England without hindrance.[44] The meetings that awaited her in London were of great importance. They would determine her future as a missionary.

# Chapter 13

# DESTINY IN THE BAPTIST MISSION ROOMS

Charlotte arrived in London on the *Palmyra* on May 7, 1827. She promptly went to No. 6 Fen Court, Fen-Church Street, the house that the Baptist Missionary Society rented for its meetings now that it no longer met in the Jamaica Coffee-house.[1] There she met with the society's executive committee.

The committee had been exchanging reports and other information with the Baptist Board of Foreign Missions, their "sister society in the United States." The committee knew that the board had sent Charlotte in 1815 as its first appointed woman missionary. Then, despite the controversy over Charlotte's appointment and its 1816 resolution to appoint no additional single women missionaries, the American Baptist Board had subsequently appointed two more.

In 1817 the board had begun ministry among Native Americans by appointing Humphrey Posey to serve the Cherokee nation. When Humphrey Posey asked the board to send reinforcements to join him in the Cherokee mission, he requested a preacher, a general superintendent, a blacksmith, a carpenter, a miller, a shoemaker, a tanner, and a female teacher and assistant.[2] Ann Cleaver responded to that request and in 1821 became the board's second woman appointee. In 1826 the board appointed Louisa A. Purchase, a Native American woman from Massachusetts, to serve within the Choctaw nation.[3]

Charlotte entered the house at Fen Court to meet with the executive committee on May 24, 1827. In the four months between her departure from India and her arrival in London, the work she had left behind had been curtailed. The girls' schools that Charlotte had pioneered and championed took the brunt of that reduction. Richard Burton, new to Digah and into whose care the schools had been entrusted, had previously remarked, "The girls give much trouble. They are difficult to collect, and difficult to keep together, even with handsome rewards."[4] Now he reported, "When my dear friend, Mrs. Rowe, left Digah, there were three native female schools, but these I have been obliged to discontinue."[5] Charlotte hoped the society would appoint her so she could return and continue ministry in India. Might the American Baptist precedent of appointing Ann Cleaver and Louisa Purchase encourage British Baptists to appoint Charlotte?

That hope was dashed.

The executive committee's minutes stated, "Mrs. Rowe, lately returned from Digah, met the Committee, who conversed with her respecting her affairs & prospects." The committee did not report the details of its conversation with Charlotte. It simply recorded the outcome: "Resolved, that in addition to the sum of £45 per annum to which she is entitled on behalf of her three children, the sum of £100 be placed at the disposal of Mrs. Rowe, in the expectation that she may be enabled hereafter to provide for herself."[6] Rather than appoint and return her to continue her ten-year ministry at Digah, the committee gave Charlotte a modest grant to aid her until she could provide for herself. In the eyes of the committee, Charlotte Rowe had traveled from Digah to Fen Court not as a missionary, but as a missionary's widow. She left Fen Court as a missionary's widow.

Although the nondenominational London Missionary Society recognized Charlotte as "an efficient missionary," the committee had received no word from Baptists in America on her behalf.[7] Her spiritual father and stalwart mission supporter, William Staughton, had concluded his Sansom Street pastorate, become president of the new Baptist institution called Columbian College, and moved to Washington, D.C. in 1823.[8] In 1824 the board had asked its standing committee in Boston to take general superintendence of the Burma mission "as a very considerable proportion of the Asiatic trade of this nation is carried on through Boston and Salem, whereby the greatest facilities are afforded for regular and constant communications with our Missionaries in the East."[9] When all the work of the "Missionary Rooms" moved to Boston in 1826, Staughton ended his twelve years as the board's first corresponding secretary and continued in the less involved role of board president. By public request, on July 16, 1826, Staughton preached in the U.S. Capitol, delivering the joint eulogy to John Adams and Thomas Jefferson, who had both died twelve days earlier on July 4. When Charlotte met with the executive committee at Fen Court, Staughton's immediate attention was focused on education, college administration, and public affairs.

The committee did receive a strong letter of advocacy for Charlotte from Dr. King in Patna who wrote of "the high opinion I entertain of Mrs. Rowe's character, her integrity & devotedness to her duty, which an acquaintance with her, of nine or ten years, justifies." King testified that Mrs. Rowe "had done much honor to the great work and labored with industry & sincerity, in the vineyard of her Lord & Master."[10] Unfortunately, King's letter of recommendation came too late. It arrived almost three years after Charlotte met with the committee.

Several factors may have influenced the committee's reluctance to appoint Charlotte. The Baptist Missionary Society's first secretary, Andrew Fuller, had died twelve years earlier, but his missiological thought remained influential. Fuller had publicly wondered, "Are women then to be reckoned as missionaries?" His unanswered musing may have inclined the committee to continue its practice of not appointing women missionaries. Many British Baptists had the same vocational and gender biases as those held by their American "sister society" and believed that missionaries needed to be ordained and that ordained persons could only be men.

Appointing Charlotte to missionary service in 1827 would most surely have caused controversy in England similar to that which had surrounded Charlotte in the United States. For example, when the society held its jubilee meeting in Kettering fifteen years later, William Brock, the prominent Baptist pastor from Norwich, addressed the women in the audience: "Ladies, it is not yours to be supreme, it is ours. It is yours to obey. But though it is ours to be supreme, yet it is a supremacy in which there is to be nothing capricious, nothing tyrannical. You are not to be our drudges today, and our toys tomorrow. You are our companions—you are our helpmates."[11]

Even women who publicly supported the cause of mission could be subject to criticism. Mary Webb, the enterprising Boston founder of the first women's missionary society in America, had found it necessary to couch her public work in cautious language:

We are aware that by thus coming out, we lay ourselves open to the remarks of the enemies of religion; but believing the path of duty to be guarded on the right hand and on the left, we feel safe. Our object is not to render ourselves *important*, but *useful*. We have no wish to go out of our province, nor do we undertake to become teachers in Israel; it is our *pleasure* to see our brethren go before, and we are content to be permitted "to glean after the reapers," and follow with our earnest prayers, their more extensive labours: *this* privilege we *must covet*.[12]

Without appointment and support from the Baptist Missionary Society, Charlotte faced a dilemma. She could no longer afford to fund her own missionary service and saw no reason to live in India if her time were to be consumed with work to support her family. Her most viable option was to return to the United States and settle her affairs in India at a distance. But first, she needed to raise funds for the voyage to America just as she had done before she had sailed to London from Digah.

Two months after meeting with the committee at Fen Court, Charlotte settled in the town of Yeovil, some one hundred thirty miles southwest of London and forty miles south of Bath.[13] Yeovil had more than doubled in three decades and had more than 5,000 people seriously overcrowding its homes and narrow, ill-paved streets. Deemed one of England's most unsanitary and unhealthy places, Yeovil was plagued "with endemic diseases resulting from squalid living conditions, substandard and hazardous working conditions, poverty, overwork and inadequate public services." A local doctor described Yeovil as "a very filthy, a very dirty, and a very stinking place."[14]

What led Charlotte to such an unpromising town? Did Joshua's mother or sisters live there? Was this where she was to bring the Burton children? Had she perhaps become acquainted with some Baptists in the town? Baptists had been in Yeovil since before the 1689 Act of Toleration when they met in a barn on South Street. After the act granted them freedom of worship, they converted the barn into a meeting house. In 1810 they erected a chapel on the site and continued to grow in number. When Charlotte arrived in 1827, they were expanding their building into a larger chapel.[15]

Irrespective of Baptist friends or Rowe or Burton relatives, Charlotte may have settled in Yeovil for economic reasons. In light of her constrained finances, Charlotte could quickly find work and inexpensive housing in

Yeovil until she could return to America. Yeovil's prime industry was glove making and leather dressing. Some 80 percent of Yeovil families worked in the glove industry, and employment was readily available.[16]

Charlotte took advantage of opportunities to meet with the friends of mission while in England. She attended an annual missionary meeting in Liverpool. On another occasion, in 1828, she attended a missionary address by an Episcopal minister. Walking home afterwards, she was overtaken by two men who were conversing about the evening's address. One questioned whether the things they had just heard were true. Charlotte spoke to the stranger saying that she had been an eyewitness and could confirm many of the preacher's statements. "This seemed to have some effect in convincing him of their truth."[17]

Little else is known about Charlotte's activities in England. She may have visited the Fordhook estate formerly owned by the Atlee family in the Parish of Acton just west of London. She presented a piece of petrified sugar cane to a woman naturalist in England.[18] She became acquainted with the city of Bath, but the duration and reason for her presence there is not recorded.

## Drama on the Ganges

While in England, Charlotte wrote an article that was published in two London newspapers, the *London Morning Herald* and the *Public Ledger and Daily Advertiser*. It was the report of her second dramatic encounter on the Ganges as she was leaving India.

After departing from Digah, Charlotte, the children, and Sarah Bacon traveled first east then south on the Ganges, stopping at Monghyr and Phoolwarree before reaching Serampore. From Serampore they continued south on the river in the slow-moving budgerow. Upon reaching Dum Dum, just north of Calcutta, she came upon a tragic sight.

There at the river's edge, lay a man's corpse with its feet touching the Ganges' holy water and its head cradled in the widow's lap. Charlotte was taken aback as she watched men preparing a funeral pyre, two young children standing beside the widow, and other women behind her prompting her to prepare to die. Charlotte ordered her oarsmen to stop: "I trembled so, that for some time I could not speak, and they all stood wonder stuck to see our budgerow putting near to them. One man stood in front of the crowd, so near that I could with ease hold conversation with him. I bowed to him in the native way, which he returned.—I begged permission to speak to him, and he said, be pleased to speak in Hindoo."[19]

When the man confirmed that the widow was about to throw herself into the fire, Charlotte received permission to speak to her. The widow, urged on by those behind her, said she was prepared to kill herself. Just then the widow's older, married daughter stepped forward with an infant in her arms. "There I beheld three generations assembled to unite in destroying the only hope of those fatherless babes, and I involuntarily clasped my hands, and burst into a flood of tears." Charlotte appealed to the widow on behalf of her children and grandchild, but with others whispering into the widow's ear, Charlotte's words were of no avail.

The widow said the Shasters assured her that after burning herself she would go to be with her dead husband. Charlotte's rejoinder showed the fruit of her study of Hinduism. "Your present Shasters are found to be false ones," she asserted. They were "not like the original ones, which say, that true fidelity is the care of your children; and God, who made both you and them, will judge you for leaving them." Furthermore, Charlotte warned the widow, "the God who made the world is the God of life: he gave you your life" and she would be judged if she destroyed the gift of life she had been given.

Charlotte then appealed to civil authority. To throw herself upon her husband's funeral pyre "was contrary to the laws of the Company, which would rather preserve the people's lives; and that if the Magistrates should seek them out, they would perhaps hang them all." The boatmen in the budgerow joined Charlotte in urging the widow to refrain from killing herself, saying that the missionaries would provide for her if she came with Charlotte. At this, the crowd grew boisterous. As Charlotte could not bear to watch the widow burn herself alive, she asked the boatmen to loosen their boat and depart.

Twelve years earlier when Charlotte and her friends formed the Sansom Street Baptist Female Society, Luther Rice had said their endeavors could save widows from death in the flames of funeral pyres. Now Charlotte had tried to do that very thing. She wrote sadly, "I afterwards learned that the woman was burned."[20] Charlotte did not say if she recalled Rice's words on that tragic day. Nevertheless, she had not passed by. She had not remained silent. Even in her final hours in India, she had offered herself as an instrument to do what she could.

# PART 3

❧

# AMERICA—THE OVERLOOKING
# OF A MISSIONARY

The new year of 1828 was only three days old when a New York City editor decided to entertain his readers with an exotic story from India. That day's issue of the *Evening Post* reprinted the *London Morning Herald* article about Charlotte Rowe's attempt to dissuade a widow from throwing herself onto her husband's funeral pyre.[1] The article identified Charlotte Rowe as "an American lady, widow of a Missionary from the British Baptist Society" whose narrative was written at the close of 1826 "on the Ganges, below Cutwa, at a place called Dum Dum." For the readers' benefit, the *Post*'s editor added that Charlotte was the daughter of the late Judge Atlee of Lancaster and sister of the distinguished Philadelphia physician, Dr. Edwin A. Atlee. The editor gave no indication that Charlotte was herself a missionary, much less America's first appointed woman missionary. Both facts would have been newsworthy. Instead of being identified by her ministry and accomplishments, Charlotte was introduced by reference to her husband, father, and brother and their roles in society.

It was the start of a process in which Charlotte White Rowe was consistently disregarded.

## Chapter 14

## REENTERING AMERICA

Charlotte and her three children traveled from Liverpool to the United States in one of the two cabins available for "a few respectable passengers" on the one-year-old, fast-sailing American ship *James Perkins*.[1] They arrived September 23, 1829, spent some days in New York City and Boston, then in mid-December settled in Philadelphia. On March 2, 1830, Charlotte received a "welcome and comfortable letter" from John Dyer. Charlotte's reply expressed no rancor for the Baptist Missionary Society's refusal to appoint her. Instead, she wished every blessing for Dyer and his family and asked to be remembered "to *all* my known acquaintances in the kindest manner."

While her letter addressed some business matters, it was largely a letter between friends. She reported that her children were now healthy. "Sissie's eyes only cause her frequent cessation from books. Judson is as full of life as possible: he would much like a visit from Hurree." The children preferred Philadelphia to any place they had seen, and Charlotte agreed, "*I* feel at home in it."

As in India, supporting her family in America required frugality and initiative. Charlotte confided to Dyer, "I have taken a house in the cheapest row in this city, renting out at 170 dollars per room. It is three stories, having 2 rooms on a floor above kitchen & cellar. Here I have been since the 17th Dec. doing our own housework to save expense." Following her pattern in Digah, she opened a small boarding school for girls in her home starting with two girls as day students. Since she did not yet have other students living with her, she took in a young married couple as boarders, concluding that "with management and industry, I hope to save what we have, and live."[2]

When winter's cold weather was over, Charlotte began seeking out old friends and acquaintances in Philadelphia. On April 5 she joined some of them at the Sansom Street Baptist Female Society's annual meeting. She noted modestly, "It was a meeting of much feeling." Thirty-five women were present as well as four men: Noah Davis, a founder and agent of the Baptist General Tract Society; Isaac McCoy, a missionary among the Native American nations; and two young ministers. Charlotte told John Dyer, "I was at the forming of this Society 16 years ago, and was one of its managers." Now at the women's request, she resumed her place in the society.[3]

Charlotte had only two relatives still living in Philadelphia. They were her cousin William Atlee, the oldest son of her uncle Samuel Atlee, and her nephew Edwin Pitt Atlee, the oldest son of her brother Edwin Augustus Atlee from whom she was estranged. Her brother Edwin had embraced Swedenborgianism and was now a leader in the movement in Cincinnati. She found Edwin Pitt Atlee to be "a most worthy young man." He was a lawyer with "a pleasant family of little folks" in whom Charlotte and her children took much delight. Edwin Pitt was also deeply involved in anti-slavery work, which must have further encouraged Charlotte.

Charlotte's life in Philadelphia was marked by simplicity. This included her clothing. Her comments on clothes suggest that Charlotte intentionally dressed somewhat out of fashion. In 1825 she had written of herself, "The only danger is, that I shall offend by my plainness."[4] She saw Joshua's "plainness of life" as a mark of his missionary character.[5] And when planning to send her daughters to England for their education, she hoped that the twins would be able to wear clothing of "plain but of good materials."[6]

There was more in Charlotte's world to influence her choice of clothes than the example of plain-clothed Quakers such as her brother Edwin. Charlotte was undoubtedly aware that Ann Judson had endured public censure concerning her clothing when she visited the United States in 1823. The July 25 issue of the *New England Galaxy* had been unsparing with its scorching accusation of Ann:

Mrs. Judson, the wife of A. Judson, a famous missionary in the East Indies, sailed from Boston a short time since, where she had been to visit her friends, and to collect *Money*, from the pious and charitable, to aid her in distributing the bread of life to the poor heathen of Asia. A lady, who was in habits of familiar intercourse with Mrs. Judson, and to whom application was made for charity, in her behalf, informs us, that the *visiting dress*, of this *self-denying* female missionary, could not be valued at less than TWELVE HUNDRED DOLLARS!! The reader may be startled at the mention of such an enormous amount laid out in a *single* dress to decorate the person of one whose affections are professedly set on heavenly things, and despising the vain and gaudy allurements of the world: it appeared to us incredible, till we heard from the lady some of the details. The Cashmere Shawl was valued at $600; the Leghorn Flat $150; Lace trimming on the gown $150, &c.; jewelry would soon make up the sum, leaving *necessary* articles of clothing out of the question. We hope the next edition of the missionary arithmetic, will inform us how many infants were robbed of their innocent, if not necessary, playthings, how many widows had denied themselves the use of sugar in tea, and butter on bread, how many poor debtors had robbed their creditors and labored without stockings and shoes, to furnish out this modern representative of the mystical Babylon.[7]

Other newspapers circulated the *Galaxy*'s criticism of Ann Judson. Theophilus Gates repeated the claim in three successive issues of *The Reformer*.[8] Fearing readers might believe the accusation if there was no rebuttal to the *Galaxy*'s article, the Boston Baptist Association appointed a committee to investigate the charges. The committee discovered that the *Galaxy*'s source was not an eyewitness but a rumor that had passed through a chain of four people. The investigators then substantiated that the shawl cost $25 and had been given to Ann in England. The leghorn flat had been purchased in Salem for not more than $8.50. The lace supposedly adorning Ann's dress was either nonexistent or "so trifling that it did not make an impression sufficient to be remembered." Ann's supposedly costly jewelry consisted of a chain and small locket bearing the likeness of a family member that she had received as a gift. All the rest of her jewelry was valued at less than $5. Ann Judson had been a guest in the homes of all five committee members, all of whom testified that she had been "distinguished for the plainness and cheapness of her dress." They had also met with her frequently in New York and Washington, and "in no instance did they see anything in her deportment or apparel which did not accord with that modesty, simplicity, and plainness, which becometh women professing godliness."[9]

The vindication concerning Ann's clothing was deemed serious enough to warrant a resolution from the Baptist Board of Foreign Missions. Moved by William Staughton and seconded by Luther Rice, the board resolved unanimously to "cordially approve the judicious means which were adopted by the Boston Baptist Association, for vindicating the character of Sister Judson, from the charge of extravagance in dress, which was maliciously alleged against her, by the Editor of an eastern newspaper."[10]

Charlotte's attention to plain clothing was similar to that of many women preachers of her era.[11] Freewill Baptist Salome Lincoln began her preaching ministry in 1827.[12] Her 1843 biography described her clothing as "plain, yet tasty, and always manifested an excellent judgment in selecting the colors. She was not extravagant; but dressed in a manner becoming her station."[13] In 1830 the widely traveled evangelist Nancy Towle preached in Philadelphia to more than three thousand people at a time.[14] Towle wrote that she sewed her own clothes and "anything superfluous— I have not allowed myself to possess. My ornaments of gold, I sacrificed— and even to a watch in my pocket, I have not commanded, during the space, I have been a pilgrim—travelling upwards."[15]

Starting in the late eighteenth and increasingly through the nineteenth century, Americans largely held the "separate spheres" ideology that asserted distinctive gender roles. The public sphere was for men while women were restricted to the private sphere. While touring the United States for nine months in 1831, French diplomat Alexis de Tocqueville took note that this ideology was intentionally promoted: "In no country has such constant care been taken as in America to trace two clearly distinct lines of action for the two sexes and to make them keep pace one with the other, but in two pathways that are always different. American women never manage the outward concerns of the family or conduct a business or take a part in political life...."[16]

Because preaching by its very nature was a public act, Salome Lincoln, Nancy Towle, Harriet Livermore, and other women in ministry were often judged as acting out of their proper sphere. Women who drew attention to themselves in public were suspected of having immoral intentions.

Some women preachers therefore sought to diminish any accusation of enticement by wearing plain clothes.

Charlotte's clothing preference, however, was not simply to avoid criticism or to mark her role as a missionary. She valued modesty and faithful stewardship of money. In her view, plain, modest clothing was appropriate for all Christians, not simply women preachers or missionaries. In her letter to John Dyer, Charlotte commented on the clothing fashions she saw in the United States: "The fashions here disgust me almost as much as those of Bath in England. We are growing too voluptuous. Elegance, elegance in all things, but simplicity seems to be the ruling sin." Even the Quakers in Philadelphia, she felt, were inconsistent. She observed that the Quakers "go abroad in a plainer attire than others, yet the voluptuousness prevalent at their weddings, parties and *jams* is beyond description. From all I can observe, we Baptists are throughout the plainest and most consistent lives, of any denomination here."[17]

## Writing about India

Charlotte's friend William Staughton died in December 1829, the very month in which she returned to Philadelphia. Although she had rejoined the Sansom Street Baptist Female Society, Dr. William T. Brantly's preaching drew her to the First Baptist Church, which she joined on August 9, 1830.[18] Like William Staughton and Henry Holcombe before him, William Brantly had been a pastor in South Carolina before coming to Philadelphia. Also like Staughton but unlike Holcombe, Brantly affirmed Charlotte's ministry as a missionary and sought to support her endeavors. He did this in part through *The Columbian Star and Christian Index*, the Baptist newspaper of which he was editor.

In January 1830, soon after settling in Philadelphia, Charlotte began writing articles for young adults in *The Columbian Star and Christian Index*. Most of her series appeared under the titles "Hints to Young Friends of Missions" and "Scenes in India—Addressed to the Young." Underscoring that her facts, illustrations, and statements were trustworthy, Charlotte chose the pen name "Honesta" and reminded readers that she was writing out of her personal experience. Brantly urged parents and children alike to digest her articles with prayerful reflection. He assured the public, "Honesta paints from impressions received on the scene of action. She has received through the testimony of the eye, those indelible convictions to which she invites public attention."[19]

Charlotte recounted things she had witnessed in India, writing of cows, oxen, buffaloes, elephants, jackals, dry and rainy seasons, the flooding Ganges, and numerous aspects of daily life. Some of her anecdotes depicted the desperation of deep poverty. She wrote of infants stolen for the ornaments they bore or sold to save them from starvation. She told of infant girls purchased for harems or forced to swallow opium until they died if not fine enough to sell. The value of boys was less influenced by their appearance for they could be sold as slaves.[20] She wrote of a young man with leprosy who was suffocated with wet sand on the Ganges.[21] She described child marriage and the act of suttee in which a widow burns herself alive on her husband's funeral pyre.[22]

Story followed story, sometimes with shocking impact. Charlotte wrote of people sleeping outside on the ground, at times so near to traveled roads that they narrowly escaped being crushed by wheels. She recounted the evening when jackals made their way among sleeping families to scavenge grains of rice left from supper. One night, meeting no resistance, one snatched an infant from the breast of its sleeping mother. After the jackals had consumed most of the body, vultures scrambled for the remains. One carried its portion to the top of a palm tree where, lacking a sufficient base on which to rest, it dropped bone and sinew onto the ground outside Charlotte's door. The next morning Charlotte's attention was called to the grisly sight. Horrified, she looked away, yet knew the pitiful fragment of the infant's body could not be abandoned where it lay. Only a person of the lowest caste would touch the dead and remove the body remnant.[23]

Notwithstanding the tragic account of the dismembered infant, Charlotte did not write to shock, thrill, or entertain. She wrote to inspire young people to lead purposeful lives.

Writing as "Honesta," Charlotte cautioned young people about seeking lives of luxury. True luxury, she maintained, was something more profound than "glittering bouquets, garniture, and costumes." She urged the young to "expend the cost of such allurements in the luxury of doing good."[24] She recounted seeing a little poor boy at an annual missionary meeting in Liverpool who brought two pounds to give to mission. When asked by the treasurer where he got the money, he explained that he went about the city collecting potato skins that he sold to an old woman for two pence a week to feed her pigs. He used half of his earnings for his own needs and the other half to support mission. Charlotte suggested that her young readers could also earn money for a good cause. They could even memorize a hymn each week and repeat it to a good lady or gentleman from whom "no doubt it would receive a reward."[25]

Previously in India, Charlotte had expressed her conviction that neither age nor poverty could keep a person from participating meaningfully in mission. Her 1823 Hindi spelling book *Mūl Sūtra* contained vocabulary lessons among which short stories such as the following were interspersed:

> A poor blind girl makes baskets day and night and donates the money she earns to missionaries for the education of '*Hindubaba log*'; another poor girl, hearing of the pitiable illiteracy of Hindu girls, makes hats for dolls and gives the money from their sale to missionaries to construct a school; one poor girl saves an 'adhela' (small copper coin) every week from her 'majoori' (wages for manual labor) for the missionaries to educate Hindu girls, and once being penniless she delivers a basket of hand-picked potatoes instead; the eight-year old daughter of indigent parents learns to stitch in order to make her weekly donation to the cause![26]

Charlotte could simply have created the stories. In light of her encounter in Liverpool, however, the stories were more likely based on incidents she had observed while doing the radical work of opening schools for girls and seeing girls attend despite opposition from their parents or others.

When writing as "Honesta" in Philadelphia, Charlotte did more than urge her readers to support mission. She challenged them to consider missionary service themselves. She suggested that they read *The Life of Henry Martyn*, a biography of the well-known Anglican missionary linguist who had departed Dinapore two years before Joshua and Betsy Rowe arrived at Digah. Charlotte offered to help those wishing to follow in Martyn's footsteps. "I will teach them to read his beautiful translations, either in the Deu Niegree (or Hindoo) character, or in the Persian character, as preparatory to their work."[27]

## Supporting A Family

Charlotte began publishing her articles in January 1830 while simultaneously opening her boarding school for young women and children. She ran the following advertisement in Brantly's newspaper:

> A CARD. MRS. C. H. ROWE, late Missionary in India, having located at No. 101 Wood street, above Seventh, gives notice to her friends and the public, that she is about opening an English School for Young Ladies and small Children; intending to admit a few select pupils as boarders. Being a native of Pennsylvania, she trusts that her fellow citizens will forward her humble efforts to support a rising family.[28]

In March, Brantly publicly endorsed Charlotte in the paper, noting her India missionary service and urging his readers to patronize her boarding school.

> BOARDING SCHOOL.—On our last page will be found Mrs. Rowe's Card, advertising her boarding and day school in this city. We solicit the particular attention of our friends to this notice. After faithfully and honorably serving the missionary cause in India, Mrs. Rowe returns to her native land, a widowed mother—with several little children dependent upon her efforts. Her superior intelligence and accomplishments well qualify her for the proposed undertaking.[29]

In April, Charlotte printed the boarding school's prospectus in the *Star*. Her school was organized into minor, second, and high classes and offered instruction in the rudiments of English, spelling, reading, grammar, writing, composition, parsing in prose and poetry, arithmetic, history, geography, use of maps, needle work, sewing, and knitting. French, piano, voice, deportment, drawing, and painting and were also offered and individually priced.

Students paid extra for their books, stationary, fuel, and meals. Charlotte could provide bed, bedding, and washing for a charge, or the student's parents could furnish them. Each pupil was to bring a towel and spoon that would be returned when they left school.[30]

Charlotte's ad invited the public to consult three well-known Philadelphians as her references. One was Rev. William T. Brantly, pastor at the First Baptist Church where Charlotte was a member. The second was her nephew, Dr. Edwin Pitt Atlee, well known in the city as a doctor and anti-slavery activist. The third referent was General William Duncan, who had been commissioned as a general during the War of 1812 and represented the city of Philadelphia in the state legislature. General Duncan was a devout Baptist and a member of First Baptist Church. His father-in-law, Judge William Moulder, had been on the board and had voted for Charlotte's appointment in 1815.

While caring for the education of eleven-year-old Charlotte and Esther and seven-year-old Judson, Charlotte also did what she could to help her three stepsons who remained in India. Joshua completed his studies at Calcutta's Fort William College and was appointed the college's English tutor. Joshua wrote to Charlotte that he increasingly felt led to missionary service but wanted to discuss that possibility with the Baptist Missionary Society himself.

William, the middle son, was an assistant teacher in William Moore's school by 1828 and hoped in the future to "get into the indigo line." Josiah, the youngest of the three, had trained as a surveyor and sent his mother a list of instruments that he needed but could not procure in India.[31] His correspondence eventually reached Charlotte in Philadelphia after being sent first to England.

Charlotte's school faced growing competition for female boarding students in the city. *Desilver's Philadelphia Directory and Strangers' Guide* for May 1831 listed various seminaries, schools, boarding-schools, academies, and at least one high school specifically for young ladies in Philadelphia at the time.[32] By August 1830, Charlotte had moved from the rented house on Wood Street into a home of her own at 156 S. 4th Street. The home had the advantage of being "peculiarly airy, having a garden and large arbors, where a school of young ladies may sit half the summer afternoon, at their work and reading."[33]

By summer 1831, Charlotte's twin daughters were twelve years old and assisting her with the school. Girls of any age were accepted as students. The school was now also admitting "little masters" up to the age of seven whose "parents may find it convenient to send them to the same school with their sisters, during the first year or two of tuition."[34]

Four years later Charlotte and her family were no longer in Philadelphia but in Lowndesboro, Alabama.[35] Her connection with Lowndesboro may have arisen through her association with William T. Brantly. Lowndes County and eight other counties on either side of the Alabama River had been settled by immigrants from Virginia and the Carolinas who had brought large numbers of slaves to raise cotton in the rich soil along the river.[36] As a South Carolinian, Brantly may have had connections with some of the families that moved to Alabama.

It is not known why Charlotte moved her family from one of the largest cities in the United States to this small Alabama town. It may have been for the sake of little Judson's health. He had almost died from illness in 1824, and northern winters may have been problematic for a child accustomed to India's warmth. In any case, on November 10, 1834, Charlotte received dismissal from her membership at First Baptist Church in Philadelphia[37] and by October 1835 was residing in Lowndesboro where she and her then seventeen-year-old daughter Charlotte were teaching English, music, and drawing in the local academy.[38] No record of Judson Ward Rowe has been found following the family's move to Alabama.

## Expanding the Boundaries of Appointments

When Charlotte moved south, the Baptist Board of Foreign Missions was entering its third decade of appointing missionaries for the Triennial Convention. From its very start in 1814, some Baptists believed the Triennial Convention's purpose should expand beyond foreign mission to send domestic missionaries within the United States and its territory. At their second meeting in 1817, the majority of the convention delegates held this opinion and amended the convention's constitution, giving the board discretion "to appropriate a portion of their funds, to domestic missionary purposes, in such parts of this country where the seed of the Word may be advantageously cast, and which mission societies on a small scale, do not effectively reach."[39]

The convention then appointed its first three domestic missionaries to serve west of the Mississippi River. James A. Ranaldson was chosen for Louisiana while John Mason Peck and James E. Webb were designated for St. Louis.

The board appointed sixteen domestic missionaries between 1817 and 1822 to serve in Missouri, Louisiana, Mississippi, Alabama, Ohio, Pennsylvania, Vermont, Virginia, North and South Carolina. Peck and Webb served under board appointment for three years (1817–1820) while the other fourteen served for an average of only one year. At its fourth meeting in 1823, the convention brought its six-year experiment with domestic mission appointments to a close.[40]

The Triennial Convention's primary work on the American frontier was not through domestic missionaries but through cross-cultural missionaries appointed to work among Indigenous American peoples. Such appointments were in keeping with the convention's original purpose of *foreign* mission inasmuch as the United States government established treaties with the Native American nations as it did with other nations. That practice continued until Congress passed the 1871 Indian Appropriations Act unilaterally declaring that "No Indian nation or tribe within the territory of the United States shall be acknowledged or recognized as an independent nation, tribe, or power with whom the United States may contract by treaty."[41]

The board had not rescinded its 1816 post-Charlotte White resolution that "it will not be expedient" to appoint single women in the future. Nevertheless, mission among the Indigenous peoples in North America proved to be an exception. By the time that Charlotte began teaching in Alabama, the board had appointed thirteen single women to missionary service in the Native American nations in North America.[42] Like Charlotte, most of the women were educational missionaries.

Also like Charlotte, three single women were appointed for service in Burma. The board appointed Helen Maria Griggs to serve in Burma on December 14, 1829, seven days after appointing Francis Mason to serve there.[43] The board undoubtedly appointed Helen as a future missionary wife, for she married Mason on May 23, 1830, the day he was ordained. The two sailed for Burma on the following day. On the other hand, the board appointed Sarah Cummings and then Caroline Jenks Harrington, both of whom sailed to Burma in 1832.[44] Tragically, a year and a half later Sarah Cummings succumbed to fever. Her early death may have strengthened the voices of those who felt the board should not appoint and send women without a husband's protection. The board apparently believed that single women were safer serving as missionaries in North America than abroad.

Meanwhile, Charlotte Rowe had not given up on missionary service. She had funded her own ministry through all her years in India and had gone to England only when it was impossible to remain at Digah without additional support. The British Society's unwillingness to make an exception to their practice of not appointing women missionaries did not end Charlotte's thoughts of continued missionary service. While teaching with her daughter in Alabama, Charlotte wrote to Lucius Bolles, Staughton's successor as the board's corresponding secretary, asking whether the board might consider appointing her son Joshua as an American Baptist missionary agent in India. Bolles wrote back to her in Lowndesboro that it would be premature to make any such commitment since Joshua had not communicated his desire to serve under American Baptists. Bolles's reply noted, "You speak in your letter of the probability of your returning to India with your daughters."[45] Apparently, Charlotte considered her return to the United States to be temporary until she had gathered enough resources to fund her return to Digah.

In 1836, one year after she began teaching in Alabama, Charlotte's thirty-seven-year-old nephew Edwin Pitt Atlee died on Christmas day. He had worked unceasingly to end slavery through his activities in the Pennsylvania Abolition Society and the National Anti-Slavery Society. In Lowndesboro, Charlotte was surrounded on every side by slaveholders. The 1830 Federal Census showed that 47 percent of Lowndes County's 9,410 residents were slaves.[46] Like William and Maria Staughton before her, Charlotte must have found life in a slaveholding society to be intolerable. Furthermore, the slavery debate had grown increasingly intense among the Baptists. Three of the first four Triennial Convention presidents had been Southern slave owners: Richard Furman (1814–1820), Robert B. Semple (1820–1831), and William B. Johnson (1841–1844). In 1822, after completing six years as the convention's first president, Richard Furman had written the classic Southern biblical defense of slavery. The convention itself tried to remain neutral, saying that convictions on slavery were matters of individual conscience. Many Baptists in the North and South, however, felt that neutrality was unacceptable. In 1843 some Baptists in the North formed the American Baptist Free Mission Society to do mission on a clearly antislavery basis. This new group would begin mission in Japan through Jonathan and Elizabeth Goble. Jonathan would become the reputed inventor of the rickshaw.[47]

In August 1844 Georgia Baptists tested the American Baptist Home Mission Society by recommending James E. Reeves for appointment as a missionary to the Cherokee nation, pointedly noting that he was a slaveholder. The society refused to appoint him. Several months later the Alabama Baptist Convention asked the Baptist Board of Foreign Missions if slaveholders could be appointed as foreign missionaries. The board replied with a decision that departed from the Triennial Convention's official neutrality. "If anyone should offer himself as a missionary, having slaves, and should insist on retaining them as his property, we could not appoint him. One thing is certain," wrote the board's president, "we can never be a party to any arrangement which would imply approbation of slavery." In 1845, Baptists in the South broke fellowship with the churches in the North and created the Southern Baptist Convention with home and foreign mission societies that would appoint slaveholders as missionaries. Following the Southern Baptist withdrawal, the Triennial Convention changed its name to the American Baptist Missionary Union (ABMU).[48]

It is not known if Charlotte left Alabama before or after the Southern Baptist split in 1845, but by 1850 she and her family had returned to the North. There she and daughter Charlotte found positions teaching in Strasburg, Pennsylvania, just eight miles southeast of Lancaster, her early childhood home.

## Back in Pennsylvania

Strasburg's identity as a cultural and educational center far exceeded anything Charlotte had found in Alabama. The town's Presbyterian ministers were prime movers in shaping that identity. In 1790 Rev. Nathaniel Sample founded the Strasburg Philosophical Society. He operated a school of theology in his parlor and started the town's first formal school, a classical academy in which he taught Greek and Latin. The following year he helped create the Strasburg Scientific Society that was said to have "aroused the interest of Ben Franklin."

The 1800s brought on "a flood of schools" in Strasburg. Rev. David McCarter, pastor of Strasburg's First Presbyterian Church, was among those contributing to the town's growth as an educational Mecca. In 1839 he founded the Strasburg Academy on 37 East Main Street. Its reputation attracted students from throughout the east coast as well as international students from Cuba and Puerto Rico. Then in 1841 McCarter founded the Strasberg Female Seminary on 17 East Main Street to offer classical education for girls.[49]

The seminary's principal had been Ann M'Cullough, but at some point the school closed.[50] Charlotte Rowe was recruited to revive it. The *Lancaster Intelligencer* announced that the school was reopened in May 1850 by the mother and daughter team of "Mrs. and Miss Rowe." The seminary's prospectus resembled that of Charlotte's first boarding school in Philadelphia by offering writing, arithmetic, grammar, geography, composition, history, piano, drawing, painting, and French. In addition, girls in the Strasburg seminary studied natural and moral philosophy, botany, physiology, rhetoric, geometry, and algebra. As was true of its academy, Strasburg's Female Seminary anticipated attracting students from a wide area. Pupils coming from a distance were expected to make partial payment in advance. The *Intelligencer* announced that the seminary was led by Mrs. C. H. Rowe, principal, and Miss C. E. Rowe, assistant teacher. Young ladies from abroad could find lodging "where the teachers are boarding."[51]

Between the time of Charlotte's teaching in Alabama and the onset of her work as principal at the Strasburg Female Seminary, the Baptist Board appointed twelve more single women missionaries for ministry within Native American nations.[52] Two of the twelve were from the Baptist church in Haverhill, Massachusetts, where Charlotte had been a member. One was Elizabeth Boynton, appointed October 1, 1838, to serve in the Creek nation. The other was Charlotte's niece, Harriet Hildreth Morse, appointed August 29, 1842, to serve in the Ojibwa mission.[53]

In addition to appointing single women to serve within the Native American nations, the board gradually began appointing them for work abroad. In 1838, four years after Sarah Cummings's death in Burma, the board appointed Rizpah Warren to work in Liberia. Similar appointments followed as single women were sent to Assam, Greece, Burma, and Siam.[54] Charlotte's niece Harriet Hildreth Morse was among those women.

Harriet had worked among the Ojibwas for two years until ill health forced her to resign. In 1847 she reapplied, and the board appointed her to serve in Siam. Harriet may have been encouraged to reapply by the Hon. James H. Duncan, the long-serving clerk of her home church in Haverhill who had become president of the Baptist Board that year.[55] On February 18, 1848, after a five-month voyage, Harriet arrived in Bangkok where she taught in a school started by the mission.[56]

During that period, the board occasionally appointed single women who were children and siblings of missionaries, sending them to work alongside their families.[57] More often the board appointed affianced women, starting in 1825 with Sarah B. Hall, who married George Dana Boardman before their departure to Burma.[58] This created the anomaly that some missionary wives were officially appointed while others were not—even though both groups were serving equally.

## Years of sorrow

Charlotte's work at the Strasburg Female Seminary was interrupted by two years that brought unanticipated sorrow in rapid succession. Charlotte's daughter Esther Anna may have continued to suffer from poor health resulting from the illness she experienced in Digah that had brought her close to death. Although "Sissie" enjoyed reading as a child, she had weak eyesight and was unable to join her sister in the teaching profession. In March 1851 Esther died unmarried at age thirty-two. Her body was brought to Lancaster for burial in the cemetery of St. James Episcopal Church near the graves of her grandparents, William Augustus Atlee and Esther Atlee.

Charlotte's sorrow was redoubled a year and a half later in October 1852 when her remaining daughter and co-teacher Charlotte Elizabeth died near Coatesville, Pennsylvania. Charlotte Elizabeth, also unmarried, died one day before her thirty-fourth birthday.[59] She was buried in the St. James cemetery next to her twin sister. A single gravestone was erected on plot #10 bearing the inscription:

Twin Sisters

Charlotte Elizabeth Rowe
Died Oct. 19, 1852
Age 33 years
Esther Anna Rowe
Died Mar. 27, 1851
Age 32 years
Daughters of
Rev. Joshua & Charlotte
Rowe
Born in Hindostan
Grandchildren of
Wm. Aug. Atlee

Presumably shortly thereafter, seventy-year-old Charlotte moved to Germantown, north of Philadelphia. Her daughters lay in the St. James cemetery in Lancaster. No record of her son Judson Ward has been found during or since this period. Lucius Bolles's 1835 letter had only mentioned her daughters, so Judson Ward may also have died by that time.

Members of Charlotte's extended family, however, were actively serving in mission. Her niece Harriet Hildreth Morse continued to teach in Bangkok, and in 1854 the husband of another niece entered a leading role on the board. Samuel Francis Smith, husband of Charlotte's niece Mary

White Smith, was pastor of the First Baptist Church in Newton Centre, Massachusetts, and editor of *The Christian Review*.[60] The hymn "My Country, 'Tis of Thee" that he wrote in 1832 was becoming increasingly popular as he began participating in the American Baptist Missionary Union.

If the decade of Charlotte's life following her parents' deaths seems to have disappeared into a thick morning fog, the decade of her life following her children's deaths seems to have receded into a hazy evening mist. Her activities in those latter years are as yet unknown. The American Baptist Board's progress and regress in appointing women missionaries, however, can be clearly traced.

*Chapter 15*


# TO APPOINT OR NOT TO APPOINT


Approval of appointing women was far from a continuous forward movement. Adoniram Judson (1814) was appointed while Ann was not. Charlotte White was appointed (1815), but then the board resolved that appointing single women missionaries was "not expedient in the future, as far as they can now Judge" (1816). The board appointed Ann Cleaver (1821) and Louisa A. Purchase (1826). Then, without amending the board's constitution to state that missionaries must be male, the board issued "rules for missionaries" (1827) stating that, "All missionaries supported by the board, shall with their wives & children, be considered as having claims on the mission fund, for equal support in similar circumstances."[1] Clearly, the 1827 language continued the expectation that appointed missionaries would be male.

In 1846, the Free Will Baptists sent Sarah P. Merrill to India as their first single woman missionary. The following year the Free Will Baptist Female Mission Society was formed in Sutton, Vermont, and sent its first missionary, Lavina Crawford, to India.

Meanwhile, the American Baptist Missionary Union was living with a paradox. It had appointed some missionary wives while other missionary wives served without appointment. The ABMU Board addressed this disparity with an 1850 resolution "that the wives of missionaries be no longer regarded as assistant missionaries and that they be held responsible for no service."[2]

Francis Wayland, a member of the Board of Managers, addressed the ABMU as it met in Philadelphia in 1854. Wayland underscored that the mission's purpose remained unchanged from its start forty years earlier, namely, to "diffuse the knowledge of the religion of Jesus Christ, by means of missions, throughout the world." Wayland opined, "It would seem, then, that preaching, that is, the oral communication of divine truth by man to man, is the means appointed by God for accomplishing the great and peculiar work of Christian benevolence."[3] His words bore the unspoken implication that if mission was primarily accomplished through preaching, and if preachers were men, then missionaries would be men. However, Wayland asserted that other means could also accomplish the goal of mission, among which education held first place. He expected "much aid in this respect from the wives of missionaries, either as teachers or superintendents." "Women," he said, "display unusual skill in teaching." That talent "may hopefully be called into requisition abroad, wherever circumstances do not render it impracticable."[4] Wayland challenged the ABMU to send women into mission by asking, "We send out printers and physicians to labor at their appropriate work, why should we not send out teachers, male and female, in the same manner?"[5]

Several months later a scene between a father and his daughter erupted in Philadelphia's Sansom Street Hall and dramatized the era's conflicting views about gender. The Fifth National Woman's Rights Convention was in progress with Rev. Henry Grew and his daughter Mary both present. Henry Grew had been a Baptist pastor in Pawtucket, Rhode Island, and Hartford, Connecticut. Mary was the half-sister of Eliza Grew, a missionary who served in Siam with her husband, John Taylor Jones. Mary Grew was seated on the platform. Her father was seated in the Hall. After Mary spoke on behalf of the convention's resolutions committee, her father rose and protested the public leadership of women at the convention. Rev. Grew quoted several Bible verses purporting to prove his assertion that God intended "that man should be superior in power and authority to woman." Mary did not challenge her father in that public setting. Instead, Lucretia Mott rose and delivered an incisive rebuttal to Grew's interpretation of scripture.[6]

In 1860 the board's executive committee reiterated its position by issuing instructions that "wives are not to be appointed as missionaries, nor in any manner controlled or guided in their duties. In a word they are to be regarded as occupying essentially the position of pastors' wives in this country." Apparently concerned that its instructions might lessen the extent or quality of work being done by missionary wives, the committee immediately added, "For zeal, self-denial and efficiency, no labors have been more distinguished, none more highly appreciated; and, if either the spirit or form of this article shall have a tendency in time to come to diminish the amount of such labor, none would regret it more than the committee."[7]

## Women Organize for Mission

In 1860, the very year in which the executive committee declared that "wives are not to be appointed as missionaries," Ellen (Huntly) Mason, the second wife of missionary Francis Mason, returned to the United States from Burma and urged the appointment of single women missionaries. When the ABMU Board of Managers failed to embrace her proposal, she turned to women of other denominations. Largely as the fruit of her advocacy, the Woman's Union Missionary Society of America for Heathen Lands was formed in 1861. This multi-denominational society had the single purpose of sending unmarried women missionaries to work among women in Asia. The society's first appointee was sent to Toungoo, Burma, in honor of Ellen Mason's influence in establishing the Woman's Union. As these single women demonstrated their abilities in Burma, India, and China, the opposition to appointing women missionaries weakened.

Half a century after Charlotte White's appointment, the board was still alternating between appointing and not appointing women missionaries through actions that either challenged or reflected the gender bias in the broader society. In 1866 the ABMU Executive Committee determined that "large discretion should be given to the Corresponding Secretary in discouraging or encouraging applications from unmarried women."[8]

Meanwhile, the multi-denominational Woman's Union Missionary Society was receiving increasing calls to appoint women for educational, evangelistic, and medical work. In 1868 some Congregational women withdrew from the Women's Union to form their own denominational society. Some Methodist and Presbyterian women likewise started separate organizations in 1869 and 1870.

The creation of the Congregationalist, Methodist, and Presbyterian woman's boards did not compel similar action by the Baptists. At this juncture, a missionary in Bassein, Burma, entered the scene. Hattie (Rice)

Carpenter and her husband, Chapin H. Carpenter, had unsuccessfully urged the board to send additional missionaries to join them in Bassein. In January 1871, Hattie wrote to her sister in Newton Centre, Massachusetts, "We are doing all we have strength for, but we see the harvest perishing for lack of reapers. I am not sure that you yourselves have not a work to do for missions at home—the forming of women's societies, auxiliary to the Missionary Union. I believe that this is the true course."[9] In response, two hundred women met at the Clarenden Street Baptist Church in Newton Centre on April 3, 1871, and formed the Woman's American Baptist Foreign Mission Society (of the East) with offices in Boston.

The following month on May 9, 1871, other Baptist women met in Chicago and formed the Woman's American Baptist Foreign Mission Society (of the West). Three years later in 1874, women in California, Oregon, and Washington formed the Woman's American Baptist Foreign Mission Society (of the Pacific Coast).

The three newly formed Baptist woman's societies took care to assure a harmonious relationship with the ABMU by working as auxiliaries that secured financial support for their missionaries and channeled their funds through the Missionary Union's treasury. The women identified the new single women missionaries, and, significantly, the ABMU Executive Committee formally appointed them.[10] Though exceptions had been made to the 1816 post-Charlotte White resolution against appointing single women, that fifty-five-year-old controversy was now officially resolved.

The woman's societies of the East and the West both appointed their first missionaries in October 1871. The Western society appointed Alvira Stevens, and the Eastern society appointed Katherine F. Evans. Both women were sent to Burma. The women also accomplished other "firsts" such as the appointment of the first single women doctors. In 1879 Dr. Caroline H. Daniels was sent to serve in Swatow, China, and Dr. Ellen "Nellie" Mitchell to serve in Burma.[11] Mitchell had previously worked for four years during the American Civil War as a nurse for the Union cause. Now at age fifty she began twenty-two years of distinguished medical ministry in Burma.[12]

In September 1881 the women opened the Baptist Missionary Training School (BMTS) in Chicago, their first school to train women for mission service. By the mid-1940s more than ten percent of American Baptist missionaries received BMTS training.

In 1886 Louise Cecelia "Lulu" Fleming became the Baptists' first appointed African American single woman missionary. The woman's society of the West supported Fleming's work as a teacher in the Congo and then her service as the mission's first African American woman doctor.

## Public Advocacy by Men

New voices were now affirming the appointment of women. In 1882 George Dana Boardman (the Younger) became president of the Missionary Union. He was the son of Burma missionaries George Dana and Sarah Boardman and was in the middle of his thirty-year pastorate at the First Baptist Church in Philadelphia. His first address urged the ABMU to send lay missionaries and specifically to send both men and women.[13]

Dr. John Nelson Murdock, the ABMU's corresponding secretary from 1866 to 1891, advocated the appointment of women missionaries. Murdock also did so as a featured speaker in ecumenical settings, such as the Centenary Conference on the Protestant Missions of the World held at London's Exeter Hall in June 1888 where the topic of women's role in mission "excited much interest."[14] So many people tried to enter the venue assigned for Murdock's paper on "Woman's work in the Foreign Field" that the session had to be adjourned and moved to the Large Hall to accommodate the crowd.

Murdock's speech was masterfully diplomatic. His opening undoubtedly reassured those who felt women's roles should be limited. "It is safe to say," he said, "that in spirit and general form the work of women in the Missions abroad ought to be like that of devout and consecrated women at home, with only such variations as the changed conditions may render necessary. The work should be that of help to the men who have been sent out to make Christ known to the heathen." Murdock used the phrase "woman's work for woman" that implied restricting women to work among women and children.

With those verbal cues in place, Murdock proceeded to discuss the role of women in various branches of mission. Education through mission schools was the first branch he addressed. "In the legitimate school work of Evangelical Missions," he said, "it may be justly claimed that women have taken a leading part."[15] His remarks about mission schools affirmed the very kind of pioneering work that Charlotte Rowe had done in Digah.

From education, Murdock turned to medicine, and from medical work he proceeded even "closer to the heart of Missions," the visiting of women who by custom and caste are kept in "prison-like seclusion" in their homes. Only women could do this "Zenana work." From home visitation, Murdock went on to speak of schools in India established for caste women and child-widows. And from schools for women he proceeded to a larger discussion of training and directing Bible-women "sent forth into surrounding towns and villages, to impart the truths of the Gospel to the women and children, with a view of leading them to a saving knowledge of Christ." Murdock claimed that the work of Bible-women exemplified the prophetic statement of Psalm 68:11, which he said the Canterbury revisers had correctly rendered as, "The Lord giveth the word, the women that publish the tidings are a great host."[16]

Having brought along his hearers as he built his case, Murdock now finally crossed the bar that limited women to work only with women and children:

> It is now no uncommon thing for single women, going in companies of two or more, to visit the regions around some central station, telling the glad tidings *to all who will hear their word*; and some of us can recall instances of the conversion of *men* through such labours. And doubtless this form of woman's work will become more general, and so more successful, as facilities for it shall open, and as experience may justify it. Why may not women now be sent on the same errand on which the angel at the sepulcher sent the astonished Mary of Magdala? It is well known that some of the most effective workers in the evangelistic movement of our time are *women*.[17]

Murdock illustrated the point with a powerful example: "One of the most successful stations in the Burman department of our own Missions in Burmah was opened by a woman, and has been led up to be one of the most prosperous and numerous Burman churches in the world, under the sole supervision of its founder." The published record of the conference speeches identified that missionary as Marilla Baker Ingalls of Thongze, Burma.[18] Murdock described at great length her ministry as "a real overseer and leader of a numerous Christian flock" who worked mostly in private. Murdock predicted that "unless we misread the signs of the times" the force and efficiency of mission would increase through more women doing similar work.

> At first the wish would sometimes arise that this woman were a man, but that wish long since was resolved into the prayer that God

will give us more men and women too, of kindred spirit and equal faculty. "The tools to him who can use them," applies to women as well as to men. It seems that the Lord is a respecter neither of persons nor of sexes. He works by whom He will to the confounding of human customs and prejudices.[19]

Murdock asserted that the plan of sending out single women missionaries was not new. He was silent about the controversy that had erupted following Charlotte White's appointment and the initial unwillingness of both American and British Baptists to appoint women like her. Indeed, Murdock may have known little if anything about her story as her appointment had taken place seventy-three years earlier and mission histories had increasingly omitted any mention of Charlotte White. Nevertheless, Murdock averred, "Single women have been employed in the Missions from the beginning, and the early annals of all the great Societies have been adorned by the names and enriched by the deeds of these devoted workers." In Murdock's view, the new phenomenon was the number of women being sent and the creation of organizations to support them.

Speaking as a mission administrator, Murdock then warned against gender competition among mission agencies.

May I be permitted to remark in passing that it will be a dark day for Missions when our Missionary organisations shall become divided on the line of sex, and people shall begin to talk of "Men's Missionary Societies" and "Women's Missionary Societies" as separate factors in the one great work, whose essential condition is that it is neither male nor female, but one—indivisibly, indistinguishably one—in Christ Jesus for the renovation of our common humanity. The day that sees them separate will see them rivals, and where then will be the unity of purpose and spirit so necessary to insure efficiency and success.[20]

This caution was not theoretical. The American Baptist Missionary Union already saw a tendency for local churches to think that the woman's societies were for women and the Missionary Union was for men. Women tended to be more committed and consistent in supporting missionaries than men within the congregations and formed missionary "circles" named for the woman missionary they supported and with whom they had a strong, personal, and participatory relationship. Their funds were given to support "their missionary" rather than to support the entire work of the

Missionary Union.

On the one hand, Murdock used paternalistic language when speaking of the woman's societies as auxiliary organizations. "Let the noble Women's Societies be helpers at home of the Parent Societies, as those who are supported by their funds are helpers of the Missionaries in charge of Mission Stations abroad—always co-operative, but never co-ordinate." Murdock echoed the separate spheres gender ideology that had emerged in the era of the American Revolution. He viewed the "headship of man in ordering the affairs of the kingdom of God" as natural and predestined. Citing Adam's creation before Eve's and the text "the head of the woman is the man," Murdock concluded that male headship was an unchangeable order of creation, a Divine ordinance. Nevertheless, he clearly urged the liberation of women from limitations that mission organizations placed on their work: "Their work must overleap the bounds which as I think, has been mistakenly fixed for it. Let it be no longer 'Woman's work for Woman,' but rather Woman's work for Mankind."[21]

In the crowd listening to Murdock's speech was Adoniram Judson Gordon, a member of the ABMU Board of Managers Executive Committee. Gordon was a strong evangelical advocate for recognition of women both as missionaries and as pastors. Several years later Gordon participated in a summer convention at which a young woman missionary was scheduled to speak in one of the public sessions about her work. "The scruples of certain of the delegates against a woman's addressing a mixed assembly were found to be so strong," Gordon noted, "that the lady was withdrawn from the programme, and further public participation in the conference confined to its male constituency."[22] The incident prompted Gordon to produce a paper titled "The Ministry of Women," which was published in *The Missionary Review of the World* in 1894. His closely reasoned paper showed how scripture validates women in ministry. It then gave examples of several contemporary American Baptist women missionaries.

One was Adele Fielde, the "brilliant missionary" who pioneered work with Bible-women in China. Gordon noted that the board recalled Fielde when some senior missionaries complained that in her work she was transcending her sphere as a woman. Gordon recounted both the charge against her and her response:

"It is reported that you have taken upon you to preach," was the charge read by the chairman: "Is it so?" She replied by describing the vastness and destitution of her field—village after village, hamlet after hamlet, yet unreached by the Gospel—and then how, with a native woman, she had gone into the surrounding country, gathered groups of men, women and children—whoever would come— and told out the story of the Cross to them. "If this is preaching I plead guilty to the charge," she said. "And have you ever been ordained to preach?" asked her examiner. "No," she replied with great dignity and emphasis—"no; but I believe I have been foreordained."[23]

Gordon also wrote of Marilla Baker Ingalls' work in Burma and recounted Murdock's approving words about Ingalls at the Centenary Conference in London:

When before the Exeter Hall Missionary Conference in 1888, Secretary Murdoch described the work of Mrs. Ingalls, of Burma, declaring that, though not assuming ecclesiastical functions, yet by force of character on the one hand, and by the exigencies of the field on the other, she had come to be a virtual bishop over nearly a score of churches, training the native ministry in theology and homiletics, guiding the churches in the selection of pastors, and superintending the discipline of the congregations, the story evoked only applause, without a murmur of dissent from the distinguished body of missionary leaders who heard it.[24]

## Confronting the "Dark Day"

One year after A. J. Gordon's article appeared, the Missionary Union admitted that the "dark day for Missions" about which Murdock had warned had arrived. A committee to assess the relations between the ABMU and the several woman's societies reported "a widely prevailing impression that the Union is a society of men only." The ABMU was often referred to as "the men's society." This was a dark day for the union because women formed the largest portion of the its constituents and in many churches were "a majority of those who contribute to the funds of the Union."[25] Inasmuch as the auxiliary societies engaged in "woman's work for woman," the Missionary Union was now financially vulnerable to women's funds being designated for women.

The committee sought to correct this impression and the associated financial vulnerability by bringing women into governance roles. Women already represented their churches as delegates to the union's annual meetings and voted on matters that were brought to meetings for discussion and decision. Many were life members. Although the ABMU's constitution did not prohibit women from serving on the Board of Managers, none had ever been elected to the board. The committee therefore brought three recommendations to the Union: first, the constitution should be revised to stipulate that no less than one fifth of the Board of Managers would be women and that the presidents of the four women's missionary societies would also be ex *officio* members of the board; second, that the executive committee should urge every church to form a missionary committee composed of both men and women to promote mission education in the congregation, collect missionary contributions, remit them to the union, and constitute an ongoing communication link between the church and the union; and finally, that the board should appoint a special committee to confer with the woman's societies about electing women to the ABMU's executive committee.[26]

The suggestion that women should serve on the union's executive committee provoked considerable discussion. A delegate from New York said that the Union, having admitted women to the Board of Managers, should be consistent and also place women on the executive committee. Dr. Murdock felt the union was proceeding too rapidly on such an important matter and moved indefinite postponement of the matter. T. J. Morgan, secretary of the American Baptist Home Mission Society, was present and noted that the union's actions would also impact his own organization. Morgan therefore urged caution out of the concern that "the action of the Union would determine the policy of the denomination in all of our societies."[27] In other words, if women made governance decisions about *foreign* mission by serving on the executive committee of the American Baptist Missionary Union, Baptists would also expect women to be able to make governance decisions about *domestic* mission by serving on the executive committee of the American Baptist Home Mission Society.

A delegate presuming to speak on behalf of women said that "the women shrink from the added responsibility proposed. They say they now have all the responsibility they wish to carry." After Murdock withdrew his motion for indefinite postponement of the matter, the recommendation to form a committee was unanimously adopted.[28]

Women had supported the Triennial Convention and its board from its inception. Among the earliest of the women's societies, the Sansom Street Baptist Female Society had provided the board with reliable financial contributions and with its first appointed woman missionary in the person of Charlotte White. Nevertheless, the Sansom Street women had not been able to represent their own society in meetings of the convention or the board. At the start, the convention's members were not individuals but mission societies or associations that sent delegates to the meetings. When the convention held its second meeting in 1817, it consisted of 187 member societies, 110 of which were female societies. Although the meeting took place in the Sansom Street Baptist Church, neither Maria Staughton nor any other woman was able to officially participate. All 65 delegates to the convention were men, including those representing the Sansom Street Baptist Female Society and similar women's societies.

The convention's constitution and that of its successor, the American Baptist Missionary Union, was amended multiple times and eventually allowed individuals, both men and women, to become members. The Baptist mission enterprise now passed a major milestone by adopting the 1895 recommendations. At last, women could participate in governance through membership on the board, a role from which Charlotte White, Maria Staughton, and all other women had been excluded for eighty years.[29]

By the 1896 annual meeting, consultation had taken place between the ABMU and the four woman's societies. The woman's societies of the East and West expressed no desire to be represented on the executive committee at that time. The woman's society of California held that women should be eligible to serve on the executive committee but did not ask that any be appointed. No response was received from the woman's society of Oregon, and no further action was taken on the matter.[30]

## Resolving the Dilemma of Missionary Wives

Single women were now being fully appointed as missionaries along with single and married men. Married women were not appointed, however, and were typically mentioned not by name but by spousal status, as in "Rev. A. F. Groesbeck and wife, of Iowa, who go to China."[31] This manner of referring to couples exemplified the view that married women were under the covering of their husbands. In this social construction of gender, wives were considered so completely under their husbands' authority that in the eyes of the law they ceased to exist. In the first volume of his *Commentaries on the Laws of England* published in 1765, English jurist Sir William Blackstone famously stated, "By marriage, the husband and wife are one person in law: that is, the very being or legal existence of the woman is suspended during the marriage."[32]

Baptists were never monolithic in their thought and had long held diverse views concerning missionary wives. Some fully embraced the separate spheres ideology. Others, like Mary Mead Clark, chafed at the patriarchal treatment of women. Clark and her husband, Edward Witter Clark, served some thirty years among the Ao Nagas in North East India starting in the 1870s. At that time, women missionaries whether married or single could serve only on committees related to women's work. Likewise, women had no right to vote when the missionaries met in conference to make recommendations to the board. Women's invisibility was symbolized by the board's practice of referring to married women by their husband's name, such as Mrs. Edward Clark, Mrs. Miles Bronson, and so on. Mary Clark took initiative to change that practice. She circulated a petition among the missionary wives asking the board in official reports and documents to identify women by their own names rather than by their husband's name. Mary's petition reportedly told the board, "We all have first names. Please use them."[33] When Mary wrote her book *A Corner in India* in 1907, many female authors were being published either under their initials, a male pen name, or their husband's name. To identify her authorship of her book, however, Mary used her full first, maiden, and married name: Mary Mead Clark. But change was slow. Even as *The Baptist Missionary Magazine* advertised Clark's new book, the Missionary Union's official journal continued its deeply engrained naming practice. Its November 1907 issue listed nineteen male missionaries who had sailed to their locations of service, each accompanied by "and wife."[34]

At the turn of the twentieth century, the board enacted what appeared to be incremental change regarding married women. By 1908 the board's missionary manual regarded the wife of a missionary not as an "assistant" but as an "associate" in his work. A wife or fiancée of a missionary was now required to undergo a medical examination and to state her religious belief and attitude toward mission work. Though still not formally appointed, wives were expected "so far as family cares will permit, to learn the language and share in the mission work." They received no compensation for their work through a separate salary.[35]

A series of organizational actions soon surpassed those incremental changes. In 1907 the Northern Baptist Convention was formed. In 1908 the American Baptist Missionary Union became a cooperating agency of the Northern Baptist Convention. In 1910 the Missionary Union changed its name to the American Baptist Foreign Mission Society (ABFMS). In 1911 the Free Will Baptists merged with the Northern Baptist Convention and the Free Will Baptist Foreign Mission Society merged with the ABFMS.

Formal conversation about appointing married women as missionaries now began within the ABFMS executive committee's sub-committee on candidates. Others also expressed their opinions to the sub-committee members as evidenced by the continually changing votes taken within the sub-committee over the course of eleven months:

April 6, 1911. After a full discussion in regard to the appointment of the wives of missionaries, it was *Voted*: To secure information from other Boards as to their practice.[36]

April 24, 1911. *Voted*: To recommend that the policy of the Society hereafter be to appoint as missionaries the wives of its missionaries, provided that the action does not involve any appropriation for salaries apart from the salaries of their husbands, and provided that they are members of Baptist churches.[37]

October 6, 1911. After discussion regard to the appointment of the wives of missionaries, it was *Voted*: To report the matter to the Board, without recommendation.[38]

October 23, 1911. *Voted*: To recommend that the policy of the Society hereafter be to appoint as missionaries the wives of its missionaries, for the term of service of their husbands, provided that the action does not involve any contract relation with them, and provided that they are members of Baptist churches; That wives of missionaries now in active service be immediately appointed missionaries of the Society, subject to the above conditions.[39]

November 13, 1911. The question of the appointment of wives of missionaries as missionaries was discussed but no formal action was taken.[40]

March 2, 1912. *Voted*: That Mr. Levy and Dr. Barbour be requested to draft a vote for presentation to the Board at Chicago regarding the appointment of the wives of missionaries as missionaries of the Society.[41]

Then in Chicago on March 7, 1912, the board voted, "That it be the policy of the Board hereafter in the appointment of missionaries to appoint both the husband and wife."[42] In that moment, 268 women were recognized not only as missionary wives but also as missionaries themselves. It had been one hundred years since Ann Judson had sailed from Salem to India without appointment by the Congregationalists, ninety-eight years since the Baptist Board had appointed Adoniram Judson but not Ann, and ninety-seven years since Charlotte White had become the first American woman to be appointed as a foreign missionary. Now at last, the practice of appointing married as well as single women had finally arrived.

In 1914 the women strengthened their mission work by merging the American Baptist woman's societies of the East and of the West into one unified Woman's American Baptist Foreign Mission Society. Since 1871, the separate societies had supported a total of 388 women missionaries. At the time of their merger, 161 women missionaries were in active service and fourteen more were under appointment.[43] The women elected Helen Barrett Montgomery as the new society's first president. Montgomery, a licensed Baptist preacher, was already a recognized author, scholar, and leader in both educational and mission settings.[44] In 1920, she was elected president of the Northern Baptist Convention, making her the first woman president of any major U.S. denomination.

In 1967 the Woman's American Baptist Foreign Mission Society completed a full merger with the ABFMS. The organization, later also known as American Baptist International Ministries, provided salaries for women as well as medical insurance and retirement benefits commensurate with those for men. It followed the egalitarian practice of listing husbands and wives in the alphabetical order of their first names rather than automatically naming the husband first. It intentionally elected both women and men to all levels of staff and governance. And in 2016 it elected the Rev. Sharon Koh as its first woman executive director, the leadership role that William Staughton had held as corresponding secretary.

*Chapter 16*

# WRITTEN OUT OF HISTORY

Ann Judson became justly well known and admired, while Charlotte White Rowe receded into almost complete obscurity. Her invisibility resulted from being repeatedly overlooked by American Baptists writing mission histories. Baron Stow's 1835 *A History of the English Baptist Mission to India* omitted her name, stating only, "After the death of Mr. Rowe, this station [Digah] was effectively maintained by the zealous exertions of his widow."[1] In 1849 William Gammell wrote *A History of American Baptist Missions in Asia, Africa, Europe and North America*. It was the first comprehensive history of the American Baptist mission and was reprinted several times. Gammell recorded Charlotte's appointment, her arrival in Calcutta in April 1816, and her marriage to Joshua Rowe of the English Baptist Mission at Digah.[2] His history did not indicate that Charlotte was the first woman to receive appointment, nor did it mention the ensuing controversy or the nature and length of her ministry in India.

David Benedict's 1850 *A General History of the Baptist Denomination in America, and other parts of the World* mentioned George H. Hough as the first pastor of the New Bedford, New Hampshire, church and noted that he resigned "to engage in the India mission."[3] As a general denominational history, the book did not intend to be a history of Baptist mission, yet it cited Hough but not Charlotte White. A decade later Benedict's book *Fifty Years among the Baptists* also omitted Charlotte as it elaborated that Hough was "one of the earliest selections of Mr. Rice for the Baptist mission in the East."[4] A notable example of the intentional exclusion of women from written records took place during this era. In 1831 the Free Will Baptist evangelist David Marks published his memoir that included references to five popular Baptist women preachers. Before releasing the 1846 posthumous reprinting of his memoir, his is wife, Marilla, removed all his references to the women.[5] It is not known whether Charlotte White's omission from David Benedict's works was accidental or deliberate.

*The Missionary Jubilee* was published in 1869 to mark the board's fiftieth anniversary. The book reported Charlotte's appointment along with George Hough, followed by the following cryptic comment: "Had not the Board been restrained by the theory that men, under a special call from God, must offer themselves for missionary service, they might doubtless have obtained more laborers.[6] The funds accumulated would have justified the appointment, in those three prosperous years, of a considerable number."[7] The critique was the only possible hint that Charlotte's appointment had caused controversy. Readers of *The Missionary Jubilee* would only realize that Charlotte was the first woman to be appointed if they combed through the book's thirty-six-page list of missionaries and compared the dates of the women's appointments.

Perhaps influenced by Benedict's books and missing *The Missionary Jubilee*'s hint, Ada C. Chaplin made no mention of Charlotte when she published *Our Gold-Mine: The Story of American Baptist Missions in India* in 1877. Chaplin asserted, "Mr. and Mrs. Hough were the first missionaries sent out by the Baptist Missionary Convention."[8] In the next twelve years Chaplin's book underwent eight editions, all of which repeated that misleading statement and omitted Charlotte.

Samuel F. Smith published *Missionary Sketches: A Concise History of the Work of the American Baptist Missionary Union* in 1879. Smith prefaced the work by noting that it had first appeared as monthly sketches in *The Examiner and Chronicle* and omitted many important names, events, and details. "The work," he cautioned, "aims to be only what its title implies."[9] Smith's *Missionary Sketches* did not mention Charlotte, his wife's aunt. Edmund F. Merriam updated Smith's book at least six times without ever correcting the omission.

In 1881 William Cathcart's voluminous *Baptist Encyclopedia* cited Hough but not Charlotte.[10]

In 1884 George Winfred Hervey published *The Story of Baptist*

*Missions in Foreign Lands.* Charlotte's name surfaced in Hervey's richly detailed history only as he recounted the controversy surrounding the 1829 appointment of Helen Maria Griggs, who later married Burma missionary Francis Mason. Hervey commented, "As at that time no maiden lady had been sent out, the abstract question of sending her, or any other maiden lady, had first to be discussed in the meetings of the Board. True, Mrs. White had before gone to India in the family of Mr. Hough, but she was a widow."[11]

Charlotte received passing mention three years later in Thomas Armitage's 1887 two volume *History of the Baptists*, namely that "in 1815 Mr. Hough, of New Hampshire, and Miss White [*sic*], of Philadelphia, were appointed missionaries."[12] Walter N. Wyeth's 1892 *A Galaxy in the Burman Sky* was somewhat more substantive, devoting a paragraph to Charlotte. It recognized her as "a part of the second gift of American Baptists to Burma," the Houghs being the other part of that gift that followed the Judsons. Wyeth reported Charlotte's marriage to Joshua Rowe and service with him in Digah for seven years until his death. Wyeth further noted that an English periodical had expressed hope that Charlotte would remain at Digah to continue her useful work, but he gave his readers no indication that she had done so. The paragraph concluded that Charlotte was a "light not lost, though assigned a different sphere."[13]

During the sixty-six years that followed *The Missionary Jubilee*, apart from the brief references in Hervey, Armitage, and Wyeth, Baptist mission histories were uniformly silent about Charlotte White. This included the reissue of Ada C. Chaplin's *Our Gold-Mine* (1889), Sophia Bronson Titterington's *A Century of Baptist Foreign Missions* (1891), and Henry C. Vedder's *A Short History of Baptist Missions* (1927), which mistakenly named Sarah Cummings as the Baptists' first single woman missionary.[14] Edmund F. Merriam intended to produce a comprehensive work to succeed William Gammell's history. Perhaps due to his repeated updating of Smith's *Missionary Sketches,* Merriam was likewise silent about Charlotte in his own book, *A History of American Baptist Missions* (1900, updated in 1913). A. H. Newman's *A Century of Baptist Achievement* (1901) was a broad overview not limited to mission history, yet it cited Hough and omitted Charlotte.[15] With this body of work preceding her, Helen Barrett Montgomery may have been unaware of Charlotte White. Montgomery was typically careful to give credit where credit was due but wrote nothing about Charlotte either in *Western Women in Eastern Lands* (1910) or in

*Following the Sunrise: A Century of Baptist Missions, 1813–1913* (1913).
Charlotte did not reappear in Baptist mission histories until 1935 in
Dana M. Albaugh's *Between Two Centuries*. After service from 1923–1927
as an American Baptist missionary in the Belgian Congo, Albaugh had
returned to the United States due to ill health. Following work in Michi-
gan and New York, he became a leader in the Home Department of the
American Baptist Foreign Mission Society. His book reviewed one hundred years of American Baptist mission in Assam, South India, Bengal-
Orissa, and South China. Albaugh reintroduced Charlotte White through
two paragraphs devoted to the controversy surrounding her appointment,
observing that the board "was almost wrecked on the perplexing problem
of the relation of women to the foreign work."[16]
Charlotte surfaced again in 1955 in Robert G. Torbet's *Venture of
Faith: The story of the American Baptist Foreign Mission Society and the
Woman's American Baptist Foreign Mission Society, 1814–1954*. The book
was written to mark the society's one hundred-fiftieth anniversary and remains the standard comprehensive history of American Baptist mission.
*Venture of Faith* provided a brief but accurate account of Charlotte's appointment, the controversy it stirred, and her marriage to Joshua Rowe
after which she served with the British Baptists.[17]
Charles L. Chaney's *The Birth of Missions in America* (1976) devoted
four sentences to Charlotte White. Chaney identified her as the first single
woman missionary. He noted that her appointment met opposition and
that she never arrived in Rangoon but met and married an English Baptist
missionary in Calcutta. Outlines of Charlotte's story appeared in H. Leon
McBeth's *Women in Baptist Life* (1979), *The Baptist Heritage* (1987), and
*A Sourcebook for Baptist Heritage* (1990) as well as in Bill J. Leonard's *Dictionary of Baptists in America* (1994). While Albaugh, Torbet, Chaney,
McBeth, and Leonard were noteworthy in reintroducing Charlotte White,
none of them dealt with her missiology or her service in India, first in
partnership with her husband and then as a widowed single parent with
six children. McBeth thought that Joshua Rowe was single, and by missing
the women appointed for service among the Native American nations, he
asserted that the first unmarried single women missionaries were not appointed until 1832. Leonard's entry simply noted that Charlotte and
Joshua met "on the mission field." Leonard was unaware of the years of
Charlotte's birth or death, and his book *Baptist Ways* (2003) mistakenly
stated that she had lived with her sister and brother-in-law in India.[18] All

of the histories overlooked Charlotte's significance as the first American woman appointed as a foreign missionary.

A wider public learned about Charlotte through the genre of women's studies. R. Pierce Beaver's article "Pioneer Single Women Missionaries" for the Missionary Research Library's *Occasional Bulletin* (1953) introduced Charlotte H. White as the first such pioneer.[19] He brought her story before an expanded audience in *American Protestant Women in World Mission: A History of the First Feminist Movement in North America* (1968). Beaver identified Charlotte as "the first woman sent overseas by an American agency for service without the aid of a husband."[20] He accurately recounted details from Charlotte's letter of application to the board, her journey to Calcutta, her marriage to Joshua Rowe, and her service at Digah after Joshua's death. Beaver's account said nothing of Charlotte's missiology or the nature of her ministry beyond being "in charge of a large school." Beaver mistakenly concluded that Charlotte "was not asking for missionary status" although she was "asking for full missionary responsibility and work."[21] In actuality, the controversy did not arise over her being sent to Asia but over her being an appointed missionary.

Dana L. Robert's *American Women in Mission: A Social History of their Thought and Practice* (1997) succinctly reported, "The Baptists were the first American mission board to appoint a single woman as a foreign missionary."[22] Robert also noted that Charlotte went with the Houghs as the first reinforcements to the Judsons, that she paid her own way, and that she married an English Baptist missionary. *American Women in Mission* did not examine Charlotte's missiological thought and practice in India.

The loss of Charlotte's story was partially because she fulfilled most of her missionary call under the society in England that had not appointed her, rather than under the board in America that had. But it was also because the Baptist Board of Foreign Missions lacked the ability or will to fashion a joint appointment with the British Baptists or to maintain a relationship with her.

Undoubtedly, Charlotte's invisibility also resulted from historians' failure to note her significance as the first woman to be appointed. Appointment was important. While it confirmed mutual organizational obligations, it also had great spiritual significance. It was an act by which the body of Christ publicly affirmed that God had called her into the ministry of mission. In that regard, it resembled ordination. For Charlotte and for other women, appointment meant calling things by their right names. It was a matter of justice.

## The Influential "Mere Instrument"

Perhaps Charlotte would have disregarded the slight and often misleading attention paid to her by her own and succeeding generations. Her unassuming view of her own importance rested in her conviction that God was present and at work. She said that each should "do the measure of good which lies in our power. It may be but little; but no more may be assigned us to perform."[23] She likened herself to a seemingly insignificant ant working with others to build a large, pyramid-like anthill on an Indian plain. Like the ant, she did "not shrink from *doing little—doing many littles*."[24] She wrote, "I feel myself to be a mere instrument in the hand of the Master workman. If he use me not, I am nothing—but in His hand, I have performed far beyond my natural strength or abilities. I have been enabled to do all, under the sense of the Sufficiency of His grace to bring me through."[25]

Without confidence that God was active in unseen ways, Charlotte could have become deeply discouraged, for after her departure the affairs at Digah appeared quite dismal. The work had ground to a halt. Her stepson Joshua wrote to her that all the native female schools at Digah had been closed.[26] Dr. King in Patna lamented, "Our dear Digah (made dear by its former inhabitants) is no more so!"[27] Missionary Thomas Penney passed Digah three times in 1830 and reported that "it had a melancholy appearance." The premises at Digah were "occupied by someone who keeps them in tolerable repair," waiting for the society to send someone to the "destitute station."[28]

Charlotte could not know that her Hindi spelling book, *Mūl Sūtra*, would outlive her as the Calcutta School-Book Society continued to reissue it. Between 1840 and 1844 it entered its fourth edition with a new printing of 1,500 copies.[29] In the next three years, more than a third of those new copies had been sold.[30] Between 1848 and 1851, the School-Book Society decided to revise the then twenty-five-year-old book. The work was entrusted to John Parsons,[31] the British Baptist missionary and Hindi scholar at Monghyr who would also revise the Hindi New Testament.[32] Schools continued to purchase several hundred copies of *Mūl Sūtra* per year. In 1862–1863 the book again took on extended life with a new printing of 2,000 more copies.[33] In 1865 it was among the Urdu and

Hindi books that Trübner & Co. of London imported to England from India.[34]

Charlotte could have been encouraged by her family's mission activity. Her stepsons Joshua and Josiah Rowe both found ways to serve in India. Joshua had hoped to assist her in re-establishing the female schools at Digah upon her return to India. Although that hope never materialized, Joshua worked at the mission press in Serampore and then became an English tutor at Fort William College. While this was not a missionary appointment, it placed Joshua in work alongside William Carey and Joshua Marshman, who were on the faculty. All Indian Christian students were required to study under Joshua Rowe while his class was optional for non-Christian, non-resident students.[35] Joshua established a school at Cherrapunjie in Meghalaya, then with his wife Rhoda taught at Bareilly and Agra.[36] His brother Josiah was a trustee of the Lall Bazar Baptist Chapel in Calcutta[37] and a member of the governing committee of the Calcutta Baptist Missionary Society, an auxiliary to the Baptist Missionary Society in London.[38] Josiah listed his profession as "housebuilder" and was the architect for the chapels at the Boys' Native Christian Institution in Entally and at the Jan Bazar in Calcutta.[39] He contributed generously to the costs of both chapels and for expansion of the Circular Road Baptist Chapel in Calcutta.[40] Charlotte's step-grandson Joshua Mardon Rowe studied Persian, Arabic, Bengali, Urdu, and Hindi to prepare for missionary service but died in Agra in 1852 at age twenty-one before being appointed.[41] Her step-granddaughter Rhoda Mardon Rowe served in Allahabad, India, with her missionary husband, Thomas Evans.[42]

Charlotte's American family was likewise active in mission. Her niece Harriet Hildreth Morse worked for seven years in Siam. After failing health forced Harriet to return to the United States in 1855, she resumed ministry among Native Americans by becoming matron at the Baptist mission school for the Delaware nation in Kansas.[43] After retiring from that ministry in 1859, she served as matron of the Industrial School for Girls in Dorchester, Massachusetts.[44] Charlotte's grandnephew Daniel Appleton White Smith (D. A. W. Smith) sailed to Burma in 1863.[45] Smith served in Burma for fifty-two years, first at Henzada and then for forty years as president of the Karen Theological Seminary at the Rangoon suburb of Insein. A thousand men trained for the ministry under his guidance.[46]

Because Charlotte had dared to open the door for women to be appointed as missionaries, her influence extended beyond the ministries of her own family. More than half of the 386 missionaries sent out by the Baptist Board in its first fifty years were wives or single women. All the single women were appointed as were a gradually growing number of the missionary wives. Women, single and married alike, finally achieved the right to full and equal missionary appointment ninety-seven years after Charlotte's controversial appointment. In the board's first two centuries, women constituted 60 percent of the 4,000 missionaries sent by American Baptists. Twenty-six percent of long-term American Baptist missionaries serving in 2017 were ordained women.

Charlotte Hazen Atlee White Rowe died Christmas Day 1863 at age eighty-two, the same day on which her first husband had died fifty-nine years earlier. Charlotte's body was carried from Philadelphia to St. James Episcopal Church in Lancaster, Pennsylvania, where her funeral service was held on December 27.[47] She was buried in plot #9 of St. James cemetery next to her twin daughters.

America's first appointed woman foreign missionary was laid to rest unheralded, in an unmarked grave.

# BIBLIOGRAPHY

UNPUBLISHED LETTERS

Biss, John. Regent's Park College, Oxford, UK.

"Letters (12) from John Chamberlain." NRA 10413 Baptist SE Asia. Angus Library and Archive, Regent's Park College, Oxford University, Oxford, UK. Cited as Chamberlain letters.

Chamberlain, M. Regent's Park College, Oxford, UK.

Furman, Richard, and James C. Furman Collection, Furman University, Greenville, SC.

King, Dr. Regent's Park College, Oxford, UK.

Rowe, Charlotte. Regent's Park College, Oxford, UK.

Rowe, Joshua. Regent's Park College, Oxford, UK.

Rowe, Joshua (the son). Regent's Park College, Oxford, UK.

Rowe, Josiah. Regent's Park College, Oxford, UK.

Smith, Hanna. Regent's Park College, Oxford, UK.

Sutcliff Papers, Angus Library and Archive, Regent's Park College, Oxford University, Oxford, UK.

Tallmadge, Matthias B. Correspondence and papers, 1715–1868. MS 612. Box 3, folder 5. New-York Historical Society, New York, NY.

PUBLISHED SOURCES

"19th Century Health." Yeoviltown.com. Accessed 23 March 2021, http://www.yeoviltown.com/history/19thcenturyhealth.aspx.

*Abstract of the Returns of the Fifth Census.* Washington: Printed by Duff Green, 1832. Accessed 18 March 2021, https://permanent.fdlp.gov/lps48050/LPS48050.pdf.

"Acknowledgment." *Calcutta Christian Observer* New Series 1/8 (August 1840): unnumbered pages following 498.

Addams-Massmann, Jennifer. "'I Felt a Power from His Wounds and Blood': Native American Women and Female Missionaries in Early Moravian Missions in North America, 1742–1765." Cambridge Center for Christianity Worldwide and World Christianities Senior Seminar, University of Cambridge, 22 November 2017. Accessed 23 March 2012, https://www.cccw.cam.ac.uk/wp-content/uploads/2017/12/Jennifer-Adams-Massmann-Nov-2017-seminar-paper.pdf.

"Address." *Massachusetts Baptist Missionary Magazine* 4/11 (September 1816): 340.

"Agra." *Baptist Magazine* 50 (September 1858): 588–89.

Albaugh, Dana M. *Between Two Centuries. A Study of Four Baptist Mission Fields—Assam, South India, Bengal-Orissa and South China.* Philadelphia: Judson Press, 1935.

Allen, Jonathan. *A Sermon Delivered at Haverhill, February 5, 1812, on the Occasion of two Young Ladies being about to embark as the wives of Rev. Messieurs Judson and Newell, going Missionaries to India.* Haverhill, MA: W. B. & H. G. Allen, 1812.

"America." *Baptist Magazine* 9 (October 1817): 388–94.

American Baptist Foreign Mission Society. *Second Annual Report of the Baptist Board of Foreign Missions for the United States.* Philadelphia: Anderson & Meehan, 1816.

American Baptist Missionary Union. *Board Records. Executive Committee Minutes.* American Baptist Historical Society, Atlanta, Georgia.

American Baptist Missionary Union. *Fortieth Annual Report* (1854); *Sixty-eighth Annual Report* (1882*); Eighty-first Annual Report* (1895); *Eighty-second Annual Report* (1896); *Eighty-third Annual Report* (1897). Boston: Missionary Rooms.

American Baptist Missionary Union. *The Missionary Jubilee: an account of the fiftieth anniversary of the American Baptist Missionary Union, at Philadelphia, May 24, 25, and 26, 1864, with commemorative papers and discourses.* Rev. ed. New York: Sheldon & Co., 1869.

American Baptist Missionary Union Missionary Register. "Single Women." Hand-written card file at American Baptist International Ministries, King of Prussia, PA.

"American Intelligence." *Baptist Magazine* 7 (October 1815): 434–35.

Armitage, Thomas. *A History of the Baptists traced by their vital principles and practices, from the time of our Lord and Saviour Jesus Christ to the year 1886.* Vol. 2. New York: Bryan, Taylor & Co., 1887.

Arnebeck, Bob. "Yellow Fever in New York City 1791–1799" (A paper presented at the 26th Conference on New York State History, June 9–11, 2005, Syracuse, NY). Accessed 19 March 2021, http://bobarnebeck.com/yfinnyc.html.

"Arrival of the Missionaries in India" [William Staughton to Thomas Baldwin, 8 October 1816]. *Massachusetts Baptist Missionary Magazine* 4/12 (December 1816): 418.

"The article published in our last number." *Reformer* 4/46 (1 October 1823): 237–38.

Atlee, Edwin. "Serampore Missionaries." *Reformer* 4/40 (1 April 1823): 73–78.

"Atlee, William Augustus." In National Cyclopaedia of American Biography.

Vol. 16. New York: James T. White & Company, 1918.

Baker, Rachel. *Devotional somnium, or, A Collection of prayers and exhortations: uttered by Miss Rachel Baker, in the City of New York, in the winter of 1815.* New York: S. Marks, 1815.

Balik, Shelby M. *Rally the Scattered Believers: Northern New England's Religious Geography.* Bloomington: Indiana University Press, 2014.

Baptist Board of Foreign Missions. *Annual Report.* 1815–1819. Philadelphia: William Fry, Printer (1815), or Philadelphia: Anderson & Meehan, Printers.

————. *Letterbook.* American Baptist Historical Society, Atlanta, Georgia.

————. *Records.* American Baptist Historical Society, Atlanta, Georgia.

"The Baptist Board Minutes." In *Transactions of the Baptist Historical Society.* Vol. 7. 1920–1921. London: Baptist Union Publication Department, 1921.

Baptist Missionary Society. *Annual Report of the Committee of the Baptist Missionary Society, Addressed to the General Meeting, held at Finsbury Chapel, Thursday, May 2nd, 1839.* London: J. Haddon. Accessed 18 March 2021, https://findit-uat.library.yale.edu/catalog/digcoll:500083.

Baptist Missionary Society. *Brief Narrative of the Baptist Mission in India: Including an Account of Translations of the Sacred Scriptures into the Various Languages of the East.* 4th ed. London: E. W. Morris, 1813.

Baptist Missionary Society. *Minutes.* Microfilm roll 1, vols. 4 and 6. Wheaton College Billy Graham Center Archives, Wheaton, IL.

Barber, Edwin Atlee. *Genealogical Record of the Atlee family.* Philadelphia: Press of Wm. F. Fell & Co., 1884.

Bassett, T. D. Seymour. "Danforth, Clarissa." In *Vermont Encyclopedia,* edited by John J. Duffy, Samuel B. Hand and Ralph H. Orth, 101. Burlington: University of Vermont Press, 2003.

Basu, Baman Das. *History of Education in India under the Rule of the East India Company.* Calcutta: Modern Review Office, 1922.

Beaver, R. Pierce. "Pioneer Single Women Missionaries." *Occasional Bulletin* 4/12 (30 September 1953): 1–7.

Beaver, R. Pierce. *American Protestant Women in World Mission. A History of the First Feminist Movement in North America.* Grand Rapids: William B. Eerdmans Publishing Company, 1968.

Benedict, David. *A General History of the Baptist Denomination in America, and other parts of the World.* 2 vols. Boston: Lincoln & Edmands, 1813. Reprinted as a single volume, New York: Lewis Colby and Company, 1850.

Benedict, David. *Fifty Years Among the Baptists.* New York: Sheldon & Company, 1860.

Bethune, Joanna. *The Life of Mrs. Isabella Graham.* New York: John S. Taylor, 1839.

Betteridge, Allen. *Deep Roots, Living Branches: A History of Baptists in the English*

*Western Midlands*. Leicester: Matador, 2010.

Black, Sarah. "Mary Sophia (Shaw) Daüble." Dorchester Industrial School for Girls. Howard Gotlieb Archival Research Center, University of Massachusetts—Boston. Accessed 2 April 2021, https://dorchesterindustrialschool-forgirls.wordpress.com/blog/mary-sophia-shaw-dauble/.

Blackstone, William. *Commentaries on the Laws of England*. Vol. 1. Boston: T. B. Wait, 1818.

"Boarding and Day School." *Columbian Star and Christian Index* 4/23 (4 June 1831): 367.

"Boarding and Day School—by Mrs. [Charlotte] Rowe." *Columbian Star and Christian Index* 3/9 (28 August 1830): 144.

"Boarding School." *Columbian Star and Christian Index* 2/13 (27 March 1830): 204.

Brackney, William H., ed. *Dispensations of Providence: The Journal and Selected Letters of Luther Rice, 1803–1830*. Rochester, NY: American Baptist Historical Society, 1984.

Brekus, Catherine A. *Strangers and Pilgrims. Female Preaching in America 1740–1845*. Chapel Hill: University of North Carolina Press, 1998.

Briggs, John. "She-Preachers, Widows and Other Women: The Feminine Dimension in Baptist Life since 1600." *Baptist Quarterly* 31/7 (July 1986): 337–52.

Burrage, Henry S. *History of the Baptists in Maine*. Portland, ME: Mark's Printing House, Printers, 1904.

"Calcutta." *Baptist Magazine* 16 (December 1824): 541–42.

Calcutta Baptist Missionary Society. *Fourteenth Annual Report*. Calcutta: Baptist Mission Press, 1833. Accessed 19 March 2021, https://findit.library.yale.edu/catalog/digcoll:2818463.

"Calcutta. Marriages." *Asiatic Journal and Monthly Miscellany* 3/14 (February 1817): 197.

Calcutta School-Book Society. *The Thirteenth Report of the Proceedings of the Calcutta School-Book Society 1840–1844*; *The Fourteenth Report of the Proceedings of the Calcutta School-Book Society 1845–1847*; *The Fifteenth Report of the Proceedings of the Calcutta School-Book Society 1848–1851*; *The Twenty-third Report of the Proceedings of the Calcutta School-Book Society 1862–1863*. Calcutta: Calcutta School-Book Society.

"A Card." *Columbian Star and Christian Index* 2/5 (31 January 1830): 80.

Carey, S. Pearce. *William Carey, D.D.: Fellow of Linnaean Society*. Philadelphia: Judson Press, 1923.

Carey, W. H. *Oriental Christian Biography, Containing Biographical Sketches of Distinguished Christians Who Have Lived and Died in the East*. 3 vols. Calcutta: Baptist Mission Press, 1850.

Carey, William. *An Enquiry into the Obligations of Christians to Use Means for the*

*Conversion of the Heathens*. Leicester: Ann Ireland, 1792.

Cathcart, William. *The Baptist Encyclopedia*. Philadelphia: Louis H. Everts, 1881.

Cattan, Louise A. *Lamps Are for Lighting*. Grand Rapids: William B. Eerdmans Publishing Company, 1972.

Chaplin, Ada C. *Our Gold-Mine: The Story of American Baptist Missions in India*. Boston: W. G. Corthell, 1877.

Chase, George Wingate. *The History of Haverhill, Massachusetts, from its first settlement in 1640, to the year 1860*. Haverhill: Published by the Author, 1861.

Chase, Gilbert. *America's Music, from the Pilgrims to the Present*. Rev. 3rd ed. Urbana: University of Illinois Press, 1992.

Clare, I. S. *Lancaster and Its People. An Account of Lancaster, PA*. Lancaster, PA: D. S. Stauffer, 1892. Chapter 1 (pgs. 12–36) available at PA-Roots.com. Accessed 23 March 2021, https://www.pa-roots.com/index.php/pacounties/lancaster-county/369-books-and-journals-lancaster-county/lancaster-and-its-people-an-account-of-lancaster-pa/1110-chapter-i-general-history-of-lancaster-lancaster-and-its-people-an-account-of-lancaster-pa.

Clifford, Geraldine J. *Those Good Gertrudes: A Social History of Women Teachers in America*. Baltimore: Johns Hopkins University Press, 2014.

Cox, Francis Augustus. *History of the Baptist Missionary Society, from 1792 to 1842*. Vol. 1. London: T. Ward & Co., and G. & J. Dyer, 1842.

Davis, Almond H. *The Female Preacher, or, Memoir of Salome Lincoln, afterwards the wife of Elder Junia S. Mowry*. Boston: A. B. Kidder, 1843.

"Decease of the Late Mrs. Evans." *Missionary Herald: Containing intelligence, at large, of the proceedings and operations of the Baptist Missionary Society* (1 April 1874): 70.

"Departure of Missionaries for Calcutta." *Massachusetts Baptist Missionary Magazine* 3/5 (March 1812): 129.

Desilver, Robert. *Desilver's Philadelphia Directory and Strangers' Guide. 1831*. Philadelphia: Robert Desilver, 1831.

Dick, Devon. *The Cross and the Machete*. Kingston, Jamaica: Ian Randle Publishers, 2009.

"Digah." *Baptist Magazine* 12 (August 1820): 302; [Joshua Rowe to John Saffery] 14 (December 1822): 535–38; 16 (May 1824): 225; 17 (September 1825): 408–409; [Richard Burton to a relative] 18 (November 1826): 538–39; 19 (June 1827): 293; [Richard Burton letter, 26 April 1827] 20 (March 1828): 138

"Digah" [Charlotte Rowe letter extract, 18 October 1824]. *Friend of India* 7/76 (November 1824): 351–52.

"Digah" [Charlotte Rowe letter extract, 7 July 1824]. *Friend of India* 7/63 (August 1824): 252.

"Dijah." *Evangelical Magazine and Missionary Chronicle* 5 (August 1827): 357.

"Dinapore" [Thomas Penney letter]. *Baptist Magazine* 23 (May 1831): 217–18.

"Dissenters' Marriages." *Oriental Baptist* 1 (September 1847): 284–85.

Dorsey, Bruce. *Reforming Men and Women: Gender in the Antebellum City*. Ithaca: Cornell University Press, 2002.

Eaton, W. H. *Historical Sketch of the Massachusetts Baptist Missionary Society and Convention 1802–1902*. Boston: Massachusetts Baptist Convention, 1903.

Eden, Emily. *'Up the Country.' Letters written to her Sister from the Upper Provinces of India*. Vol. 1. London: Richard Bentley, 1866.

Ellmaker, J. Watson. "Col. Samuel J. Atlee." *Journal of Lancaster County Historical Society* 2 (1898): 140–45. Accessed 23 March 2021, https://lancasterhistory.org/images/stories/JournalArticles/vol2no5pp140_145_204600.pdf.

Everest, Allan S. *Moses Hazen and the Canadian Refugees in the American Revolution*. Syracuse: Syracuse University Press, 1976.

Everts, W. W. *Historical Discourse Delivered on the One Hundred and Twenty-fifth Anniversary of the First Baptist Church of Haverhill, Mass., by Rev. W. W. Everts, Jr., Pastor, May 9, 1890*. Haverhill: Chase Brothers, Printers, 1890.

"Extract of a letter from Mr. [Richard] Burton to the Secretary, dated Digah, May 3d, 1826." *Baptist Magazine* 19 (February 1827): 89.

"Extract of a Letter from Mr. [Joshua] Rowe to a Young Lady in New York, Dated June 5, 1818." *American Baptist Magazine and Missionary Intelligencer* 2/3 (May 1819): 107–109.

"Extract of a Letter from Mr. [Joshua] Rowe to Mr. [John] Saffery, dated Digah, April 3, 1820." *Baptist Magazine* 12 (December 1820): 528–30.

"Extract of a Letter from Mr. [Joshua] Rowe to Mr. [John] Saffery, dated Digah, Jan. 4, 1821." *Baptist Magazine* 13 (September 1821): 417–19.

"Extract of a Letter from Mr. [Joshua] Rowe to Mr. [John] Saffery, dated Digah, Oct. 1819." *Baptist Magazine* 12 (August 1820): 352.

"Extract of a letter from Mr. [Joshua] Rowe to Mr. [John] Saffery of Salisbury." *Baptist Magazine* 7 (July 1815): 294.

"Extract of a letter from Mrs. C. [Charlotte] H. White (now Mrs. Rowe) to her correspondent in Philadelphia, dated Serampore, May 2, 1816." *Christian Herald and Seaman's Magazine* 3/3 (12 April 1817): 35–36.

"Extract of a letter from Mrs. [Charlotte] Rowe, dated Digah, Oct. 17, 1817." *Latter Day Luminary* 1/2 (May 1818): 95.

"Extract of a letter from Mrs. [Charlotte] Rowe, dated Digah, Oct. 1824." *Baptist Magazine* 17 (August 1825): 362–63.

"Extract of a letter from Mrs. [Charlotte] Rowe, dated June 5th, 1825." *Baptist Magazine* 18 (November 1826): 397.

"Extract of a Letter from Rev. Dr. [William] Staughton, dated Philadelphia, Dec. 29, 1815." *Baptist Magazine* 8 (April 1816): 171–72.

"Extract of a Letter from Rev. George H. Hough, to one of the Editors, dated Serampore, April 27, 1816." *American Baptist Missionary Magazine and Intelligencer* 1/3 (May 1817): 93–95.

"Extract of a letter from the Rev. Dr. [William] Carey, dated Serampore, June 29, 1813." *Latter Day Luminary* 1/9 (August 1819): 439.

"Extracts of a Letter from Mr. [Joshua] Rowe, dated April 10, 1822." *Baptist Magazine* 15 (April 1823): 173–75.

"Extracts from a letter written by the Rev. Andrew Fuller to the Rev. Messrs. Mardon, Biss, Moore, and Rowe, with their wives, on their departure from England." *Oriental Baptist* 7 (November 1853): 321–23.

First Baptist Church, Philadelphia, Pennsylvania. *Register of membership, baptisms and marriages, 1772–1844.* Philadelphia Congregations Early Records. Accessed 19 March 2021, https://philadelphiacongregations.org/records/items/show/364.

"The First Baptist Missionary to the Heathen in Bengal." *Oriental Baptist* 7 (April 1853): 118.

"For the substance of the following account of the Annual Meeting of the Calcutta Auxiliary Baptist Missionary Society…." *Baptist Magazine* 19 (April 1827): 194–95.

Freeman, Curtis W. *A Company of Women Preachers: Baptist Prophetesses in Seventeenth Century England.* Waco: Baylor University Press, 2011.

"From Mr. [John] Lawson, dated Calcutta, June 23d, 1817." *Latter Day Luminary* 1/2 (May 1818): 94–95.

"From Mrs. [Charlotte] Rowe to Mrs. S——[Maria Staughton], Digah, Hindosthan, April 13, 1817." *Latter Day Luminary* 1/1 (February 1818): 48–49.

"From Mrs. [Charlotte] Rowe. Digah on the Ganges, Hindostan. Dec. 9th, 1816." *American Baptist Magazine and Missionary Intelligencer* 1/8 (March 1818): 296–98.

"From the New England Galaxy of July 25th." *Reformer* 4/45 (1 September 1823): 209–10.

"From the Same [Charlotte H. Rowe] to the Corresponding Secretary. Digah, April 21, 1817." *Latter Day Luminary* 1/1 (February 1818): 49–50.

Fuller, Andrew Gunton. *The Complete Works of Rev. Andrew Fuller, With a Memoir of His Life.* Vol. 2. Boston: Lincoln, Edmands & Co., 1833.

Gammell, William. *A History of American Baptist Missions in Asia, Africa, Europe and North America.* Boston: Gould, Kendall and Lincoln, 1849.

"Generosity." *Massachusetts Baptist Missionary Magazine* 4/11 (September 1816): 274.

Gifford, Martha J. "How It Began: How the Moulmein Christian Hospital Got Its Start: Baptist Missionaries in Burma." Denison Digital Resource Commons, Denison University Libraries. Accessed 19 March 2021,

http://cdm15963.contentdm.oclc.org/cdm/ref/collec-
tion/p15963coll18/id/28.

Gilchrist, John Borthwick. *The Stranger's Infallible East-Indian Guide, or Hindoostanee Multem in Parvo, as a Grammatical Compendium of the Grand,
Popular, and Military Language of all India (Long, but Improperly, Called the
Moors or Moorish Jargon*. London: Black, Kingsbury, Parbury, and Allen,
1820.

Gordon, A. J. "The Ministry of Women." *Missionary Review of the World* 17/12
[New Series 7/12] (December 1894): 910–21.

"The Grass Tabernacle, or the Baptist Chapel at Dinapore." *Missionary Herald:
Containing intelligence, at large, of the proceedings and operations of the Baptist
Missionary Society* (1 October 1879): 295–97.

Hervey, George Winfred. *The Story of Baptist Missions in Foreign Lands*. St.
Louis: C. R. Barns Publishing Co., 1884.

Hill, Samuel S., ed. *Religion in the Southern States: A Historical Study*. Macon:
Mercer University Press, 1983.

"Hindi Literature." *Trübner's American and Oriental Literary Record* 8 (21 October 1865): 150.

Holcombe, Henry. *The Whole Truth, Relative to the Controversy Betwixt the
American Baptists*. Philadelphia: J. H. Cunningham, 1820.

Honesta [Charlotte Rowe]. "Heathen Children's Society." *Columbian Star and
Christian Index* 4/15 (9 A5pril 1831): 235.

Honesta. "General Record." *Columbian Star and Christian Index* 4/16 (16 April
1831): 243–44.

Honesta. "Hints to Young Friends of Missions." *Columbian Star and Christian
Index* 2/5 (31 January 1830): 68–69; 2/8 (20 February 1830): 114; 2/12 (20
March 1830): 178–79; 2/15 (10 April 1830): 226–27.

Honesta. "Hints to Young Well-Wishers of Missions to the Heathen in the
East." *Columbian Star and Christian Index* 2/2 (9 January 1830): 27–28.

Honesta. "Scenes in India—By an Eye Witness. Addressed to the Young." *Columbian Star and Christian Index* 2/21 (22 May 1830): 324–26; 3/3 (17 July
1830): 33–35.

Honesta. "Scenes in India. Addressed to the Young." *Columbian Star and Christian Index* 2/24 (12 June 1830): 372–73.

Honesta. "Scenes in India—Designed for the Young." *Columbian Star and
Christian Index* 3/12 (18 September 1830): 178–79.

Honesta. "Tears." *Columbian Star and Christian Index* 4/10 (5 March 1831):
155.

Horne, Melvill. *Letters on Missions: Addressed to the Protestant Ministers of the
British Churches*. Bristol: Bulgin & Rosser, 1794.

Hough, Mrs. [Phoebe]. "On Melancholy." *Latter Day Luminary* 1/3 ([Fourth

Annual Report of the Board; May 1818): 159.

Hunt, Shally. *Prisoner of Hope*. East Sussex, UK: Shally Hunt, 2012.

"India and Foreign Mission Society of Haverhill, (Mass.)." *Massachusetts Baptist Missionary Magazine* 4/7 (September 1815): 223.

India Office Family History Search. British Library. London, England. Online search tool at http://indiafamily.bl.uk/ui/home.aspx.

"Interesting Intelligence from India" [William Carey to William Staughton, 20 October 1812]. *Massachusetts Baptist Missionary Magazine* 3/2 (September 1813): 322.

Ives, Ansel W. "A Remarkable Case of Devotional Somnium." *Transactions of the Physico-medical Society of New York.* New York: Collins & Co. 1817.

Jaffrelot, Christophe. "Sanskritization vs. Ethnicization in India. Changing Identities and Caste Politics before Mandal." *Asian Survey* 40/5 (September–October 2000): 756–66.

Johnson, Oliver. *A Home in the Woods: Pioneer Life in Indiana*. Indianapolis: Indiana University Press, 1951.

Johnston, James, ed. *Report of the Centenary Conference on the Protestant Missions of the World*. 2 vols. London: James Nisbet & Co., 1889.

Judson, Edward. *The Life of Adoniram Judson*. Philadelphia: American Baptist Publication Society, 1883.

Kaye, John William. *The Administration of the East India Company: A History of Indian Progress*. London: Richard Bentley, 1853.

Keay, John. *The Honourable Company. A History of the English East India Company*. London: HarperCollins Publishers, 1993.

Klein, H. M. J., and William F. Diller. *The History of St. James' Church (Protestant Episcopal) 1744–1944*. Lancaster: Vestry of St. James' Church in Lancaster, Pennsylvania, 1944.

Knowles, James D. *Life of Mrs. Ann H. Judson, late missionary to Burmah; with an account of the American Baptist Mission to that Empire*. Philadelphia: American Sunday School Union, 1830. Reprint, Boston: Gould, Kendall, and Lincoln, 1846.

Leonard, Bill J. *Baptist Ways. A History*. Valley Forge, PA: Judson Press, 2003.

"Letter from Dr. [William] Staughton to Mr. [Joseph] Ivimey" [24 October 1812]. *Baptist Magazine* 5 (February 1813): 83–84.

"Letter from Mr. [Gordon] Hall" [to Dr. Morse, 22 February 1812]. *Panoplist and Missionary Magazine United* 4/11 (April 1812): 522.

"Letter from Mrs. [Ann] Judson to Mrs. S—— [Maria Staughton], dated Rangoon Mission-house, April 29th, 1819." *Latter Day Luminary* 2/11 (February 1820): 39–41.

"Letter from Mrs. [Charlotte] Rowe. Digah on the Ganges, Hindostan" [9 December 1816]. *Christian Herald and Seaman's Magazine* 5/4 (16 May 1818): 112–14.

"List of Donations." *Massachusetts Baptist Missionary Magazine* 3/3 (September 1811): 94–95.

"List of Missionary Stations." *Baptist Magazine* 18 (Supplement 1826): 620–25.

Loskiel, George Henry. *The History of the Moravian Mission among the Indians in North America: From its Commencement to the Present Time.* London: T. Allman, 1838.

Loveless, Alton E., comp. *Free Will Baptist Early Women Ministers and Leaders.* Columbus, OH: FWB Publications, 2016.

Lovett, Richard. *The History of the London Missionary Society, 1795–1895.* Vol. 1. London: Henry Frowde, 1899.

Lynd, Samuel W. *Memoir of the Rev. William Staughton, D. D.* Boston: Lincoln, Edmands, & Co., 1834.

MacDougall, Hamilton C. *Early New England Psalmody: An Historical Appreciation 1620–1820.* Brattleboro: Steven Daye Press, 1940.

Mais, Charles. *The Surprising Case of Rachel Baker, Who Prays and Preaches in her Sleep.* New York: Whiting and Watson, 1814.

*Manual of the American Baptist Missionary Union for the Use of Missionaries and Missionary Candidates.* Boston: Ford Building, 1908.

Marshman, Joshua Clark. *The Life and Times of Carey, Marshman and Ward, embracing the History of the Serampore Mission.* Vol. 2. London: Longman, Brown, Green, Longmans, & Roberts, 1859.

Mason, Francis. *A Cenotaph to a Woman of the Burman Mission: or, Views in the Missionary Path of Helen M. Mason.* New York: Lewis Colby, 1851.

Masood, Ehsan. *Science & Islam: A History.* London: Icon Books, 2009.

"Massachusetts, Town Clerk, Vital and Town Records, 1626–2001," database with images, FamilySearch. "Nathaniel H. White and Charlotte H. Atlee." Accessed 23 March 2021, https://familysearch.org/ark:/61903/3:1:33S7-9RSP-NB2?cc=2061550&wc=Q4DM-N3V%3A353349801%2C353505001%2C : 25 October 2020, Worcester > Rutland > Births, marriages, deaths 1719-1814 > image 221 of 293; citing Massachusetts Secretary of the Commonwealth, Boston. Massachusetts, Town Clerk, Vital and Town Records, 1626–2001.

McBeth, H. Leon. *The Baptist Heritage: Four Centuries of Baptist Witness.* Nashville: Broadman Press, 1987.

McBeth, H. Leon. *Women in Baptist Life.* Nashville: Broadman Press, 1979.

"Meeting of the Board in Baltimore, April 28, 1819." *Latter Day Luminary* 1/7 (May 1819): 382–83.

"Memoir of Rev. William Batchelder." *American Baptist Magazine and Missionary Intelligencer* 1/10 (July 1818): 353–57.

Minor, Linda. "The Story of David Atlee Phillips (Part IV)." *Quixotic Joust* (blog), 7 August 2016. Accessed 19 March 2021, http://quixoticjoust.blogspot.com/2016/08/the-story-of-david-atlee-phillips-part.html.

"Missionaries." *American Baptist Magazine* 13/1 (January 1833): 13–14.

"Missionaries at Serampore." *Reformer* 2/24 (1 December 1821) 283–84.

Montgomery, Helen Barrett. *Following the Sunrise: A Century of Baptist Missions, 1813–1913.* Philadelphia: American Baptist Publication Society, 1913.

Moody, Robert E., and Leverett Saltonstall. "Leverett Saltonstall: A Diary beginning Jany. A.D. 1806." *Proceedings of the Massachusetts Historical Society* 89 (1977): 127–77.

Morrison, Doreen. *Slavery's Heroes: George Liele and the Ethiopian Baptists of Jamaica 1783–1865.* CreateSpace Independent Publishing Platform, 2014.

"Mr. Hough to Rev. Mr. Winchell, Rangoon, Jan. 1818." *American Baptist Magazine and Missionary Intelligencer* 1/12 (November 1818): 449–50.

"Mrs. Judson." *Reformer* 4/47 (1 November 1823): 262–63.

Myers, John Brown, ed. *The Centenary Volume of the Baptist Missionary Society, 1792–1892.* 2nd ed. London: The Baptist Missionary Society, 1892.

"New Native Places of Worship." *Calcutta Christian Observer* 7/71 (April 1838): 232.

Newell, Harriet. *Memoirs of Mrs. Harriet Newell, Wife of the Rev. S. Newell, American Missionary to India, who died at the Isle of France, Nov. 30, 1812, aged nineteen years.* 5th ed. Edinburgh: Ogle, Allardice, & Thomson, 1817.

Newell, Harriet. *The Life and Writings of Mrs. Harriet Newell.* Philadelphia: American Sunday School Union, 1831.

Newman, A. H. *A Century of Baptist Achievement.* Philadelphia: American Baptist Publication Society, 1901.

Nordbeck, Elizabeth C. "Origins of the Christian Denomination in New England." United Church of Christ. Accessed 19 March 2021, https://www.ucc.org/about-us_hidden-histories-2_origins-of-the-christian.

"Note by the Editors." *Reformer* 2/22 (1 October 1821): 232.

"On the Duties and Privileges of Female Members of a Gospel Church," *Baptist Magazine* 2 (November 1810): 556–59.

"Opening of Dr. Staughton's New Baptist Meeting House, Philadelphia." *Massachusetts Missionary Magazine* 3/8 (December 1812): 254–55.

"Ordination of Missionaries." *Massachusetts Missionary Magazine* 3/5 (March 1812): 159.

*Origination and Constitution of the Sansom Street Baptist Female Society for Promoting Evangelical Missions: Formed June 27, 1814.* Philadelphia: R. P. & W. Anderson, 1814.

Osborn, Bob. "Baptist Chapel." In *A to Z of Yeovil's History.* Accessed 23 March 2021, http://www.yeovilhistory.info/bapchap.htm.

"Passengers from India." *Asiatic Journal and Monthly Register for British India and its Dependencies* 23/138 (June 1827): 888.

The Peerage. A genealogical survey of the peerage of Britain as well as the royal families of Europe. Accessed 23 March 2021, http://www.thepeer-age.com/p35304.htm#i353039.

"Personal and Other Notes. Sailed." *Baptist Missionary Magazine* 87/11 (November 1907): 482.

"Political Awareness." Yeoviltown.com Accessed 2 April 2021, http://www.yeoviltown.com/history/political.aspx.

Pond, Jean Sarah. *Bradford. A New England Academy.* Bradford, MA: Bradford Academy Alumnae Association, 1930.

Powell, J. H., and Kenneth R. Foster. *Bring Out Your Dead: The Great Plague of Yellow Fever in Philadelphia in 1793.* Philadelphia: University of Pennsylvania Press, 1993.

Record Book, Minutes of the ABFMS Board of Managers. 1912. American Baptist Historical Society, Atlanta, Georgia.

Record Book II, ABFMS Board of Managers. Sub-committee on Return of Missionaries, Candidates and Home Salaries. American Baptist Historical Society, Atlanta, Georgia.

Reed, Jonas. *A History of Rutland: Worcester County, Massachusetts, from its Earliest Settlement, with a Biography of its First Settlers.* Worcester: Mirick & Bartlett, Printers, 1836.

Reese, W. H., artist, and Frederick Kuhl, printer. "Philadelphia Horse & Carriage Bazaar, S.E. Corner of Ninth & George, between Walnut & Chesnut [*sic*] Sts. Philadelphia. / On Stone by W. H. Rease No. 17 Sth 5th St. Phila." Lithograph. Library Company of Philadelphia Digital Collections. Accession No. P.2173. Accessed 23 March 2021, https://digital.librarycompany.org/islandora/object/digitool:65312.

"Relating to the want of Hindoostanee School-Books." *Calcutta School-Book Society's Proceedings. Second Report.* Calcutta: School and Mission Presses, 1819.

"Remarks on the Foreign Mission." *Massachusetts Baptist Missionary Magazine* 3/12 (December 1813): 353–55.

"Report of the Baptist Mission." *Missionary Register* (June 1816): 204.

"Report of Baptist Mission in India." *Missionary Register* 1/10 (October 1813): 354–58.

"Report of the English Baptist Missionary Society." *Religious Intelligencer for the Year Ending May, 1826* 10/33 (14 January 1826): 511–14.

Rippon, John. *The Baptist Annual Register, for 1790, 1791, 1792, and part of 1793. Including Sketches of the State of Religion among Different Denominations of Good Men at Home and Abroad.* London: Messrs. Dilly, Button, and Thomas, 1793.

Robert, Dana L. *American Women in Mission: A Social History of Their Thought and Practice.* Macon: Mercer University Press, 1997.

Robinson, J. "Memoir of the Late Rev. William Robinson, of Dacca." *Oriental*

*Baptist* 7 (November 1853): 329–36.

Rogers, William, and William Staughton. "Foreign Mission Societies." *Massachusetts Baptist Missionary Magazine* 4/1 (March 1814): 5–6.

Rowe, Charlotte H. Papers. Angus Library, Regent's Park College, Oxford, UK.

Rowe, Joshua. *An account of the Life and experience of Joshua Rowe.* Papers. Angus Library, Regent's Park College, Oxford, UK.

Rowe, Joshua. *Journal of Voyage from Bristol to New York in Brig Hannah, Capt. August Ryan of Newbury Port. 1804* [no page numbers; a handwritten document of four two-column sheets]. Papers. Angus Library, Regent's Park College, Oxford, UK.

Rowe, Joshua. Papers. Angus Library, Regent's Park College, Oxford, UK.

Russell, Horace O. *Foundations and Anticipations. The Jamaica Baptist Story: 1783–1892.* Columbus, GA: Brentwood Christian Press, 1993.

Safford, Mrs. Henry G. [Marietta]. *The Golden Jubilee.* New York: Woman's American Baptist Foreign Mission Society, 1921.

"Sailing of the Missionaries from Philadelphia." *Massachusetts Baptist Missionary Magazine* 4/9 (March 1816): 274–76.

Sangari, Kumkum. "The 'Amenities of Domestic Life': Questions on Labour." *Social Scientist* 21/9–11 (September–October 1993): 3–46. Accessed 19 March 2021, https://www.jstor.org/stable/3520425.

Sansom Street Baptist Church. *Records.* American Baptist Historical Society, Atlanta, Georgia.

Sellers, Charles Coleman. *Theophilus, the Battle-axe: A history of the lives and adventures of Theophilus Ranson Gates and the Battle-Axes.* Philadelphia: Press of Patterson & White Co., 1930.

Semple, Robert B. *A History of the Rise and Progress of the Baptists in Virginia.* Richmond: John O'Lynch, 1810.

Shannon, David T., ed. *George Liele's Life and Legacy. An Unsung Hero.* Macon: Mercer University Press, 2012.

Singh, Ameeta. "The Role of Missionaries in abolition of sati custom in India with special reference to Serampore Missionary." *IOSR Journal of Humanities and Social Science* 10/20 (ver. 2) (October 2015): 52–55.

Smith, George. *The Life of William Carey: Shoemaker & Missionary.* New York: E. P. Dutton & Co., 1909.

Smith, Samuel F. *Missionary Sketches. A Concise History of the Work of the American Baptist Missionary Union.* Boston: W. G. Corthell, 1879.

Stanley, Brian. *The History of the Baptist Missionary Society 1792–1992.* Edinburgh: T&T Clark, 1992.

"Stations Occupied by European Troops in the Benares Division, Including Dinapore, Hazareebauqh, and Benares." In *Army Medical Department. Statistical, Sanitary, and Medical Reports for the Year 1862.* London: Harrison and Sons, 1864.

Staughton, William. *The Baptist Mission in India: Containing a Narrative of its Rise, Progress, and Present Condition*. Philadelphia: Hellings and Aitken, 1811.

Stewart, I. D. *The History of the Freewill Baptists: For a Half Century*. Vol. 1. Dover: Freewill Baptist Printing Establishment, 1862.

Stow, Baron. *A History of the English Baptist Mission to India*. New York: American Sunday School Union, 1835.

Stowe, David M. "Hall, Gordon." In *Biographical Dictionary of Christian Missions*, edited by Gerald H. Anderson, 275. New York: Macmillan Reference USA, 1998.

Thompson, Evelyn Wingo. *Luther Rice: Believer in Tomorrow*. Nashville: Broadman Press, 1967.

Timpson, Thomas. *Memoirs of British Baptist Female Missionaries; with a Survey of the Condition of Women in Heathen Countries*. London: William Smith, 1841.

"To George Washington from Charlotte de La Saussaye Hazen, 3 August 1795," *Founders Online*, National Archives, Accessed March 23, 2021, https://founders.archives.gov/documents/Washington/05-18-02-0329. [Original source: *The Papers of George Washington*, Presidential Series, vol. 18, *1 April–30 September 1795*, ed. Carol S. Ebel, 500–501. Charlottesville: University of Virginia Press, 2015.]

Tocqueville, Alexis de. *Democracy in America. Part the Second, The Social Influence of Democracy*. New York: J. & H. G. Langley, 1840.

Torbet, Robert G. *Venture of Faith: The Story of the American Baptist Foreign Mission Society and the Woman's American Baptist Foreign Mission Society, 1814–1954*. Philadelphia: Judson Press, 1955.

Towle, Nancy. *Vicissitudes Illustrated, in the Experience of Nancy Towle, in Europe and America*. Charleston: James L. Burges, 1832.

Vail, Albert L. *Mary Webb and the Mother Society*. Philadelphia: American Baptist Publication Society, 1914.

Vail, Albert L. *The Morning Hour of American Baptist Missions*. Philadelphia: American Baptist Publication Society, 1907.

Vedder, Henry C. *A Short History of Baptist Missions*. Philadelphia: Judson Press, 1927.

"Very Dear Brethren" [William Carey and Richard Burton to the Society, 4 December 1826]. *Baptist Magazine* 19 (June 1827): 293.

Vinton, John Adams. *Life of Deborah Sampson the Female Soldier in the War of the Revolution*. Boston: J. K. Wiggin & Wm. Parsons Lunt, 1866.

Ward, William, to William Staughton. 23 December 1812. *Massachusetts Baptist Missionary Magazine* 3/2 (September 1813): 326.

Webb, Mary. "An Address from 'the Boston Female Society, for Missionary

Purposes,' to Females professing godliness." *Massachusetts Baptist Mission-ary Magazine* 3/9 (March 1813): 281–83.

Weeks, Stephen B. *History of Public School Education in Alabama*. Washington: Government Printing Office, 1915.

Wenger, Edward Steane. *The Story of the Lall Bazar Baptist Church. Calcutta. Being the History of Carey's Church from 24th April 1800 to the Present Day.* Calcutta: Edinburgh Press, 1908.

Whelan, Timothy D., ed. *Baptist Autographs in the John Rylands University Library of Manchester, 1741–1845*. Macon: Mercer University Press, 2009.

White, Daniel Appleton. *The Descendants of William White, of Haverhill, Massachusetts: Genealogical Notices*. Boston: American Printing and Engraving Company, 1889.

Williams, Charles. *The Missionary Gazetteer: Comprising a geographical and statistical account of the various stations to the Church, London, Moravian, Wesleyan, Baptist, and American, Missionary Societies, &c. &c. &c. with their progress in Evangelization and Civilization*. London: Frederick Westley and A. H. Davis, 1828.

Winthrop, John. *The History of New England from 1630 to 1649*. Vol. 1. Boston: Little, Brown & Company, 1853.

Wolf, Carla. "Strasburg—A Town of Trains and Heritage." *Amish Country News* (Spring 2019): 34–35. Available at https://issuu.com/amishcountrynews/docs/spring19_acn_digital.

Wyeth, Walter N. *A Galaxy in the Burman Sky: A Memorial*. Philadelphia: W. N. Wyeth, 1892.

Yates, William. *Memoirs of Mr. John Chamberlain, Late Missionary in India*. London: Wightman and Cramp, 1826.

# ACKNOWLEDGMENTS

Charlotte White Rowe likened her ministry in India to planting seeds in people's lives and said that she would likely be unaware of the fruit that those seeds might produce in years to come. I expect that most of the people who have encouraged my research and writing are unaware that their seeds of questions, suggestions, information, assistance, and inspiration have grown to help produce this biography. It is my pleasure to express this appreciation for their kind influence.

My research into Charlotte's life began while I was executive director of the American Baptist Foreign Mission Society, also known as American Baptist International Ministries (IM), the agency that in 1815 risked sending Charlotte White to Asia as America's first appointed woman foreign missionary. Cathy Holmes, my IM colleague and administrative assistant, planted seeds of insight from her more than three decades of service as an educator in "her country" of India. She helped me see the value of reclaiming and sharing the story of Charlotte's life and ministry. She also challenged me to follow Charlotte's footsteps in India. With assistance from Benjamin Chan and James Williams at IM, Cathy became the guru of logistics who led the 2019 visit to India in which eight other friends also participated. No painting or image of Charlotte is known to exist. Therefore, our journey of discovery in Kolkata, Serampore, Patna, Digah and Danapur gained even greater importance in helping Charlotte's story come alive. And it wouldn't have happened without Cathy.

People in India and the UK contributed seeds of information that greatly assisted the research process. A rich treasure of details about Charlotte and Joshua Rowe emerged from documents in the Angus Library at Regents College in Oxford, UK.

Whether we are researchers or interested members of the general public, we all owe a great debt of gratitude to archivists and institutions that preserve and make source materials available to us. Thank you to librarian Emma Walsh and staff for granting access and graciously guiding me through Charlotte and Joshua Rowe's unpublished letters in the Angus

Library.

Samaresh Nayak (Balasore) facilitated our 2019 India visit. Sudipta Nanda, (Kolkata) guided us to Carey Baptist Church (formerly Lall Bazar Baptist Chapel) where Charlotte White had seen the Rice and Judson baptismal site, to the William Carey house at Serampore where Charlotte had first stayed on her arrival in India, and to St. John's Anglican Church where she and Joshua Rowe were married. Members of the Serampore College administration and faculty received us warmly and introduced us to the archivist whose search confirmed the absence of Rowe source materials in the College archives. Christopher Bachmann (Patna) led us to the Danapur Cantonment where we saw the former brick church that replaced the "Grass Tabernacle" in which Joshua Rowe preached. He led our exploration of the Cantonment cemetery where heavily matted jungle vegetation prevented us from locating Joshua Rowe's gravestone. He guided us a mile from the Cantonment to the bank of the Ganges where the Baptist mission had stood and long ago disappeared into the waters, a casualty of the river's encroachment.

Many people in the US have sown seeds of encouragement that helped bring Charlotte's biography to fruition. Then executive director Deborah van Broekhoven and staff of the American Baptist Historical Society in Atlanta, Georgia guided me to valuable source materials of the Baptist Board of Foreign Missions, the American Baptist Missionary Union, Sansom Street Baptist Church and First Baptist Church of Philadelphia. Deborah's enthusiasm as a researcher and historian encouraged me in this project. Portions of my research first appeared in the article "Reclaiming Charlotte White Rowe, America's First Appointed Woman Missionary" in the *American Baptist Quarterly* (Summer 2019). I am grateful to executive director Priscilla Eppinger for permission to use the material in this biography. Staff of the Wheaton College Billy Graham Center Archives in Wheaton, Illinois, made microfilmed records of the British Baptist Missionary Society available that provided insight into the society's actions regarding Charlotte Rowe. Thomas R. Ryan, president and CEO of LancasterHistory in Lancaster, Pennsylvania, helped us gain entry to the Danapur Cantonment grounds in India with his letter of introduction that confirmed the importance of the Cantonment and its cemetery to this research.

Carol Bauer stimulated my research into the lives of her ancestors, William and Maria Staughton, the successful advocates of Charlotte's appointment. Many historic institutions enrich Philadelphia, one of which is the Library Company of Philadelphia founded in 1731 by Benjamin Franklin. The library staff provided access to documentation of the Sansom Street Baptist Female Society for the Propagation of Evangelical Missions, the society founded by Maria Staughton, Charlotte White, and other women of the Sansom Street congregation.

My research also led me to St. James Episcopal Church in Lancaster, PA, Charlotte's home church during her early childhood. Ann Webber, one of Charlotte's relatives in the Atlee family and a member of St. James, led me to the gravesite of Charlotte's twin daughters in the church cemetery. Parish secretary Karen King located the records of Charlotte's funeral and burial at St. James. I am grateful to Cordelia Moyse for introducing Charlotte to the present generation at St. James during the church's 275th Anniversary and to rector David Peck and the congregation for warmly embracing Charlotte as a daughter of the church. I applaud David's vision and leadership to place a fitting headstone to mark Charlotte's grave in the St. James cemetery.

Frederick S. Downs, former professor of church history at Eastern Theological College in Jorhat, Assam and professor of the history of Christianity at United Theological College in Bangalore, Karnataka, India, generously critiqued an early draft of this biography. His insightful comments were informed by his life's work in India and supported my conviction regarding the importance of this research.

Kathy Brown began early to share Charlotte's story among American Baptist women. Lonnie and Laura Bruce encouraged me to bring this work to publication. Eight friends likewise encouraged me by planting seeds of their unique perspectives as fellow pilgrims on our 2019 journey to India: Wendy Bernhard, Lorna Hansen, Joyce McVicker, Cordelia Moyse, Debra Mulneix, Carolyn Predmore, Marcia Ricketts and Marcia Street. And I thank Mercer University Press for publishing Charlotte's story and making it available both to scholars and general readers.

I am very aware that my research, travel and writing have all taken me away from my home and family, sometimes even when I have been physically present in their midst. I dedicate this book with love to my wife Janelle who graciously encouraged me during these past six years as I have worked to discover and tell Charlotte's story.

And finally, I am grateful to Charlotte Hazen Atlee White Rowe. With faith, courage and tenacity she shared good news about God's love, provided educational opportunities for girls as well as boys, respected the Indigenous people among whom she worked, and maintained an unassuming regard for her own importance. In so doing, she embodied that which the prophet Micah said God requires of us: do justice, love kindness and walk humbly before God.

# NOTES

INTRODUCTION
[1] Lynd, *Memoir of the Rev. William Staughton*, 182.

CHAPTER 1
[1] Barber, *Atlee Family*, 13–15.
[2] Ibid., 21.
[3] Ibid., 21–22.
[4] Klein and Diller, *History of St. James' Church*, 51.
[5] "Atlee, William Augustus," 140.
[6] Ellmaker, "Col. Samuel J. Atlee," 140–45.
[7] Barber, *Atlee Family*, 126.
[8] I. S. Clare, *Lancaster and its People*, 12–36.
[9] Everest, *Moses Hazen*, 97, 176.
[10] Minor, "The Story of David Atlee Phillips (Part IV)."
[11] Barber, *Atlee Family*, 23.
[12] Powell and Foster, *Bring Out Your Dead*, 12.
[13] "Yellow Fever," *Independent Gazetteer*, 14 September 1793, 3.
[14] Minor, "The Story of David Atlee Phillips (Part IV)."
[15] Everest, *Moses Hazen*, 122, 144–45, 162; "To George Washington from Charlotte de La Saussaye Hazen, 3 August 1795," NARA.
[16] Pond, *Bradford*, 18–19.
[17] Reed, *History of Rutland*, 174.
[18] "Massachusetts, Town Clerk, Vital and Town Records, 1626–2001."
[19] Ibid.
[20] Barber, *Atlee Family*, 80–81; White, *Descendants of William White*, 32.
[21] White, *Descendants of William White*, 30–31.
[22] Balik, *Rally the Scattered Believers*, 45.
[23] "Memoir of Rev. William Batchelder," 357.
[24] Charlotte H. White to the Baptist Board of Foreign Missions, 13 June 1815, in Baptist Board of Foreign Missions, *Second Annual Report* (1816), 112.
[25] "Memoir of Rev. William Batchelder," 335–37.
[26] Moody and Saltonstall, "Leverett Saltonstall," 147–48.

[27] MacDougall, *Early New England Psalmody*, 61.
[28] Chase, *America's Music*, 115.

CHAPTER 2
[1] Loskiel, *History of the Moravian Mission*, 63.
[2] Adams-Massmann, "I Felt a Power from his Wounds and Blood," 1.
[3] Russell, *Foundations and Anticipations*, 9.
[4] Rippon, *Baptist Annual Register*, 1:335.
[5] Ibid., 335.
[6] Ibid., 333–34.
[7] Morrison, *Slavery's Heroes*, 79.
[8] Shannon, ed., *George Liele's Life and Legacy*, 165–67.
[9] Dick, *Cross and the Machete*, 102.
[10] Klein and Diller, *History of St. James' Church*, 52.
[11] Ibid., 54.
[12] Klein and Diller, *History of St. James' Church*, 69.
[13] Charlotte H. White to the Baptist Board of Foreign Missions, 13 June 1815, in Baptist Board of Foreign Missions, *Second Annual Report* (1816), 112.
[14] Vail, *Mary Webb and the Mother Society*, 33.
[15] Burrage, *History of the Baptists in Maine*, 114.
[16] Eaton, *Historical Sketch of the Massachusetts Baptist Missionary Society*, 21.
[17] Baptist Board of Foreign Missions, *Second Annual Report* (1816), 93.
[18] "India and Foreign Mission Society of Haverhill, (Mass.)," 223.
[19] "List of Donations," 95.
[20] Keay, *Honourable Company*, 14.
[21] Ibid., 39.
[22] Ibid., 130ff., 148ff., 193ff.
[23] John Chamberlain to Rev. Andrew Fuller, July 1802, Chamberlain letters.
[24] Yates, *Memoirs of Mr. John Chamberlain*, 87.
[25] J. Rowe, *Journal of Voyage*.
[26] Whelan, ed., *Baptist Autographs*, 118.
[27] Baptist Missionary Society, *Brief Narrative of the Baptist Mission in India*, 55.
[28] Lynd, *Memoir of the Rev. William Staughton*, 60.
[29] Stow, *History of the English Baptist Mission to India*, 100–101.
[30] Everts, *Historical Discourse*, 28.
[31] Newell, *Life and Writings*, 9.
[32] Everts, *Historical Discourse*, 28.
[33] Newell, *Life and Writings*, 144.

[34] "Letter from Mrs. [Ann] Judson to Mrs. S—— [Maria Staughton]" [29 April 1815], 41.

[35] Knowles, *Memoir of Ann H. Judson* (1846), 44.

[36] Ibid., 43.

[37] G. W. Chase, *History of Haverhill*, 642.

[38] Knowles, *Memoir of Ann H. Judson* (1846), 46.

[39] Newell, *Memoirs*, 73, 77–78, 82.

[40] Knowles, *Memoir of Ann H. Judson* (1846), 48.

CHAPTER 3

[1] Reese and Kuhl, "Philadelphia Horse & Carriage Bazaar" (lithograph).

[2] "Opening of Dr. Staughton's New Baptist Meeting House," 254–55.

[3] Vail, *Morning Hour*, 107, 130–31.

[4] Hill, ed., *Religion in the Southern States*, 132.

[5] "Letter from Dr. [William] Staughton to Mr. [Joseph] Ivimey" [24 October 1812], 84.

[6] Betteridge, *Deep Roots*, 108, 110.

[7] S. Pearce Carey, *William Carey*, 93.

[8] Arnebeck, "Yellow Fever in New York City."

[9] Lynd, *Memoir of the Rev. William Staughton*, 40.

[10] Ibid., 228.

[11] Ibid., 37.

[12] Clifford, *Those Good Gertrudes*, 31.

[13] Lynd, *Memoir of the Rev. William Staughton*, 42.

[14] Ibid., 58–59.

[15] Ibid., 178.

[16] Ibid., 68.

[17] Allen, *Sermon Delivered at Haverhill*, 19.

[18] Ibid., 19–20.

[19] Ibid., 21.

[20] Ibid., 24.

[21] A well-known etching of the service shows the clergy observing the kneeling Ann Judson but laying hands only upon the men.

[22] Harriet Atwood married Samuel Newell just days after the commissioning service. Samuel Nott married Roxana Peck in Franklin, Connecticut, en route to Philadelphia. Roxana was prevented by the weather and her wedding preparations from attending the service in Salem.

[23] "Departure of Missionaries for Calcutta," 129.

[24] "Ordination of Missionaries," 159.

[25] "First Baptist Missionary to the Heathen in Bengal," 118.

[26] Ibid., 119.

[27] Thompson, *Luther Rice*, 52–54.

[28] Stowe, "Hall, Gordon," 275.

[29] Bethune, *Life of Mrs. Isabella Graham*, 52.

[30] W. H. Carey, *Oriental Christian Biography*, 1:182.

[31] Ibid., 183.

[32] Ibid., 184.

[33] Basu, *History of Education in India*, 5.

[34] W. H. Carey, *Oriental Christian Biography*, 1:185–86.

[35] Ann Judson to her parents and sisters, 21 June 1813, in Baptist Board of Foreign Missions, *First Annual Report* (1815), 36.

[36] Knowles, *Life of Mrs. Ann H. Judson* (1830), 76.

[37] Judson, *Life of Adoniram Judson*, 112–21; "Meeting of the Board in Baltimore, April 28, 1819," 382–83.

[38] Timpson, *Memoirs of British Baptist Female Missionaries*, 208.

CHAPTER 4

[1] "Departure of Missionaries for Calcutta," 129.

[2] Yates, *Memoirs of Mr. John Chamberlain*, 90.

[3] Brackney, *Dispensations of Providence*, 47n.5.

[4] Ibid., 47.

[5] Singh, "Role of Missionaries in abolition of sati custom in India," 53. See also Briggs, "She-Preachers, Widows and Other Women," 352.

[6] "Letter from Mr. [Gordon] Hall," 522.

[7] W. H. Carey, *Oriental Christian Biography*, 2:416–20.

[8] Thompson, *Luther Rice*, 62.

[9] Brackney, ed., *Dispensations of Providence*, 53.

[10] The church is now the William Carey Baptist Church.

[11] "Interesting Intelligence from India" [William Carey to William Staughton, 20 October 1812], 322.

[12] William Ward to William Staughton, 23 December 1812, 326.

[13] The convention continues to exist as the American Baptist Foreign Mission Society, also known as American Baptist International Ministries. The chief executive position of corresponding secretary is now called executive director.

[14] McBeth, *Women in Baptist Life*, 82. McBeth identified Charlotte H. White as the first donor but did not cite his source. See McBeth, *Baptist Heritage*, 351.

[15] The details of the meeting that follow are recorded in the pamphlet *Origination and Constitution of the Sansom Street Baptist Female Society for Promoting Evangelical Missions: Formed June 27, 1814.*

[16] "Remarks on the Foreign Mission," 353; Rogers and Staughton, "Foreign Mission Societies," 5.

[17] Rogers and Staughton, "Foreign Mission Societies," 5.

[18] Lynd, *Memoir of the Rev. William Staughton*, 37.

[19] Ibid., 229–31.

[20] American Baptist Missionary Union, *Missionary Jubilee*, 21.

[21] Carey, *Enquiry into the Obligations of Christians*, 75, 83 (emphasis added).

[22] Benedict, *General History of the Baptist Denomination in America* (1850), 411.

[23] Ibid. (1813), 1:4.

[24] "American Intelligence," 435.

[25] Baptist Board of Foreign Missions, *Records 1814–1828* (11 April 1815), 26.

[26] Baptist Board of Foreign Missions, *First Annual Report* (1815), 29.

[27] Charlotte H. White to the Baptist Board of Foreign Missions, 13 June 1815, in Baptist Board of Foreign Missions, *Second Annual Report* (1816), 112.

CHAPTER5

[1] Charlotte H. White to the Baptist Board of Foreign Missions, 13 June 1815, in Baptist Board of Foreign Missions, *Second Annual Report* (1816), 112.

[2] Holcombe, *Whole Truth*, 9.

[3] Ibid., 9 (emphasis original).

[4] G. Smith, *Life of William Carey*, 152.

[5] Hunt, *Prisoner of Hope*, 157–60.

[6] Baptist Board of Foreign Missions, *First Annual Report* (1815), 53.

[7] Holcombe, *Whole Truth*, 10.

[8] Ibid., 27.

[9] "On the Duties and Privileges of Female Members of a Gospel Church," 556–59.

[10] Baptist Board of Foreign Missions, *Records* (26 July 1815), 33.

[11] Holcombe, *Whole Truth*, 9.

[12] Vinton, *Life of Deborah Sampson*, xviii.

[13] "Extract of a Letter from Rev. Dr. [William] Staughton" [29 December 1815], 171–72.

[14] In *A Company of Women Preachers*, Curtis W. Freeman names fourteen seventeenth-century English Baptist women preachers and reprints writings from seven of them.

[15] Winthrop, *History of New England from 1630 to 1649*, 352–53.

[16] Brekus, *Strangers and Pilgrims*, 59–60.

[17] Ibid., 4, 62–63.

[18] Semple, *History of the Rise and Progress of the Baptists in Virginia*, 374.

[19] Brekus, *Strangers and Pilgrims*, 9.

[20] Nordbeck, "Origins of the Christian Denomination in New England."

[21] Bassett, "Danforth, Clarissa," 101.

[22] Stewart, *History of the Freewill Baptists*, 306.

[23] Ibid., 307.

[24] Ibid., 338.

[25] Charlotte White to Elizabeth Talmadge, 18 March 1816, in Tallmadge correspondence and papers.

[26] Baker, *Devotional somnium*, 16.

[27] Ibid., 18–19.

[28] Mais, *Surprising Case of Rachel Baker*, 6ff.

[29] Ibid., 9–10.

[30] "Moral Phenomenon," *Natchez Gazette*, 21 June 1815, 3, a reprint from the *National Advocate* (New York).

[31] Baker, *Devotional somnium*, 173–74, 206, 209, 225.

[32] Baker, *Devotional somnium*, 186–87.

[33] Acts 2:17-18.

[34] Baker, *Devotional somnium*, 218–19.

[35] Ibid., 221–22.

[36] Ibid., 283.

[37] Ibid., 20.

[38] Ibid., 236–37.

[39] Mais, *Surprising Case of Rachel Baker*, 11.

[40] Baker, *Devotional somnium*, 285.

[41] Mais, *Surprising Case of Rachel Baker*, 10.

[42] Ives, "Remarkable Case of Devotional Somnium," 411; "Extract of a letter to Dr. Spalding, of N. York," *New-York Evening Post*, 5 September 1817, 2.

[43] The number of women preachers increased between 1817 and 1845. In *Strangers and Pilgrims*, Catherine A. Brekus names at least eighty-seven women who began preaching after the controversy over Charlotte White's appointment in 1815, twenty of whom were Baptists.

[44] Johnson, *Home in the Woods*, 31, 48.

[45] Clifford, *Those Good Gertrudes*, 37.

[46] Baptist Board of Foreign Missions, *Records* (26 July 1815), 33.

CHAPTER 6

[1] Brackney, ed., *Dispensations of Providence*, 128.

[2] The replies from the members are found in the *Records of the Baptist Board of Foreign Missions, Records 1814–1828*, archived at the American Baptist Historical Society in Atlanta, Georgia.

[3] Holcombe, *Whole Truth*, 10.

[4] Ibid., 10.

[5] Baptist Board of Foreign Missions, *Records* (13 September 1815), 36.

[6] Holcombe, *Whole Truth*, 11.

[7] Baptist Board of Foreign Missions, *Second Annual Report* (1816), 65.

[8] Staughton, *Baptist Mission in India*, 69.

[9] "Generosity," 274.

[10] "Address," 340.

[11] "Generosity," 274.

[12] Phebe Hough, like Ann Judson, was not appointed.

[13] Holcombe, *Whole Truth*, 12.

[14] Baptist Board of Foreign Missions, *Second Annual Report* (1816), 66.

[15] Ibid., 66.

[16] Ibid., 113; Holcombe, *Whole Truth*, 10.

[17] Baptist Board of Foreign Missions, *Second Annual Report* (1816), 113–16.

[18] "Instructions," Baptist Board of Foreign Missions, *Second Annual Report* (1816), 114. Emphasis added.

[19] Sansom Street Baptist Church, Church Minutes (2 November 1815).

[20] *Origination and Constitution*, 89.

[21] Baptist Board of Foreign Missions, *Second Annual Report* (1816), 65–66.

[22] "Sailing of the Missionaries from Philadelphia," 275.

[23] Ibid., 276.

[24] Lynd, *Memoir of the Rev. William Staughton*, 183.

[25] Hough, "On Melancholy," 159.

[26] American Baptist Missionary Union Missionary Register, "Single Women."

[27] Lynd, *Memoir of the Rev. William Staughton*, 179.

[28] 1 Corinthians 9:22.

[29] Lynd, *Memoir of the Rev. William Staughton*, 180.

CHAPTER 7

[1] J. Rowe, *Account of the Life and Experience of Joshua Rowe*, Angus Library.

[2] Cox, *History of the Baptist Missionary Society*, 287.

[3] Hanna Smith to John Sutcliff, 3 April 1802 (letter begun in February and completed in April), Sutcliff papers, Angus Library.

[4] S. Pearce Carey, *William Carey*, 47.

[5] Robinson, "Memoir of the Late Rev. William Robinson," 329–36. Robinson and Chater were commissioned on 12 March 1806.

[6] Joshua Rowe to John Sutcliff, 10 November 1803, Sutcliff papers, Angus Library.

[7] "Extract of a letter from Mr. [Joshua] Rowe to Mr. [John] Saffery of Salisbury" [1 November 1814], 294.

[8] Whelan, ed., *Baptist Autographs*, 117n.58.

[9] "Extracts from a letter written by the Rev. Andrew Fuller to the Rev. Messrs. Mardon, Biss, Moore, and Rowe" [1 January 1804], 321–23.

[10] Joshua Rowe to John Sutcliff, 10 November 1803, Angus Library.

[11] Joshua Rowe to John Sutcliff, 3 January 1804, Angus Library.

[12] Joshua Rowe to John Sutcliff, 3 January 1804, Angus Library.

[13] J. Rowe, *Journal of Voyage*. Details of the voyage from Bristol to New York are drawn from this journal.

[14] *New York Evening Post*, 5 May 1804, 1.

[15] Ibid., 21 April 1804, 3.

[16] Joshua Rowe to John Sutcliff, 24 May 1804, Angus Library.

[17] Ibid.

[18] Ibid.

[19] Joshua Rowe to John Sutcliff, 4 December 1804, Angus Library. Details of the voyage from New York to Madras are from this letter.

[20] Joshua Rowe to John Sutcliff, 1 March 1805, Angus Library. Details of the voyage from Madras to Calcutta are drawn from this letter.

[21] "Extract of a letter from the Rev. Dr. [William] Carey, dated Serampore, June 29, 1813," 439.

[22] "Report of Baptist Mission in India," 358; Joshua Rowe to John Saffery, 24 December 1812, Angus Library.

[23] Williams, *Missionary Gazetteer*, 224.

[24] Keay, *Honourable Company*, 236.

[25] Kaye, *Administration of the East India Company*, 681, 685, 687.

[26] Eden, *'Up the Country,'* 20.

[27] Keay, *Honourable Company*, 454–55.

[28] "Extract of a letter from Mr. [Joshua] Rowe to Mr. [John] Saffery of Salisbury" [1 November 1814], 294–95.

[29] Joshua Rowe to John Saffery, 1 November 1814, Angus Library.

[30] Ibid.

PART 2

1 "Arrival of the Missionaries in India" [William Staughton to Thomas Baldwin, 8 October 1816], 418.

2 Ibid.

CHAPTER 8

1 "Extract of a Letter from Rev. George H. Hough, to one of the Editors, dated Serampore, April 27, 1816," 93.

2 Kaye, *Administration of the East India Company*, 640–46; Lovett, *History of the London Missionary Society*, 108–109.

3 Bombazet is "thin plain or twill-woven worsted cloth with smooth finish used for dresses and coats" (https://unabridged.merriam-webster.com/una-bridged/bombazet).

4 "Extract of a letter from Mrs. C. H. White (now Mrs. [Charlotte] Rowe) to her correspondent in Philadelphia" [2 May 1816], 36.

5 Ibid., 36.

6 "Extract of a Letter from Rev. George H. Hough to one of the Editors, dated Serampore, April 27, 1816," 93.

7 "Calcutta. Marriages," 197. The Rowe-White marriage date transcribed by the British Library is stated in India Office Family History Search as 18 June 1816 (http://indiafamily.bl.uk/ui/FullDisplay.aspx?RecordId=014-000241128). One source may be in error, or the marriage may have taken place on June 11 and been recorded a week later.

8 "Dissenters' Marriages," 284–85.

9 The India Office Family History Search locates the weddings of the following Carey children at St. John's: Felix Carey to Amelia Pope (2 November 1821), Jonathan Carey to Anna Pearce (14 September 1824), and Lucy Carey to Samuel Pearce Brunsdon (21 March 1826). Similarly, Baptist missionary William Robinson and Mrs. Mary Lish (24 April 1827) were wed at St. John's.

10 Rowe, *Journal of Voyage*, 11 April 1804.

11 Joshua Rowe to William Burls, 12 November 1805, Angus Library.

12 John Chamberlain to Joseph Ivimey, 23 September 1816, Chamberlain letters, Angus Library.

13 Fuller, *Complete Works*, 2:610.

14 John Biss to Andrew Fuller, 15 November 1805, Angus Library.

15 Beaver, *American Protestant Women*, 66–67.

16 Baptist Board of Foreign Missions, *Third Annual Report* (1817), 169.

17 Ibid., 170.

18 Acts 18:18, 26.

19 Baptist Board of Foreign Missions, *Records* (22 June 1816).

[20] Baptist Board of Foreign Missions, *Third Annual Report* (1817), 169.

[21] "From the Same [Charlotte H. Rowe] to the Corresponding Secretary" [Charlotte Rowe to William Staughton, 21 April 1817], 50.

[22] Data from American Baptist International Ministries as of September 2017.

[23] Baptist Board of Foreign Missions, *Fifth Annual Report* (1819), 390.

CHAPTER 9

[1] Honesta, "General Record," 244.

[2] "From the Same [Charlotte H. Rowe] to the Corresponding Secretary" [William Staughton, 21 April 1817], 50.

[3] Joshua Rowe to John Saffery, 9 August 1809, Angus Library.

[4] Yates, *Memoirs of Mr. John Chamberlain*, 368.

[5] Ibid., 386.

[6] "Missionary Intelligence," 298.

[7] Ibid.

[8] "Mr. Hough to Rev. Winchell, Rangoon" [George Hough to Winchell, January 1818], 450.

[9] "From Mrs. Rowe to Mrs. S——, Digah" [Charlotte Rowe to Maria Staughton, 13 April 1817], 49.

[10] The Baptist Mission educated Eurasian children in schools in Sirdhana, Agra, Digah, Serampore, and Ceylon ("Report of the Baptist Mission," 204).

[11] "Relating to the want of Hindoostanee School-Books," 34.

[12] "From Mr. [John] Lawson, dated Calcutta, June 23d, 1817," 94.

[13] "Extract of a letter from Mrs. [Charlotte] Rowe" [17 October 1817], 95.

[14] Joshua Rowe to John Dyer, 12 October 1820, Angus Library; Williams, *Missionary Gazetteer*, 222.

[15] Joshua Rowe to John Sutcliff, 25 December 1812, Angus Library.

[16] "Extract of a letter from Mr. [Joshua] Rowe to Mr. [John] Saffery" [4 January 1821], 417.

[17] Charlotte Rowe to [perhaps John Dyer], 22 September 1824, Angus Library.

[18] *Encyclopedia Britannica*, s.v. "Nawab" https://www.britannica.com/topic/nawab; *Encyclopedia Britannica*, s.v. "Zamindar," https://www.britannica.com/topic/zamindar; Jaffrelot, "Sanskritization vs. Ethnicization in India," 757.

[19] "Digah" [Joshua Rowe to John Saffery, 1 January 1822], 536.

[20] "Letter from Mrs. [Charlotte] Rowe. Digah on the Ganges, Hindostan" [9 December 1816], 113.

[21] "Digah" [Joshua Rowe to John Saffery, 1 January 1822], 538.

[22] Joshua Rowe to John Sutcliff, 19 October 1810, Angus Library.

[23] Wyeth, *Galaxy in the Burman Sky*, 37–38.

[24] "Extracts of a Letter from Mr. [Joshua] Rowe, dated April 10, 1822," 173.

[25] Joshua Rowe to John Dyer, 4 July 1822, Angus Library.

[26] Joshua Rowe to John Dyer, 8 October 1822, Angus Library.

[27] Charlotte Rowe to Ann Murray, 30 October 1822, Angus Library.

[28] Charlotte Rowe to John Dyer, 21 October 1824, Angus Library.

[29] "Extract of a Letter from Mr. [Joshua] Rowe to a Young Lady in New York, Dated June 5, 1818," 107–108.

[30] Ibid., 108.

[31] "Grass Tabernacle, or the Baptist Chapel at Dinapore," 296.

[32] Joshua Rowe to Rev. John Dyer, 21 July 1821, Angus Library.

[33] Joshua Rowe to John Sutcliff, 15 October 1821, Angus Library.

[34] Joshua Rowe to John Dyer, 21 July 1821, Angus Library.

[35] "Extract of a letter from Mrs. [Charlotte] Rowe, dated June 5th, 1825," 397.

[36] Joshua Rowe to John Dyer, 5 January 1820, Angus Library.

[37] "Extract of a Letter from Mr. [Joshua] Rowe to Mr. [John] Saffery, dated Digah, April 3, 1820," 529.

[38] Joshua Rowe to John Dyer, 1 July 1820, Angus Library.

[39] Joshua Rowe to Carey, Marshman, and Co., 10 January 1821, Angus Library.

[40] "Extract of a Letter from Mr. [Joshua] Rowe to Mr. [John] Saffery, dated Digah, April 3, 1820," 529.

[41] Joshua Rowe to John Dyer, 21 July 1821, Angus Library.

[42] Joshua Rowe to John Dyer, 12 October 1820, Angus Library.

[43] Joshua Rowe to John Dyer, 3 January 1822, Angus Library.

[44] Joshua Rowe to John Sutcliff, 1 March 1805, Angus Library.

[45] Joshua Rowe to John Dyer, 10 April 1822, Angus Library.

CHAPTER 10

[1] This and all following correspondence quoted between Charlotte Rowe and Edwin A. Atlee is from Atlee, "Serampore Missionaries," 73–78.

[2] Joshua Rowe to John Saffery, 20 August 1822, Angus Library.

[3] Atlee, "Serampore Missionaries," 75.

[4] Sellers, *Theophilus*, 18.

[5] Ibid., 47.

[6] "Note by the Editors," 23 (emphasis original).

[7] "Missionaries at Serampore," *Reformer*, 1 December 1821, 284.

[8] Atlee, "Serampore Missionaries," 73.

[9] Atlee, "Serampore Missionaries," 77.

[10] Joshua Rowe to John Dyer, 17 April 1823, Angus Library.

CHAPTER 11

[1] Charlotte Rowe to John Dyer, 26 August 1825, Angus Library.

[2] Ibid.

[3] Charlotte Rowe to John Dyer, 10 September 1824, Angus Library.

[4] Charlotte Rowe to John Dyer, 21 October 1824, Angus Library.

[5] Charlotte Rowe to John Dyer, 10 September 1824, Angus Library.

[6] Ibid.

[7] Charlotte Rowe to John Dyer, 24 October 1824, Angus Library.

[8] Charlotte Rowe to John Dyer, 21 October 1824, Angus Library.

[9] Charlotte Rowe to John Dyer, 10 September 1824, Angus Library.

[10] Ibid.

[11] Charlotte Rowe to John Dyer, 29 August 1825, Angus Library.

[12] "Stations Occupied by European Troops," 293.

[13] Charlotte Rowe to John Dyer, 22 September 1824, Angus Library.

[14] Charlotte Rowe to Ann Rowe [Joshua Rowe's mother], 9 September 1824, Angus Library.

[15] Peerage, http://www.thepeerage.com/p35304.htm#i353039.

[16] Charlotte Rowe to John Dyer, 16 March 1826, Angus Library.

[17] Charlotte Rowe to John Dyer, 22 October 1824, Angus Library.

[18] "Digah," Charlotte Rowe letter extract, 18 October 1824, 351.

[19] Hindu arithmetic places numbers above one another, adding the columns from left to right, and placing the sum above rather than below the columns. Multiplication and division are also computed left to right.

[20] Charlotte Rowe to John Dyer, 22 October 1824, Angus Library.

[21] Ibid.

[22] "Extract of a letter from Mrs. [Charlotte] Rowe, dated Digah, Oct. 1824," 362–63.

[23] Charlotte Rowe to John Dyer, 21 October 1824, Angus Library.

[24] Charlotte Rowe to John Dyer, 10 September 1824, Angus Library.

[25] Joshua Rowe to Andrew Fuller, 7 December 1808, Angus Library.

[26] Joshua Rowe to John Saffery, 9 October 1822, Angus Library.

[27] Charlotte Rowe to John Dyer, 26 August 1825, Angus Library.

[28] Joshua Rowe to John Dyer, 3 January 1822, Angus Library.

[29] Joshua Rowe to William Ward, 26 November 1821, Angus Library.

[30] Joshua Rowe to John Dyer, 17 April 1823, Angus Library.

[31] Charlotte Rowe to Ann Rowe [Joshua Rowe's mother], 10 September 1824, Angus Library.

[32] Ibid.

[33] Charlotte Rowe to John Dyer, 24 January 1826, Angus Library.

[34] "From Mrs. Rowe. Digah on the Ganges, Hindostan. Dec. 9th, 1816," 297.

[35] Honesta, "Scenes in India—By an Eye Witness" (17 July 1830), 34–35.

[36] Charlotte Rowe to Ann Rowe [Joshua Rowe's mother], 10 September 1824, Angus Library.

[37] "Digah" [Charlotte Rowe letter extract, 18 October 1824], 352.

[38] "Digah" [Charlotte Rowe letter extract, 7 July 1824], 252.

[39] Ibid.

[40] "Digah" (September 1825), 408.

[41] Charlotte Rowe to John Dyer, 29 August 1825, Angus Library.

[42] Ibid.

[43] An open or enclosed sedan chair borne by two or four bearers.

[44] Honesta, "Scenes in India—Designed for the Young," 178.

[45] Charlotte Rowe to John Dyer, 24 January 1826, Angus Library.

[46] Charlotte Rowe to John Dyer, 16 March 1826, Angus Library.

[47] Honesta, "Scenes in India—Designed for the Young," 178.

[48] Charlotte Rowe to John Dyer, 29 August 1825, Angus Library.

[49] Charlotte Rowe to John Dyer, 13 July 1826, Angus Library.

[50] "For the substance of the following account," 195.

[51] Masood, *Science & Islam*, 197.

[52] Baptist Missionary Society Minutes (16 June 1825), Minute 218.

[53] Gilchrist, *Stranger's Infallible East-Indian Guide*, i, vii, xv, xvi.

[54] Charlotte Rowe to John Dyer, 24 January 1826, Angus Library (emphasis original).

[55] Gilchrist, *Stranger's Infallible East-Indian Guide*, xxv.

[56] Ibid., ix–x.

[57] Ibid., 89.

[58] G. Smith, *Life of William Carey*, 94.

CHAPTER 12

[1] "Letter from Mrs. [Ann] Judson to Mrs. S—— [Maria Staughton]" [29 April 1819], 41.

[2] "Extract of a Letter from Mr. [Joshua] Rowe to Mr. [John] Saffery, Dated Digah, Oct. 1819," 352.

[3] Charlotte Rowe to John Dyer, 12 September 1824, Angus Library.

[4] Charlotte Rowe to John Dyer, 21 October 1824, Angus Library.

[5] Charlotte Rowe to John Dyer, 24 October 1824, Angus Library.

[6] Charlotte Rowe to John Dyer, 13 July 1826, Angus Library.

[7] Charlotte Rowe to John Dyer, 31 December 1824, Angus Library.

[8] Charlotte H. White to the Baptist Board of Foreign Missions, 13 June 1815, in Baptist Board of Foreign Missions, *Second Annual Report* (1816), 112.
[9] Charlotte Rowe to John Dyer, 13 July 1826, Angus Library (emphasis original).
[10] Joshua Rowe to Carey, Marshman, and Co., 10 January 1821, Angus Library.
[11] "Digah" (May 1824), 225.
[12] "Calcutta," 542.
[13] Baptist Missionary Society Minutes (16 September 1824), Minute 59.
[14] "Report of the English Baptist Missionary Society," 513.
[15] "List of Missionary Stations," 622.
[16] Charlotte Rowe to John Dyer, 12 September 1824, Angus Library.
[17] Charlotte Rowe to Ann Rowe [Joshua Rowe's mother], 10 September 1824, Angus Library (emphasis added).
[18] G. Smith, *Life of William Carey*, 92.
[19] Ibid., 95
[20] Joshua Rowe to Andrew Fuller, 26 February 1805, Angus Library.
[21] Joshua Rowe to John Dyer, 15 July 1819, Angus Library.
[22] Charlotte Rowe to John Dyer, 21 October 1824, Angus Library.
[23] Charlotte Rowe to Ann Rowe [Joshua Rowe's mother], 10 September 1824, Angus Library.
[24] Charlotte Rowe to John Dyer, 24 January 1826, Angus Library.
[25] Charlotte Rowe to John Dyer, 24 October 1824, Angus Library.
[26] Charlotte Rowe to John Dyer, 31 December 1824, Angus Library.
[27] Charlotte Rowe to John Dyer, 24 January 1826, Angus Library.
[28] Charlotte Rowe to Ann Rowe [Joshua Rowe's mother], 10 September 1824, Angus Library.
[29] Charlotte Rowe to John Dyer, 26 August 1825, Angus Library.
[30] Charlotte Rowe to John Dyer, 24 January 1826, Angus Library.
[31] "Digah" [Richard Burton to a relative, 13 April 1826], 539.
[32] "Extract of a letter from Mr. [Richard] Burton to the Secretary, dated Digah, May 3d, 1826," 89.
[33] Charlotte Rowe to John Dyer, 13 July 1826, Angus Library.
[34] Honesta, "General Record," 243.
[35] Charlotte Rowe to John Dyer, 13 July 1826, Angus Library.
[36] "Digah" (June 1827), 293.
[37] Honesta, "General Record," 243.
[38] Ibid.
[39] M. Chamberlain to John Dyer, 4 November 1826, Angus Library.
[40] Honesta, "Hints to Young Friends of Missions" (20 March 1830), 178.

[41] "Very Dear Brethren" [William Carey and Richard Burton to the Society, 4 December 1826], 293.
[42] Honesta, "General Record," 243.
[43] "Passengers from India," 888.
[44] Honesta, "Heathen Children's Society," 235.

CHAPTER 13
[1] "Baptist Board Minutes," 55–57.
[2] Baptist Board of Foreign Missions, *Records* (7 May 1821), 38.
[3] American Baptist Missionary Union, *Missionary Jubilee*, 262.
[4] "Extract of a letter from Mr. [Richard] Burton to the Secretary," 89.
[5] "Digah" [Richard Burton letter, 26 April 1827], 138.
[6] Baptist Missionary Society Minutes (24 May 1827), Minutes 201, 202.
[7] "Dijah," 357.
[8] Columbian College is now George Washington University.
[9] Baptist Board of Foreign Missions, *Records* (27 September 1824), 172.
[10] Dr. King to Baptist Missionary Society, 19 November 1829, Angus Library.
[11] *Baptist Magazine*, 1842, 385, quoted in Stanley, *History of the Baptist Missionary Society*, 228.
[12] Webb, "An Address from 'the Boston Female Society, for Missionary Purposes,'" 282.
[13] Joshua Rowe (the son) to Charlotte Rowe, 16 January 1828, Angus Library.
[14] "19th Century Health," http://www.yeoviltown.com/history/19thcentury-health.aspx.
[15] Osborn, "Baptist Chapel," http://www.yeovilhistory.info/bapchap.htm.
[16] "Political Awareness," http://www.yeoviltown.com/history/political.aspx.
[17] Honesta, "Scenes in India. By an Eye Witness. Addressed to the Young" (22 May 1830), 324–25.
[18] Honesta, "Tears," 155.
[19] "Narrative by Mrs. Charlotte H. Rowe," *London Public Ledger and Daily Advertiser*, 3 September 1827, 2; "Narrative by Mrs. C. Rowe," *London Morning Herald*, 23 October 1827.
[20] "Narrative by Mrs. Charlotte H. Rowe," *London Public Ledger and Daily Advertiser*, 3 September 1827, 2.

PART 3
[1] "Narrative by Mrs. C. Rowe," *London Morning Herald*, 23 October 1827, reprinted in the *New York Evening Post*, 3 January 1828, 2.

CHAPTER 14

[1] "The Union Line of Packets for New York," *Liverpool (England) Mercury*, 6 February 1829; "Marine News," *Charleston (SC) Mercury*, 1 October 1829; "For Freight or Charter," *Charleston (SC) Daily Courier*, 10 November 1829.

[2] Charlotte Rowe to John Dyer, 4 April 1830, Angus Library.

[3] Ibid.

[4] Charlotte Rowe to John Dyer, 26 August 1825, Angus Library.

[5] Charlotte Rowe to John Dyer, 21 October 1824, Angus Library.

[6] Charlotte Rowe to John Dyer, 13 July 1826, Angus Library.

[7] "Mrs. Judson," *National Standard* (Middlebury, Vermont), 11 November 1823, 1.

[8] "From the New England Galaxy of July 25th," 209–10; "The article published in our last number," 237–38; "Mrs. Judson," 262–63.

[9] "Vindication of Mrs. Judson," *Vermont Watchman and State Journal*, 30 December 1823, 4.

[10] Baptist Board of Foreign Missions, *Records* (27 October 1823), 132.

[11] Brekus, *Strangers and Pilgrims*, 197, 202–203.

[12] Loveless, *Free Will Baptist Early Women Ministers and Leaders*, 69.

[13] Davis, *Female Preacher*, 21.

[14] Towle, *Vicissitudes*, 84.

[15] Ibid., 228.

[16] Tocqueville, *Democracy in America*, 212.

[17] Charlotte Rowe to John Dyer, 5 April 1830, Angus Library.

[18] First Baptist Church, Philadelphia, *Register of membership, baptisms and marriages*, 77–78.

[19] Honesta, "Hints to Young Friends of Missions" (20 February 1830), 124.

[20] Honesta, "Hints to Young Well-Wishers of Missions to the Heathen in the East," 28.

[21] Honesta, "Scenes in India—By an Eye Witness. Addressed to the Young" (22 May 1830), 326.

[22] Honesta, "Scenes in India. Addressed to the Young," 372–73.

[23] Honesta, "Scenes from India—By an Eye Witness" (17 July 1830), 34.

[24] Honesta, "Hints to Young Friends of Missions" (31 January 1830), 68.

[25] Honesta, "Hints to Young Friends of Missions" (20 February 1830), 114.

[26] Sangari cites the stories as an example of altruistic middle class women reformers projecting altruism on poor laboring children: "The constituted altruism of the poor combines with the altruism of the missionaries; their unrelieved labour is intended to inspire Hindu girls and bears no relation to accumulation, mobility, future leisure or change in caste hierarchies" ("The 'Amenities of

Domestic Life,'" 25–26). Charlotte persisted in starting girls' schools, however, because she believed literacy and education were tools for economic, social, intellectual, and spiritual change and advancement.

[27] Honesta, "Hints to Young Friends of Missions" (10 April 1830), 227.

[28] "A Card," 80.

[29] "Boarding School," 204.

[30] "Boarding and Day School—by Mrs. Rowe," 144.

[31] Josiah Rowe to Charlotte Rowe, 15 April 1827, Angus Library.

[32] Desilver, *Desilver's Philadelphia Directory*, 182.

[33] "Boarding and Day School—by Mrs. Rowe," 144.

[34] "Boarding and Day School," 367.

[35] Also spelled Loundesboro.

[36] Weeks, *History of Public School Education in Alabama*, 15.

[37] First Baptist Church, Philadelphia, *Register of membership, baptisms and marriages*, 77–78.

[38] American Baptist Missionary Union Missionary Register, "Single Women."

[39] "America," 390.

[40] Baptist Board of Foreign Missions, *Records* (3 May 1823), 96.

[41] 25 U.S. Code § 71—Future treaties with Indian tribes. Legal Information Institute, Cornell Law School, accessed 2 April 2021, https://www.law.cornell.edu/uscode/text/25/71.

[42] After Ann Cleaver (1821, Cherokees) and Louisa A. Purchase (1826, Choctaws), the board appointed Susan Thompson (1828, Shawanoes), Mary Rice (1830, Ojibwas), Amanda W. Stannard (1830, Potawatomi), Sarah Rayner (1832, Cherokees), Cynthia Brown (1833, Ojibwas), Sarah Brown (ca. 1833, Ojibwas), Mary A. Colburn (1834, Creeks), Eleanor Macomber (1834, Ojibwas), Mary Bond (1835, Ottawas), Sarah C. Day (1835, Potawatomi, Ottawas), and Sarah Hale Hibbard (1835, Cherokees) (American Baptist Missionary Union, *Missionary Jubilee*, 236–72).

[43] Mason, *Cenotaph to a Woman of the Burman Mission*, 18.

[44] "Missionaries," 13.

[45] Lucius Bolles to Charlotte Rowe, 30 December 1835, Baptist Board of Foreign Missions, *Letterbook*, 10, American Baptist Historical Society, Atlanta, GA.

[46] *Abstract of the Returns of the Fifth Census*, 39.

[47] Montgomery, *Following the Sunrise*, 182.

[48] In 1910 the American Baptist Missionary Union (ABMU) changed its name to the American Baptist Foreign Mission Society (ABFMS). In 1972 the ABFMS became also known as the Board of International Ministries (BIM). In

2009 the ABFMS became also known as American Baptist International Ministries (IM).

[49] Wolf, "Strasburg—A Town of Trains and Heritage," 34–35.

[50] "Strasburg Female Seminary," *Baltimore Sun*, 9 July 1845, 4.

[51] "Strasburg Female Seminary for Young Ladies," *Lancaster Intelligencer*, 22 October 1850, 2.

[52] They were Lucy Taylor (1836, Creeks), Sylvia Case (1837, Delawares), Mary Walton (circa. 1837, Potawatomi), Elizabeth Boynton (1838, Creeks), Elizabeth F. Churchill (1838, Shawanoes), Mary Leach (1839, Ojibwas), Abigail Webster (1840, Shawanoes), Elizabeth S. Morse (1842, Delawares), Harriet Hildreth Morse (1842, Ojibwas), Jane Kelly (1843, Shawanoes), Lydia Lillybridge (1846, Ojibwas), and Elizabeth Parke Gookin (1850, Delawares) (American Baptist Missionary Union, *Missionary Jubilee*, 236–72).

[53] Harriet Hildreth Morse was the youngest of seven children born to David Morse and Rebecca (White) Morse. Rebecca White was sister to Nathaniel White, Charlotte's first husband (White, *Descendants of William White*, 28, 32, 67–68).

[54] Rizpah Warren (1838, Liberia), Rhoda Bronson (1839, Assam), Harriet E. Dickson (1839, Greece), Miranda Vinton (1841, Burma), Julia A. Lathrop (1843, Burma), Emily Waldo (1843, Greece), Harriet Hildreth Morse (1847, Siam), H. Elizabeth T. Wright (1849, Burma), and Mary Sophia Shaw (1850, Assam) (American Baptist Missionary Union, *Missionary Jubilee*, 236–72) (Black, "Mary Sophia [Shaw] Daüble").

[55] Everts, *Historical Discourse*, 49–50.

[56] American Baptist Missionary Union, *Missionary Jubilee*, 260.

[57] Rhoda Bronson (1839), daughter of Miles and Ruth Bronson; Marinda Vinton (1841), sister of Justus Vinton; Sarah Mason (1859), daughter of Francis and Helen Mason.

[58] Sarah B. Hall (appt. 1825) married George Dana Boardman; Helen Maria Griggs (appt. 1829) married Francis Mason; Eliza Wilcox (appt. 1832) married Moses Merrill; Barbara McBain (appt. 1833) married Eugenio Kincaid following Almy Kincaid's death; Ann P. Gardner (appt. 1834) married Elisha Abbott; Elizabeth Pearson (appt. 1836) married Charles R. Kellam; Maria Maine (appt. 1838) married Coroden H. Slafter; Judith Leavitt (appt. 1840) married John Taylor Jones; Mary Ann Osborn (appt. 1845) married Daniel J. MacGowan; Sarah J. Sleeper (appt. 1847) married John Taylor Jones following Judith Jones' death; Mrs. E. H. Greer was appointed in 1847 with her husband, Thomas W. Greer; Laura C. Irish (appt. 1848) married Calvin Cowing Moore; Marilla Baker (appt. 1851) married Lovell Ingalls.

[59] "DIED," *Philadelphia Public Ledger*, 26 October 1852, 2.

[60] Mary White Smith was the older of the two children born to Jonathan Kimball Smith and Anna White. Anna White was sister to Nathaniel White, Charlotte's first husband (White, *Descendants of William White*, 32).

CHAPTER 15

[1] Baptist Board of Foreign Missions, *Records* (27 April 1827), 269.

[2] American Baptist Missionary Union, *Executive Records* (1850).

[3] American Baptist Missionary Union, *Fortieth Annual Report*, 30.

[4] Ibid., 33.

[5] Ibid., 34.

[6] Dorsey, *Reforming Men and Women*, 179.

[7] American Baptist Missionary Union, *Records*, Executive Committee Minutes (3 April 1860).

[8] American Baptist Missionary Union, *Records*, Executive Committee Minutes (30 January 1866).

[9] Safford, *Golden Jubilee*, 6.

[10] Ibid., 9.

[11] Ibid., 246, 254.

[12] Gifford, "How It Began."

[13] American Baptist Missionary Union, *Sixty-eighth Annual Report*, 7.

[14] Johnston, *Report of the Centenary Conference*, 1:xxxvii.

[15] Johnston, *Report of the Centenary Conference*, 2:161.

[16] Ibid., 2:163.

[17] Ibid. (emphasis added)

[18] Ibid., 2:164.

[19] Ibid.

[20] Ibid., 2:165.

[21] Ibid., 2:167.

[22] Gordon, "The Ministry of Women," 910.

[23] Ibid., 920.

[24] Ibid.

[25] American Baptist Missionary Union, *Eighty-first Annual Report*, 17.

[26] Ibid., 19.

[27] Ibid., 20.

[28] Ibid.

[29] Ibid., 32. The first women elected to the Board of Managers in 1895 were Elizabeth (Mrs. E. R.) Stillwell of Ohio, Susan (Mrs. James B.) Colgate of New York, Elizabeth (Mrs. Henry R.) Glover of Massachusetts, Mary L. (Mrs.

Charles H.) Banes of Pennsylvania, and Fanny (Mrs. James S.) Dickerson of Illinois.

[30] American Baptist Missionary Union, *Eighty-second Annual Report*, 10.
[31] American Baptist Missionary Union, *Eighty-third Annual Report*, 10.
[32] Blackstone, *Commentaries on the Laws of England*, 441.
[33] Dr. Frederick S. Downs reported to the author.
[34] "Personal and Other Notes. Sailed," 482.
[35] *Manual of the American Baptist Missionary Union*, 13.
[36] Record Book II, Sub-committee on Return of Missionaries, Candidates and Home Salaries, 48.
[37] Record Book II, 49.
[38] Record Book II, 53.
[39] Record Book II, 54.
[40] Record Book II, 55.
[41] Record Book II, 60.
[42] Minutes of the ABFMS Board of Managers (1912 Record Book), 327.
[43] Torbet, *Venture of Faith*, 204–205.
[44] Cattan, *Lamps Are for Lighting*, 32.

CHAPTER 16
[1] Stow, *History of the English Baptist Mission to India*, 248.
[2] Gammell, *History of American Baptist Missions*, 32–33.
[3] Benedict, *General History*, 411.
[4] Benedict, *Fifty Years among the Baptists*, 129.
[5] Brekus, *Strangers and Pilgrims*, 296–97.
[6] For example, Eliza Yoer moved from Charleston to attend school in Philadelphia in 1815 and began preparing for mission service under Staughton's guidance. She returned to Charleston when not appointed. See hand-written statement on the inner cover of Henry A. Tupper's *The Foreign Missions of the Southern Baptist Convention* (Philadelphia: ABPS, 1880). Also, a Miss Dunning from New York was interviewed in 1817 and found suitable for service in Serampore (Matthias Tallmadge to Richard Furman, 30 May 1817, Richard Furman and James C. Furman Collection).
[7] American Baptist Missionary Union, *Missionary Jubilee*, 100–101.
[8] Chaplin, *Our Gold-Mine*, 75.
[9] S. F. Smith, *Missionary Sketches*, 3.
[10] Cathcart, *Baptist Encyclopedia*, 166.
[11] Hervey, *Story of Baptist Missions*, 408.
[12] Armitage, *History of the Baptists*, 2:815.

[13] Wyeth, *Galaxy in the Burman Sky*, 33.

[14] Vedder, *Short History of Baptist Missions*, 105.

[15] Newman, *Century of Baptist Achievement*, 179.

[16] Albaugh, *Between Two Centuries*, 31–32.

[17] Torbet, *Venture of Faith*, 188–89.

[18] Leonard, *Baptist Ways*, 176.

[19] Beaver, "Pioneer Single Women Missionaries," 3–4.

[20] Beaver, *American Protestant Women*, 63.

[21] Ibid., 64.

[22] Robert, *American Women in Mission*, 55.

[23] Honesta, "Scenes in India—By an Eye Witness" (22 May 1830), 324.

[24] Honesta, "Hints to Young Well-Wishers of Missions to the Heathen in the East," 27 (emphasis original).

[25] Charlotte Rowe to John Dyer, 21 October 1824, Angus Library.

[26] Joshua Rowe (the son) to Charlotte Rowe, 16 January 1828, Angus Library.

[27] Dr. King to the Baptist Missionary Society, 19 November 1829, Angus Library.

[28] "Dinapore" [Thomas Penney letter], 218.

[29] Calcutta School-Book Society, *Thirteenth Report of the Proceedings*, 11.

[30] Calcutta School-Book Society, *Fourteenth Report of the Proceedings*, 22.

[31] Calcutta School-Book Society, *Fifteenth Report of the Proceedings*, 9.

[32] Myers, ed., *Centenary Volume of the Baptist Missionary Society*, 304–304.

[33] Calcutta School-Book Society, *Twenty-third Report of the Proceedings*, 14.

[34] "Hindi Literature," 150

[35] Marshman, *Life and Times of Carey, Marshman and Ward*, 399, 450.

[36] W. H. Carey, *Oriental Christian Biography*, 3:526.

[37] Wenger, *Story of the Lall Bazar Baptist Church*, 182.

[38] Calcutta Baptist Missionary Society, *Fourteenth Annual Report*, iii.

[39] Baptist Missionary Society, *Annual Report*, 11.

[40] "New Native Places of Worship," April 1838, 232; "Acknowledgment," 498.

[41] W. H. Carey, *Oriental Christian Biography*, 3:527–28.

[42] "Decease of the Late Mrs. Evans," 70; "Agra," 588.

[43] Everts, *Historical Discourse*, 54.

[44] White, *Descendants of William White*, 68.

[45] Daniel Appleton White Smith was the son of Mary White Smith and her husband, Samuel Francis Smith. Mary White Smith was the daughter of Anna White and her husband, Jonathan Kimball Smith. Anna White was sister to Nathaniel White, Charlotte's first husband (White, *Descendants of William White*, 30–33).

[46] Torbet, *Venture of Faith*, 472.
[47] "Deaths," *Lancaster Examiner and Herald*, 30 December 1863, 3.

# INDEX

Judson, Ann 13, 29-31, 35-37, 39-40, 45, 71, 75, 137-38, 160-62, 175, 188, 189, 191, 193
Juggernaut 130
Kellam, Charles R. 235 n. 58
Kelly, Jane 234 n. 52
Kincaid, Almy 235 n. 58
Kincaid, Eugenio 235 n. 58
King Bodawpaya 51
King, Dr. 146, 153, 194
King George III 3-4, 15, 89
King James I 18
Kirkland, Col. Moses 13
Knowles, James D. 42-43
Koh, Sharon 188
Krishna Pal 80-81
language acquisition 133-35
Lathrop, Julia A. 235 n. 54
Lawson, Frances 19, 31, 37-38
Lawson, John 19, 31, 37-38, 104
Lazarus 44
Leach, Mary 234 n. 52
Leavett, Judith 235 n. 58
Leonard, Bill J. 192
Leslie, Rev. and Mrs. 146, 149
Levy, Mr. 187
Lexington & Concord 4
Lewis, Margaret 33
Liberia 235fn54
Liele, George 12-14, 54
Liele, Hannah 12-14, 33-34, 54, 88
Lillybridge, Lydia 234 n. 52
Lincoln, Salome 162
Lish, Mary 225 n. 9
Livermore, Harriet 162
Lock, Hannah 56
Lockhart, Miss 41
London Missionary Society 33, 38, 83, 98, 152
Loveless, Sarah Farquhar 33-36, 88, 105

Loveless, William C. 33-36, 88
Lowndesboro, AL 167ff.
Luke, St. 100-101
Mack, Martin 11
MacGowan, Daniel 235 n. 58
Macomber, Eleanor 234 n. 42
Madison, Pres. James 28
Madras Presidency 18
Mah Noo 108
Mahican (Mohican) nation 11
Maine, Maria 235 n. 58
Mais, Charles 60
Malaysia 35
Mardon, Mary 19, 84-85
Mardon, Rhoda 19, 84-85, 90, 98
Mardon, Richard 19, 84-87, 90, 98
Marks, David 190
Marks, Marilla 190
Marshall, Daniel 55
Marshall, Martha Stearns 55
Marshman, John 96
Marshman, Joshua 28, 112, 140, 142, 195
Martha 44
Martyn, Henry 165
Mary 44
Mary of Magdala 180
Mason, Ellen Huntly 177
Mason, Francis 169, 177, 191, 235 nn. 57, 58
Mason, Helen Maria (Griggs) 235 nn. 57, 58
Mason, Sarah 235 n. 57
Massachusetts Baptist Missionary Society 17, 25
May, Robert 31, 38
Maylin, Joseph 19-20, 28
Maylin, Elizabeth M'Cutchen 41
McBain, Barbara 235 n. 58
McBeth, Leon 192
McCarter, David 171
McCoy, Isaac 160